Developing Educational Leadership

Published in Association with the British Educational Leadership, Management and Administration Society

This series of books published for BELMAS aims to be directly relevant to the concerns and professional development needs of emergent leaders and experienced leaders in schools. The series editors are Professor Harry Tomlinson, Leeds Metropolitian University and Dr Hugh Busher, School of Education, University of Leicester.

Titles include:

Performance Management in Education: Improving Practice (2002)
Jenny Reeves, Pauline Smith, Harry Tomlinson and Christine Ford

Strategic Management for School Development: Leading your School's Improvement Strategy (2002)
Brian Fidler

Subject Leadership and School Improvement (2000)
Hugh Busher and Alma Harris with Christine Wise

Living Headship: Values and Vision (1999)
Edited by Harry Tomlinson

School Culture (1999)
Edited by Jon Prosser

School Improvement After Inspection? School and LEA Responses (1998)
Edited by Peter Earley

Policy, Leadership and Professional Knowledge in Education (1998)
Edited by Michael Strain, Bill Dennison, Janet Ouston and Valerie Hall

Managing Continuous Professional Development in Schools (1997)
Edited by Harry Tomlinson

Choices for Self-managing Schools: Autonomy and Accountability (1997)
Edited by Brian Fidler, Sheila Russell and Tim Simkins

Developing Educational Leadership:

Using Evidence for Policy and Practice

Edited by

Lesley Anderson and Nigel Bennett

SAGE Publications
London • Thousand Oaks • New Delhi

Contents

Series Editor's Preface

Lesley Anderson and Nigel Bennett were instrumental in organising the highly successful BELMAS (British Educational Leadership, Management and Administration Society) International Research Conference in 2000 and have gone on to edit two books that have their genesis in papers presented at this event. 'Developing Educational Leadership: evidence-informed policy and practice', the first to be published, explores the particularly important issue of how policy and practice can be productively informed by evidence from research. The requirement to provide a stronger justification for policy development, when the research evidence is inevitably premature, provides an interesting opportunity for those seeking to understand and influence policy development. The nature and quality of this research evidence and the process by which this informs, but does not determine, policy is explored here in theory and in practice, as are the processes by which higher quality evidence could be achievable. The relationship between research, policy and practice has never been of greater significance. Lesley Anderson and Nigel Bennett have selected papers presented at the BELMAS Research Conference in 2000 and asked the presenters to refocus those which contribute most fully on exploring this evidence-informed policy and practice theme. Such a project supports the BELMAS mission and this book clarifies and enhances its significance.

The BELMAS series explores precisely this relationship between practice and research, but has recently concentrated, perhaps excessively, on practice. The series editors are pleased that this book re-establishes the importance of the wider focus on linking research and practice. The editors have ensured that the significance of evidence-informed policy and practice is understood both in its broader context and in its particular application to educational leadership. The structuring of the collection and the judicious selection of authors who have considerable and complementary areas of expertise are purposeful and challenging. The collection has been strongly edited to ensure it has important benefits for all in the field and that there is a coherence and flow in the chapter sequencing. The new systematic reviews at Evidence for Policy and Practice Information and Co-ordinating Centre (EPPI-Centre) at the University of London's Institute of Education and the new research thrust at the National College for School Leadership (NCSL) demonstrate how central are the issues explored here. BELMAS is pleased to be associated with this excellent thematic collection of papers and with these major national developments.

Harry Tomlinson
Leeds Metropolitan University

Acknowledgements

A version of the chapter by Levačić and Glatter was published in the journal, *Educational Management and Administration* in January 2001. The editors are grateful to Professor Peter Ribbins, editor of the journal at the time, for permission to include the paper here.

We wish to express our sincere thanks to Tina McCay for her work on the manuscript and to Marianne Lagrange and Saleha Nessa of Sage Publishing for their support and assistance throughout the preparation of the book. We also gratefully acknowledge the financial support provided by BELMAS for the preparation of the index.

Notes on Contributors

Lesley Anderson is Director, Postgraduate Professional Development in the Faculty of Education and Language Studies and a lecturer in the Centre for Educational Policy and Management at the Open University. Her research interests include school autonomy and resource management. She has been an active member of the British Educational Leadership, Management and Administration Society (BELMAS) for many years and has held the posts of Vice Chair and Honorary Secretary. For the past eight years, she has been a member of BELMAS Research Committee.

Les Bell is Professor of Educational Management and Director of the Doctorate of Education Programme at the Centre for Educational Leadership and Management, School of Education, University of Leicester. He taught in both primary and secondary schools before moving into teacher training and higher education. He was Director of the School of Education and Community Studies, and later Dean of Education, Health and Social Studies, at Liverpool John Moores University. He was appointed to the Chair of Educational Management at Leicester in 1999 and now teaches the Doctoral Programme in South East Asia and the UK. He has written extensively on educational management and leadership. His research interests include the impact of government education policy on primary school headteachers, the nature of schools as organisations and cultural diversity in educational management.

Nigel Bennett is a senior lecturer in the Centre for Educational Policy and Management at the Open University, where he is responsible for its Doctorate in Education students. He is director of the IMPPEL project that is examining ways of assessing the impact of leadership continuing professional development (CPD) on practice, and co-editor (with Lesley Anderson) of a book on alternative concepts of leadership, also published in 2003.

Ray Bolam is semi-retired although continues to work as Professor of Education in the School of Social Science at Cardiff University and as Visiting Professor at the universities of Bath and Leicester. At Cardiff University, he was Head of the School of Education (1996–99) and Director of the National Professional Qualification for Headteachers (NPQH) Centre for Wales (1996–2001). From 1992 to 1994 he was Professor of Education at the University of Swansea and, prior to that, Senior Research Fellow at the University of Bristol where he was Director of the government-funded, National Development Centre (NDC) for School Management Training from 1983 to 1990. His research, development and evaluation projects and his publications have focused on school improvement, school leadership, professional development and the management of change. He has acted as consultant to the Organisation for Economic Co-operation and Development (OECD), the British Council, the European Commission and for various governments and national and international agencies in Africa, Asia, Australia, Europe and North America. He is currently a consultant with United Nations Educational Scientific, and Cultural Organisation (UNESCO) working on secondary education in the context of the post-Dakar Framework.

Marianne Coleman is a senior lecturer in educational management and a Research Tutor at the Institute of Education, University of London, and was previously at the University of Leicester. She has a continuing involvement in distance learning. She has written and researched extensively in the field of educational management and has a particular research interest in women in educational management and leadership.

Philippa Cordingley is the founder and the Chief Executive of the Centre for the Use of Research and Evidence in Education (CUREE). As adviser to the Department for Education and Skills (DfES), the National Union of Teachers, the National College for School Leadership and as Chief Professional Adviser on research to the Teacher Training Agency from 1995 to 2001 she has instigated, designed and developed a range of strategies, policies and support programmes to increase teacher interest in, access to and use of research. With CUREE colleagues, she has also developed innovative techniques for linking research on web sites, via, for example, creating and maintaining the GTC Research of the Month web site and developing the DfES's Research Informed Practice web site. Philippa has written extensively on what is involved in enabling teachers to make effective use of research and evidence.

Leela Cubillo is a lecturer in educational management at University College, Worcester. She worked as a Research Associate for the first review conducted by the Educational Leadership and Management Review Group and reporting to the Evidence for Policy and Practice Information and Co-ordinating Centre (EPPI-Centre).

Chris Dark is headteacher of Peers School in Oxford. He has worked as a head of department and a year head in comprehensive schools in Hampshire, Surrey and the Isle of Wight. He has an M.Sc in Education from the University of Oxford. Chris has been guest speaker at a range of national conferences including those organised by the National Society for the Prevention of Cruelty to Children, National Children's Bureau and the National Conference for Special

Educational Needs. He has also chaired public consultations and appeared on television. In 1998 to 2000 Chris was involved in a collaborative European Economic Community (EEC) project concerned with the integration of students with special needs into the mainstream schools in the Ural Mountains of Russia. He is a member of BELMAS Research Committee and the Secondary Headteachers' Association and a fellow of the Royal Society for Arts.

Philip Davies is currently on secondment from Oxford University to the Cabinet Office where he is Director of Policy Evaluation in the Strategy Unit. Philip helped develop, and then directed, the Masters programme in Evidence-Based Health Care at the University of Oxford. His work in the Cabinet Office is aimed at providing a strong capacity for evidence-based policy analysis and strategic thinking at the centre of government. His main areas of research interests are in education, health care, political sociology and public policy.

Charles Desforges taught science and mathematics in secondary schools for 12 years and then moved into teacher education and educational research, teaching at the universities of Lancaster, East Anglia and Exeter. He was appointed a professor of education at Exeter in 1987. He subsequently served as Dean of Education, Director of the School of Education and Deputy Vice Chancellor with special responsibility for teaching strategy. From 1999 to 2002 he was Director of the Economic and Social Research Council (ESRC) Teaching and Learning Research Programme. He has published extensively on classroom learning and was sometime editor of the *British Journal of Educational Psychology*. He is a member of the National Education Research Forum (NERF) and chairs the Priorities Group for NERF. Recently retired, he now works as a consultant on teaching and learning.

Ron Glatter is Professor of Educational Management in CEPAM, the Centre for Educational Policy and Management, at the Open University, UK. He was Director of CEPAM for several years. He is currently a Vice-President of the British Educational Leadership and Management Society (BELMAS), of which he was founding Secretary and later national Chair. He has contributed to the work of a number of international bodies including the OECD's Centre for Educational Research and Innovation (CERI). His major interests and publications are in educational governance, leadership and management, in particular the impact of reform initiatives on educational provision.

Helen Gunter is Reader in Educational Leadership and Management within the School of Education at the University of Birmingham. Before entering higher education, Helen was a secondary school teacher (history and politics) and manager for 11 years. She has teaching and research interests in education management, biographical methodology and the professional development of teachers. Helen has published articles and books on theory, educational leadership and appraisal. Her particular research interest is in the history of the field of education management.

Angela Harden is a research officer in the Evidence for Policy and Practice Information and Co-ordinating Centre (EPPI-Centre) based within the Social Science Research Unit at the University of London's Institute of Education. She has conducted many systematic reviews and has reported both substantive findings of these and associated methodological work in several journal articles and book chapters. Her current research interests are focused on meeting the challenges involved in including 'qualitative' research in systematic reviews. Her previous work has included primary research examining sex education and the provision of sexual health services for young people.

Rosalind Levačić is Professor of Economics and Finance of Education at the Institute of Education, University of London. Her main interests are financial and resource management in schools and systems of financing schools.

Jacky Lumby is Professor of Educational Leadership and Director of Research at the International Institute for Educational Leadership. She was previously a senior lecturer in educational management and Deputy Director at the Educational Management Development Unit at Leicester University. She has taught in a range of educational settings, including secondary schools, community and further education. Prior to moving into higher education, she worked in a Training and Enterprise Council with responsibility for the development of managers in both business and education. Most recently, her primary interest has been leadership and management in further education. Research projects include the management of sixth form colleges in the UK, vocational education in China, South Africa and Hong Kong and human resource management in South African schools. She has published widely on leadership and management in schools and colleges in the UK and internationally.

Peter Ribbins is Emeritus Professor in Educational Management at the University of Birmingham. During his 25 years there he has held a number of senior posts including Dean of the Faculty of Education and Continuing Studies. He has also worked as a local education authority (LEA) officer, a schoolteacher and, briefly, in industry. He has published some 25 books and over 100 articles and chapters. He was a founder member of the Standing Committee for Research in Educational Leadership and Management (SCREM). At the time of writing he is Editor of *Educational Management and Administration* and Chairman of BELMAS. His interest in evidence-informed policy and practice (EIPP) derives from many years of research into educational leaders and leadership and, more recently, from a growing fascination with issues to do with the mapping of this field.

Judy Sebba is a Senior Adviser, Standards and Effectiveness Unit (SEU), responsible for developing the research strategy and quality of research relating to schools. She was previously at the University of Cambridge where she was involved in a number of projects on evaluating the use of School Effectiveness Grants for Education Support and Training (GEST), post-inspection action planning in special and primary schools, school improvement and inspection and special needs. She represents the SEU on the Working Group for special educational needs (SEN).

James Thomas has been developing tools and methods for conducting systematic reviews at the Evidence for Policy and Practice Information and Co-ordinating (EPPI) Centre since its establishment in 1995. He supports people in the UK and internationally to write systematic reviews and promotes evidence-informed decision-making through teaching critical appraisal skills. He is also currently undertaking historical research on certain aspects of social policy in the 1930s.

Will Wale has wide experience of teaching and school management spanning 23 years including nine years as a head of department. Since 1994, he has held senior leadership roles in two secondary schools and is currently Deputy Headteacher at Queen's Park Technology College, Blackburn. He is also an Associate Tutor in the Educational Management Development Unit at the University of Leicester, working with distance learning postgraduate students following the MBA degree course in Educational Management. His main research interest is in the relationship between leadership and improvement in secondary schools in the UK.

Introduction

LESLEY ANDERSON AND NIGEL BENNETT

Evidence-informed policy and practice (EIPP) emerged as a concept in the late 1990s in response to sustained political pressure on public service providers to demonstrate that they were providing both good quality and appropriate services. National political parties were, and still are, advocating the introduction of private companies into public service provision on the grounds that the profit imperative would make them more efficient and, through appropriate contractual arrangements, more effective. However, such assertions had little empirical evidence to justify them and both sides of the debate saw a need to generate such information. This situation provided the immediate stimulus for the growth of interest in EIPP as the means to enable public policy to be determined from a more informed basis in general and with the specific intention to improve practical provision and public services.

This interest in EIPP, in general as well as specifically in education, is also associated with a number of longer-term factors that relate to what Davies, Nutley and Smith (2000) describe as the 'rise of evidence' during the twentieth century. In relation to policy, they point out that during this time there has been a massive increase in the number of organisations seeking explicitly to advise or influence policy development and that, increasingly, governments have become receptive to certain types of evidence. Such organisations include pressure groups, university researchers, 'think-tanks', professional bodies and statutory organisations, all of which attempt to influence policy-makers through the assembly and presentation of 'evidence'. Moreover, in recent times, there has also arisen an increasing public and political scepticism towards the way in which public services are delivered. Gone are the days when doctors, teachers, police officers and other professionals were trusted unquestioningly in their decisions and actions. By the end of the twentieth century, reassurance was, and still is, sought by the increasingly educated and informed public about the way in which their taxes are spent. Hence, not only is there an expectation of policy development being informed by evidence, there is also a presumption that the actions taken to implement those policies will be the most appropriate and effective in achieving their declared goals. It is expected that this concept of 'best practice' will also be informed by evidence, and evidence in the shape of targets and 'league tables' has become a means by which government departments judge the effectiveness of public services such as hospitals, local government, schools and colleges. All this has been made possible with the increased availability of all types of data, largely though significant advances in information technology and, related to this, growth in the size and capabilities of the research community. However, other factors such as the need to improve productivity and international competitiveness and an increasing emphasis on scrutiny and accountability of government have also been influential.

The interest in EIPP in education in the UK is set within the context of concern about educational standards. The later decades of the last century saw governments introduce a variety of policies aimed to bring about the desired improvement. However, despite the range of information designed to demonstrate the extent to which schools and colleges were delivering on the targets set, there was a persistent criticism about the evidence being brought forward to justify the government's claim that educational achievement was rising. One potential source of evidence to confirm or deny such claims and criticisms was educational research, and this has led to wide-ranging scrutiny of the relationship between educational research findings and the evidence for the success or otherwise of these policies. Writing about educational potential, Fitz-Gibbon (2000) describes the research–policy and practice relationship as fraught with disputes that are both methodological and philosophical in nature. While research findings from diverse sources are brought to bear on educational debates, she points out that there is a distinct lack of robust evidence from rigorous experimental trials available to inform policy-making and practice.

In terms of educational research, policy and practice, the election of a Labour government in 1997 was significant. Not only did the Blair government come to power with an agenda of 'education, education and education', its stated philosophy was the pragmatic 'what matters is what works'. Thus, Labour's first period of office saw a huge range of initiatives relating to educational research, all of which were intended to improve the evidence base for policy formulation and service delivery practice. These initiatives include the creation of bodies like the General Teaching Council, the National College for School Leadership (NCSL), the National Educational Research Forum, the Centre for the Economics of Education and the Centre for the Wider Benefit of Learning.

At the same time as a new pragmatism entered government, investigations into the nature of educational research led to the publication of two reports (Hillage et al., 1998; Tooley, 1998) which were critical of its quality and the use made of it. The Tooley report reflected Fitz-Gibbon's criticism of a lack of robust experimental data, arguing that of the (limited) number of research reports examined very few met the canons of objective social scientific research. Hillage et al. were less critical and saw greater justification for more subjective research, but it was still seen that educational research had insufficient influence on both policy and professional educational practice.

Such criticisms have a clear epistemological dimension. Any discussion that examines the quality of research has to make certain assumptions about what counts as 'good' research and 'sound' evidence, and the 1990s saw politicians and some senior educators being critical of educational research for having *too much* impact on professional practice. When he was Secretary of State for Education, Kenneth Clarke hit out at what he regarded as the harmful impact of 'barmy theory' on teaching practice. Similarly, Chief Inspector Chris Woodhead's first annual OFSTED lecture in 1995 was an attack on the well-established concept of reflective practice and he declared with satisfaction that such ideas had died in the face of the 'objective' data being generated by the schools inspection system. Much of the criticism was levelled at qualitative research, often in-depth case studies which, by their nature, are not generalisable and do not necessarily share a common methodology. One of Woodhead's claims was that the use of a set framework for conducting school inspections created a generalisable national data set on the condition of English schooling. Thus, it seems that he does not accept the widely argued social science view that the methods employed in a research study affected the nature, though not necessarily the quality, of the data generated.

In an attempt to redress these issues, the government and others have looked outside education for guidance and have been influenced by the work of the Cochrane Collaboration on evidence informed strategies in medicine. The outcome is that the government is now promoting EIPP in education and has set expectations that the research community will respond accordingly. In February 2000, the Secretary of State for Education and Employment was quoted as straightforwardly stating the case:

> It should be self-evident that decisions on Government policy *ought* to be informed by sound evidence. Social science *ought* to be contributing a major part of that evidence base ... Too often in the past policy has not been informed by good research: a former Permanent Secretary once ruefully described the old DES (Department of Education and Science) as a knowledge-free zone.
>
> (Blunkett, 2000, p. 1)

This view of the relationship between research, policy and practice is a strongly rational one that emphasises generalisability and unambiguous research findings as the basis of action. It could be criticised for underplaying the significance of values as a basis for action, the individuality of specific contexts, and the nature of tacit knowledge that writers in the fields of management and professional development have explored. Unsurprisingly, however, educational researchers in the UK have not been slow to take up the government's challenge to provide practically relevant research, and discussion about EIPP is vibrant. For example, extensive sessions on EIPP have regularly featured in the programmes of recent Annual Conferences of the British Educational Leadership, Management and Administration Society (BELMAS)[1] and the British Educational Research Association (BERA). Moreover, with support from the Department for Education and Employment, the Evidence for Policy and Practice Information and Co-ordinating (EPPI)-Centre has been set up at the University of London's Institute of Education. Through the EPPI-Centre, review groups on various aspects of education have been established and systematic reviews have been undertaken and are ongoing. One of these groups is concerned with educational leadership and management – the primary focus of this book.

The origins of this book lie in presentations and discussions at the BELMAS Sixth International Research Conference held in Cambridge in March 2000 and discussions between its organisers after the event. The editors were two of the three members of the conference organising committee.[2] Earlier versions of some of the chapters were presented at this conference, either as part of a double symposium on EPPI in education or as individual papers that were prepared and presented, at that time, without an explicit EPPI focus. The EPPI symposium emerged as a key feature of the conference and inspired us to persuade other conference paper presenters to redraft their papers along an 'EPPI line'. The result is a set of chapters that vary in both focus and attitude towards the principles of EPPI and the ways in which central government has pursued the principle in the educational leadership field.

The book is divided into two parts. It begins by considering the background to the current interest in EPPI and explores the central meaning of the term. In the Chapter 1, Charles Desforges sets the scene in education with specific reference to teaching and learning. He surveys recent thinking in the field and uses the findings as a backdrop to discuss four significant challenges that face policy-makers and educators if evidence is brought to bear on practices close to teaching and learning.

In Chapter 2, Judy Sebba draws on her experience of working within the Department for Education and Skills and considers the government strategy for research in education in response to the Hillage et al. review that was undertaken in 2000. In doing this, she highlights the need to improve the quality of the evidence base as well as access to existing evidence. Sebba also identifies and considers a range of issues that emerge in developing and improving the relationship between educational research, policy and practice.

In Chapter 3, Philip Davies addresses the important question about the difference between systematic reviews and current practice in educational research. He starts from the basis that one purpose of systematic reviews is to attempt to overcome some of the problems inherent in single studies, especially their specificity in terms of context, samples selected and the time frames when undertaken. He argues that the tendency for single studies to exaggerate the effect of policy interventions can be compensated for by systematic reviews of *all* the available evidence on some topics.

In this chapter, Davies outlines different approaches to reviewing existing literature and evidence, and makes the case for the superiority of critically appraised systematic reviews that attempt to be as comprehensive as possible, whilst weeding out primary studies that do not meet high methodological standards of validity, reliability and relevance. He also considers the work of organisations such as the Cochrane and Campbell Collaborations, which prepare, maintain and disseminate systematic reviews of the effectiveness of interventions in health care, education, crime and justice, and social welfare.

The principles and more practical details of systematic reviews are discussed in the next chapter by James Thomas and Angela Harden. Employed as core members of the EPPI-Centre, they describe the development of the Centre's activities and the system for facilitating evidence-informed policy and practice through systematic reviews.

Rosalind Levačić and Ron Glatter provide the final chapter in this part. They examine the potential for EIPP in relation to educational leadership and management and, hence, provide the context for the second part of the book. Levačić and Glatter set out a model of EIPP in the relation to all the main stakeholders and discuss some of the issues that emerge from this analysis. They also consider the factors that may promote or inhibit the development of EIPP in educational leadership and management. They argue that there is considerable potential in evidence-informed policy and practice and, on this basis, go beyond a conceptual discussion to present a set of proposals for developing EIPP in educational leadership and management, including some ideas about the possible role of BELMAS in supporting an EIPP agenda. Thus, the scene is set for Part Two.

In the second part, the focus is on EIPP in the field of educational leadership. The first chapter (Chapter 6) in this part emanates from the educational leadership and management EPPI-Centre review group. The authors, Bell, Bolam and Cubillo, were lead players in the first review undertaken by this group and they report here on both the process and the outcomes of the activity. The approach they adopted was to regard this first round of reviewing as a learning experience. While valuing the opportunity to be involved at this early stage, it is evident that Bell, Bolam and Cubillo have reservations about the process and its outcomes.

In Chapter 7, Philippa Cordingley focuses on practice and practitioners. She starts from the assertion that the process of using research and evidence to inform practice is always complex and this is particularly true in the case of interactive school classrooms where decisions and activities have to respond to multiple variables almost instantaneously. The discussion here includes the issue of teachers' tacit knowledge and the factors influencing them in changing it. Cordingley's view is that the way to make sense of this complexity in order to enhance teaching and learning is through engagement in, and with, research. In this chapter, she also considers the role of school research co-ordinators and how school-based research consortia and the activities of the National Teacher Research Panel have built on the work of teacher researchers and contribute to the enhancement of educational leadership and management.

In the next chapter Marianne Coleman continues along the line of practitioner researchers and provides examples of the ways in which they play a role in the development and execution of a research agenda, particularly one that relates to individual and institutional development and organisational change. Drawing on data reported in Middlewood, Coleman and Lumby (1999), she considers how individual schools or colleges appear to support or hamper practitioner researcher as well as the effectiveness of such research in terms of its impact on the individual, the school or college and the links with institutional improvement. Coleman goes on to develop a schema of the different levels of change that may occur as a result of practitioner research.

Jacky Lumby's chapter characterises the nature of research in the learning and skills sector. She argues that it is limited in range and scope, and that a high proportion is descriptive and exhorts colleges to replicate 'good practice'. Lumby considers how far the literature reflects the values and perspectives of particular groups and the need for research that can support practice by recognising its complexity and the range of values within the sector.

In Chapter 10, Chris Dark provides a practical account of ways in which data and information is used to inform practice in a secondary school. As the headteacher, he argues that national education policy in recent years has become increasingly 'top down' and that as funding becomes increasingly targeted to specific actions with measurable outcomes, school decision-making becomes grounded in a managerial perspective. Thus, he puts a premium on developing sound evidence bases and their use to inform both policy and practice.

A personal perspective of practitioner research is provided by Will Wale in Chapter 11. The chapter is structured around research into school leadership that he undertook as part of his studies for a master's degree. However, rather than just reporting his findings, he uses the experience as the vehicle for his chapter and reports on the process of identifying and developing his research ideas through the literature, the nature of the evidence he generated and how it can be used to inform policy and practice.

In the final chapter, Peter Ribbins and Helen Gunter consider the various recent reviews of educational researcher and comment on the EPPI-Centre systematic review response. They argue that without a map of the field of leadership studies, the systematic review approach will not satisfy the critics or expectations. Indeed, they go on to suggest that such a map is not only necessary to systematic reviewers, but is a vital tool for other organisations concerned with enhancing educational leadership and management, such as the NCSL.

NOTES

1. BELMAS was formerly known as BEMAS (British Educational Management and Administration Society).

2. Fergus O'Sullivan, University of Lincoln, was the third member of the conference organising committee.

REFERENCES

Blunkett, D. (2000) *Influence or Irrelevance: Can Social Science Improve Government?* Secretary of State's ESRC Lecture, 2 February, London: DfEE.

Davies, H.T.O., Nutley, S.M. and Smith, P.C. (2000) 'Introducing evidence-based policy and practice in public services', in Davies, H.T.O., Nutley, S.M. and Smith, P.C. (eds) *What Works? Evidence-Based Policy and Practice in Public Services*, Bristol: Policy Press.

Fitz-Gibbon, C. (2000) 'Education: realising the potential', in Davies, H.T.O., Nutley, S.M. and Smith, P.C. (eds) *What Works? Evidence-Based Policy and Practice in Public Services*, Bristol: Policy Press.

Hillage, J., Pearson, R., Anderson, A. and Tamkin, P. (1998) *Excellence in Research on Schools*. London: DfEE.

Middlewood, D., Coleman, M. and Lumby, J. (eds) (1999) *Practitioner Research in Education: Making a Difference*, London: Paul Chapman Publishing.

Tooley, J. with Derby, D. (1998) *Educational Research – a Critique: A Survey of Published Educational Research*. London: Office for Standards in Education.

PART ONE

PART ONE

1

Evidence-Informed Policy and Practice in Teaching and Learning

CHARLES DESFORGES

INTRODUCTION

Teaching has always been a process informed by evidence. Anyone who has ever tried it will be familiar with those continuous monitoring processes necessary to run a productive classroom in pursuit of learning. Teachers attend to a wide range of data on questions such as, 'are the pupils engaged with the work set, do they comprehend the lesson content, what does the level of noise indicate – busyness or distraction?' In regard to particular classroom interactions, questions arise such as, 'how long should I wait for responses after asking a question, have the pupils got the point, shall I move onto a new topic or is more practice indicated?'

These questions are resolved through the exercise of expertise or wisdom on the basis of evidence. Much of the evidence is ephemeral whilst some if it is objective. It ranges from an awareness of distractions through to the careful examination of test scores for indication of learning difficulties. The evidence is interpreted in terms of the teacher's experience, style, values and implicit beliefs or theories about teaching and learning. Some teachers, for example, are much more sensitive than others about levels of classroom noise and will intervene earlier to quieten what others would accept as 'working atmosphere'. Either way teaching was, and is, evidence-informed.

Some fairly obvious questions can be raised about this quotidian evidence-informed practice. For example, is the 'right' evidence (i.e. valid evidence) being collected? Is a quiet class necessarily a learning class? Does evidence of busyness stand as valid evidence of comprehension or even task engagement? Are the teacher's interpretative processes rigorous and relevant to the task in hand? For example, does a score of 10/10 on an arithmetic test necessarily indicate pupil competence? It might indicate copying. Do the interpretations warrant subsequent decisions? For fear of losing classroom order and pace, teachers wait only microseconds for answers to their questions. Would it be wiser, more productive, to wait longer?

3

The questions are well known and have long been recognised and formalised in the movements known as the 'reflective practitioner' or 'teacher as researcher'. The significance of the questions and procedures for examining them have generated an extensive literature in the grander movement of 'action research' which attempts to improve practice through the careful, evidence-based examination of classroom action and its underlying assumptions, beliefs and theories. Action research and its subsystems (e.g. 'teacher as researcher') rest on a value system, which assumes continuous improvements in praxis if continuous effort is invested in theory/practice cycles of investigation running on 'data'. The aspiration is to formalise teachers' intuitive, everyday practices of running on 'awareness'.

Over several recent decades a separate educational research industry has emerged. It has operated, sometimes in partnership, sometimes in collision with the reflective practitioner movement. In this industry, people designated as researchers have worked with or on teachers in effect to identify 'what works' in teaching. Generally identified as 'black box' studies, the aspiration has been to describe and explain how the processes of policy and practice are connected to desired educational outcomes. The aim is to establish, on a scientific basis, principles (if not laws) of good practice. In contrast to the reflective practitioner approach, the adoption of scientific method is explicit. Equally explicit is the adoption of people as 'subjects' of the research. Less explicit is the assumption of people as 'objects' and research results as 'objective'.

The first of these approaches has been characterised as 'research in teaching', whilst the second has been named 'research on teaching'. Both approaches, somewhat caricatured above, have always attracted critics. Critics within each paradigm have been concerned with the refinement of methods. Critics across the paradigms have been occupied in 'paradigm wars' contesting the alternative assumptions about epistemology and ontology. Increasingly, however, critics beyond both paradigms have achieved greater public salience by raising questions about the achievements of both paradigms. Where, it is asked, is the evidence of any accumulating knowledge base in the field? Where is the evidence of educational enhancement predicated on outputs of educational research whatever its epistemological provenance?

The impact of this recent body of criticism has been exacerbated by the increased salience of education in the government's league table for policy priorities. Where once 'defence of the realm' and the 'economic system' were the core concerns of governments, it seems now that all is 'education, education, education'. This shift in policy focus has been precipitated by the increasing pace of social change brought about, in the main, by revolutionary changes in the speed of information processing, which has enhanced long-established tendencies towards globalised economics and the intensification of economic competition. It is recognised that in the context of such rapid change the best bet for achieving prosperity and personal fulfilment resides in our capacity for learning. Learning has become the core concept of our time. This places new demands on educational systems, for ever-increasing efficiency and effectiveness.

We must learn, and learn quickly, new lessons about teaching and learning. It is taken for granted that this entails extensive embellishment of evidence-informed practice. In the face of challenges ahead, common custom and practice, intuition, subjective or ideological posturing and informal reflection are simply not acceptable to political leaders of any country with aspirations towards prosperity. The only acceptable way ahead, in these minds, is through a sustained commitment to evidence-informed best practice.

This posture raises anxieties in the minds of many. Rather than being rational, it is criticised as being deeply embedded in the political psyche. It is said to rest heavily on the assumptions of technical rationality, that implicit kitemark of all modern managerial systems. It seems to draw implicitly on the scientific approach to knowledge creation notwithstanding a general dyslexic and schizoid understanding of science. Perhaps most of all it is said to rest on politicians' fear of loss of control – hence loss of their remaining legitimacy – in the face of rapid change. That being said, whatever anxieties might be felt about the provenance of evidence-informed policy (EIP), the alternative is indefensible. A commitment to EIP is not a strike against creativity or wisdom or judgement. At worst it is no more than a challenge to make the very best of these processes. Put starkly, a stand against evidence is a posture in favour of ignorance. The problems with EIP are not in the 'what' but in the 'how'.

DEVELOPMENTS IN PRACTICE

A move toward EIP necessitates at least the following:

- The identification of core or high leverage questions. It will not be possible to address every question in the field. How will we identify the questions, the answers to which get us the biggest return on effort in terms of desired outcomes per hour spent?
- The means of accumulating high quality evidence on 'what works, for whom and under what circumstances'.
- The means of reviewing, organising and systematising the evidence to discern warrantable conclusions for the multi-faceted settings which characterise education.
- The means of transforming evidence into system-wide practices. However good the evidence and however systematic the patterns in it, research outputs effect nothing in and of themselves. Newton's Laws of Motion never moved anything.

We see the logic of these necessities steadily being played out in policy. There has been an increase in foresight exercises and research agenda prioritising. There has been a dramatic increase in the establishment of research reviewing bodies including, for example, the Campbell Collaboration, the Evidence for Policy and Practice Information and Co-ordinating Centre (EPPI-Centre) and the Economic and Social Research Council's (ESRC) Centre for Evidence-Based Policy. There has been a marked increase in a strategic interest in EIP including that signified in the policies and practices of the General Teaching Council (GTC) and the Teacher Training Agency (TTA). Research has been heavily implicated in several national strategic teaching programmes (National Literacy and Numeracy Strategies and the Key Stage 3 strategy, for example). This all looks rather ad hoc but as a minimum we can see the pieces of a jigsaw emerging. Most significantly, the establishment of the National Educational Research Forum (NERF) stands to bring coherence, increased salience and increased impact to this policy area.

SOME PROBLEMS

The institutional developments described above are necessary to progress in the field. However, they will by no means be sufficient for the promotion of EIP. As already argued, it is essential to focus on powerful questions, to develop methods to generate high-quality evidence, and to have systems for reviewing, evaluating and disseminating the conclusions of research. It is at this point, however, that deeper problems may be identified in the pursuit of EIP and it is to some of these problems I now turn.

PRACTITIONERS IN SYSTEMS

Teachers' practices are shaped by their knowledge, attitudes and beliefs. Figure 1.1 shows some of the sources of this schematic knowledge and their relation to practice in action.

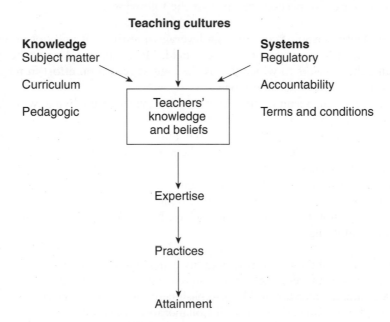

Figure 1.1   Forces shaping practice

Figure 1.1 is best read from the bottom up. The objective of teaching is to enhance pupil attainment through their engagement in learning processes. Pupils are directly influenced only by their teachers' practices. Practices – teaching in action – are determined by teachers' expertise. Expertise refers to the teachers' wisdom and judgement in making specific decisions at all stages of the teaching process, i.e. in the planning, interaction and evaluation phases. Expertise mediates between the teacher's knowledge and belief systems and the reading of the situation to hand. Expertise is an interpretative process drawing in part on a corpus of formal and tacit knowledge. In regard to teaching subject matter, teachers have an extensive grasp of the academic material per se. In addition, they have knowledge of a wide range of ways and means by which the subject is represented in curriculum materials. Teachers also hold a body of related pedagogic knowledge which refers to, for example, those concepts which are difficult to learn, or those methods of relating pupils' current knowledge to available curriculum representations.

Teachers are not solitary conduits for curriculum delivery. Although much of their work is played out in classrooms, they are members of teams and of wider systems of more or less collegiality. Teachers have an extensive understanding of their terms and conditions of work and of the regulatory and accountability systems in which they operate. These bodies of knowledge including, for example, their understanding of inspection systems, or of public examinations and testing regimes, are known to be very salient in shaping practices. They are high-profile, high-stakes corpuses of knowledge.

In addition to the public systems knowledge, teachers work in a profession which, like all professions has its own culture and subcultures. Teaching cultures represent the taken for granted ways of doing things. Subcultural differences between academic disciplines for example, or between primary and secondary schools are known to be manifest in striking differences in teaching and related practices.

The bodies of knowledge and belief, roughly sketched here, constitute the major focus of teachers' decision-making about their practice. The salience of this corpus of knowledge has long been recognised in the 'research in education' movement which encouraged, through action research, teachers to go beyond the examination of immediate classroom action and to delve deeply into the assumptions on which it is predicated. How will bodies of research evidence, however well established and authenticated, find a hearing? Teachers are inundated with messages about teaching from the sources sketched above. Can new sources expect to be heard? What significance will be given to information outside that supplied from accountability systems?

These questions have implications for how research findings might reach teachers. Should they, for example, appear through their impact on inspection processes? Or in the form of improved artefacts for teaching and learning? I shall return to these matters under the heading of 'Transformation'.

HOW MINDS WORK

If research evidence confirms and supports current practice, we can expect no problems in its appropriation. But what can we expect in the valuable cases where evidence challenges current practice and understanding? What happens when 'new' knowledge clashes with 'old' knowledge? This is a key question in the field. The assumption in EIP fields is that practice and/or understanding shifts in the direction of new evidence. Nothing could be further from the truth. The question is very familiar to researchers in the psychology of thinking and there is extensive research on the topic particularly in regard to the thinking of everyday life, to children's learning and to the development of theories by scientists. This research has been reviewed and the lessons are clear and consistent (Chinn and Brewer, 1993). There is a very long trail to be negotiated before new evidence alters 'old' understandings. Some of the route is shown in Figure 1.2.

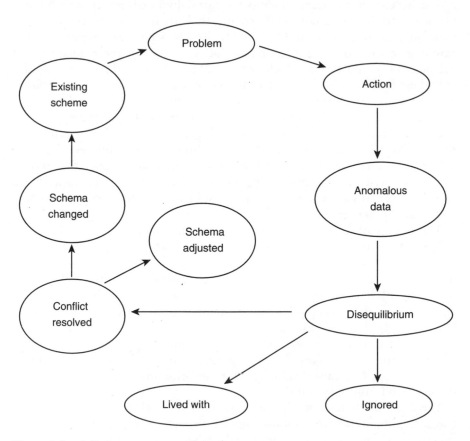

Figure 1.2   Adjustment to anomalous data

Figure 1.2 indicates that in the course of practice, we generally have established ways (extant schema) which guide our action. If anomalous data are presented (e.g. evidence challenging our cherished practice) intellectual disequilibrium is produced. We might feel unsettled. Research on people's reaction to this experience shows that the most common ways of dealing with this anxiety are to reject or ignore the anomalous data. The source of the data might be considered inadequate, biased or disreputable. The data might be explained away ('it happened in Wigan and we all know what that means'). The data might be accepted but sidestepped. A 'so what' posture is adopted. The history of science is often described in terms of a steady progress of theoretical advance. It could equally be written as a story of wasted opportunities as vanity, jealousy, cowardice, idleness, special pleading, lack of creativity and ethical bankruptcy have combined to deny the implications of challenging new evidence. This is not to say that new evidence should invariably be accepted entailing the immediate abandonment of old theory. That way lies madness. New evidence should invariably be challenged, but there are professional ways of doing this. Human minds however, have it seems, a taste for conservatism, propped up by denial or obfuscation. Only when the evidence is overwhelming and its practical and theoretical significance easily expedited are the majority of minds prepared to be convinced of its relevance. Schemas at this stage become adjusted to new circumstance and the cycle starts again.

A significant implication of this understanding of how minds work is that presenting people with evidence will not by any manner of means, be taken to necessitate changes of mind let alone of practice. Evidence-informed practice will take a lot more than evidence.

KNOWLEDGE TRANSFORMATION

This term refers to an issue otherwise known as knowledge use, knowledge transfer or knowledge application. Each term is a metaphor for the problem of understanding how knowledge acquired in one setting is best profited from in problem-solving in another setting. The problem is not at all well understood (Desforges, 2000). Studies in the history of science and technology have clearly shown that there are huge time lags between the discovery of scientific findings and their application in useable, material technologies (Dugan and Dugan, 2000). The following conditions have been implicated in technological developments from a scientific knowledge base: Application requires, at least,

- a body of well-established scientific knowledge;
- good engineering skills and artefacts;
- extensive financing of ideas;
- liberal accountability regimes allowing for diversity and experimentation;
- competition and a market for effective ideas.

Knowledge transformation is, in this context, a knowledge-led problem-solving process constrained by social, cultural, economic and political forces. It has been well said that it took the medical profession 300 years to learn to wash its hands. From the first realisation of the facts of spreading disease through doctors' handling of patients through to twentieth century procedures for aseptic medical work, centuries of scientific, technical, economic and social commitment were necessary. Painfully, sepsis is still the biggest killer in hospital systems. How much more difficult will the process of knowledge transformation be when, as is the case in education, it is more likely that the research base will be converted into advanced human practices rather than material technologies. Educational research will ask us to change our ways rather than put new tools in our hands.

None of the conditions for knowledge transformation set out above, obtains in education. There is almost no knowledge base linking teaching to learning. There is little or no experience of human engineering that sustains changes in behaviour on the basis of evidence. The financing of educational knowledge transformation is scant. Accountability regimes are draconian and there is no market for ideas. If material technology is used as analogy for knowledge transformation the prospects for EIP are exceedingly bleak.

IMPLICATIONS

The enhancement of EIP will, of course, necessitate the establishment and validation of an appropriate evidence base. But whilst necessary, this is by no means a sufficient condition. In fact, by far the greater challenges come later in the plot. It is salutary to note that the national teaching strategies for literacy and numeracy have been imposed on schools. The development of EIP, given the above analysis, is more likely to be achieved through manipulation of the inspection regime and through statutory measures than through processes of persuasion, or professional development based on professional responsibilities.

REFERENCES

Chinn, C.A. and Brewer, W.F. (1993) The role of anomalous data in knowledge acquisition, *Review of Educational Research*, Vol. 63, No. 1, pp. 1–51.

Desforges, C. (2000) *Putting Educational Research to Use through Knowledge Transformation*, London: LSDA.

Dugan, S. and Dugan, D. (2000) *The Day the World Took Off: The Roots of the Industrial Revolution*, London: Channel 4 Books.

2

A Government Strategy for Research and Development in Education

JUDY SEBBA

INTRODUCTION

In this chapter the development of evidence-informed policy is considered in the context of the government's strategy for research and development in education. The idea of using evidence in policy-making is not new. Nutley and Webb (2000) note that Keynes was a great proponent of the importance of ideas and knowledge in policy-making, arguing that policy-makers should make rational decisions based on knowledge and 'reasoned experiment'. In 1997, with the election of a new government as Davies, Nutley and Smith (2000) note, came the espoused philosophy of 'what matters is what works'. In a much quoted annual ESRC lecture given by David Blunkett, the Secretary of State for Education at that time, it was stated:

> It should be self-evident that decisions on Government policy ought to be informed by sound evidence. Social science ought to be contributing a major part of that evidence base ... Too often in the past policy has not been informed by good research: a former Permanent Secretary once ruefully described the old DES [Department of Education and Science] as a knowledge-free zone.

> (Blunkett, 2000, p. 1)

Since 1997 government departments in England have embarked on a process of modernising government which has promoted the use of evidence in the policy process. The newly set up Centre for Management and Policy Studies in the Cabinet Office and the Civil Service College within it have developed a programme for senior civil servants and ministers designed to promote a better understanding of evidence and how it should be used. Does this really signal a retreat from political ideology and a new commitment to the use of evidence in policy-making? This is the context in England in which this chapter considers the use of evidence in policy-making in relation to schools. Developing evidence-informed practice is not addressed in this chapter as,

11

although also part of the government's research strategy, it is addressed in the chapter by Cordingley.

THE DEBATE ABOUT EDUCATIONAL RESEARCH AND DEVELOPMENT

In 1996 David Hargreaves gave the Teacher Training Agency's Annual Lecture (Teaching as a research-based profession: possibilities and prospects) in which he compared the quality of educational research unfavourably with that of medicine. He argued that educational research is non-cumulative, that there is an unhelpful distinction between researchers and users, that promotion in education has been de-coupled from both practitioner expertise and knowledge of research and that educational research is poor value in terms of improving the quality of education in schools. This was not a new debate and, indeed, Hargreaves himself had described 'educational research as generally disappointing' in an earlier publication (Hargreaves, 1994, p. 50) but it fuelled an ongoing discussion within the research community. Over the next few years the quality and impact of educational research was considered in detail in many sources (e.g. Edwards, 2000; Furlong, 1998; Gray, 1998; Mortimore and Mortimore, 1999; Pring, 2000; Rudduck and McIntyre, 1998; Winch, 2001).

In 1998 two reviews of educational research were published. The first commissioned by OFSTED (Tooley and Darby, 1998) was an analysis of the quality of research publications, while the second (Hillage *et al.*, 1998) was commissioned by the Department for Education and Employment to analyse the direction, organisation, funding, quality and impact of educational research. The Hillage *et al.* study reviewed the literature, interviewed over 40 stakeholders, held focus group discussions, ran a call for evidence and collected documentary evidence. They concluded that the relationship between research, policy and practice needed to be improved. They suggested that the research agenda was too supplier-driven and that this was exacerbated by the process of research funding. The review noted that the overemphasis on short-term evaluations at the expense of exploration and development in government-sponsored research meant that research was following, rather than leading, policy.

The Hillage *et al.* review made clear that the shortcomings in the quality of some research was limiting its use. They noted that the research that addressed issues relevant to policy and practice was too small scale, incapable of generating findings that are generalisable, insufficiently based on existing knowledge and inaccessible. Pressure on researchers to produce empirical findings in published journals of international repute reflects different priorities, those partly controlled by the Research Assessment Exercise (RAE) which has determined research funding to universities in recent years, to those which 'users' in the system need to inform policy and practice. Dissemination of findings was described in the Hillage *et al.* report as 'rampant ad hocery' with little evidence of a strategy or concerted approach. The report concluded that a lack of interest and understanding of research among policy-makers and practitioners, the absence of a capacity to use findings and lack of a system for using evidence in policy-making limited the impact of research on policy and practice.

The review had a mixed reception with critiques provided, for example, by Atkinson (2000) who argued that it was too instrumental due to its government sponsorship and Swann and Pratt (1999) who suggested that the report offered a central control agenda rather than an empowerment agenda. Other researchers were critical of the methodology describing it as 'quick and dirty' or considered that it was too easy to blame the researchers predominantly for problems that the authors had acknowledged needed to be addressed by all stakeholders. Furthermore, some felt that the impact of research was greater than that described in the report but not recognised where it was implicit rather than explicit. An example of this is when teacher educators refer to teaching practices without making specific reference to the research that has informed them.

Funders, users and some researchers welcomed it. Goldstein (2000) agreed with the thrust of some of the conclusions while damning the evidence from which they were drawn. Swann and Pratt acknowledged the importance of the issues it raised and, while not agreeing with it, noted that far from criticising educational researchers it highlighted the failings of policy-makers to make good use of research. The Department for Education and Employment drew up an action plan to address each of the recommendations in the report. The subsequent Department for Education and Skills (DfES) research strategy reflected further developments of this action plan.

The wider international context should be acknowledged. Furlong and White (2002) have undertaken a review of current educational research capacity in Wales commissioned by the Universities Council for the Education of Teachers (Cymru). The National Research Council in the USA published a study (Shavelson and Towne, 2001) to examine and clarify the nature of scientific inquiry in education and how the federal government can best foster and support it. The Scottish Educational Research Association (Kirkwood, 2002) is considering how best to encourage further developments of a research strategy for Scotland. Many of the issues identified in the Hillage *et al.* review, and reflected in the DfES's research strategy, are noted in all these reports and are in no sense unique to England.

DEVELOPING A GOVERNMENT RESEARCH STRATEGY

The review of educational research identified two underlying themes which needed to be addressed: better use of the current evidence base and greater investment in a high-quality evidence base for the future. Each of the components in the research strategy contribute to one or both of these overarching aims. The DfES research budget has more than doubled since 1997 and one-third of the expenditure in 2001–02 was invested in strategic, longer-term initiatives some of which are described in this chapter, with the remaining two-thirds spent on individual research projects.

Elsewhere in this book, Thomas and Harden and Bell, Bolam and Cubillo address the major initiative in the government strategy for promoting systematic reviews. This is both investing in the future evidence base and making better use of current evidence. In particular, it is aimed at ensuring that policy-makers and practitioners can draw on synthesised, quality-assured findings rather than be potentially misled by using a single study. The chapter by Cordingley addresses another strand in the strategy, that of developing evidence-informed practice in the teaching profession and the role of the National Teacher Research Panel. Hence, this chapter focuses on other aspects of the government's strategy including developing dedicated research centres, longitudinal studies, the work of the National Educational Research Forum and initiatives contributing to improving the dissemination and impact of research.

DEVELOPING DEDICATED RESEARCH CENTRES

The Hillage *et al.* review identified the need for research centres of excellence. Consultation suggested that concentrating more resources in a few centres based in single institutions would contribute little to the development of research capacity. Hence it was decided to invest in 'dedicated' research centres, dedicated in their focus on a particular area, but cross-institutional and interdisciplinary, drawing on the key researchers in a given field wherever they are based. These centres involve collaborative teams of researchers from different disciplines and institutions working on a longer-term research programme for three to five years.

Dedicated research centres enable sustained work in priority areas to establish better quality evidence and continuity. A sustained programme of research also enables theoretical advances to develop alongside shorter-term practical and evaluative research. Research capacity can be built through the different disciplines working together and thereby extending their skills, and through studentships and attachments. The centres provide a focal point for information and discussion for other researchers, ministers, civil servants and practitioners, encouraging debate, challenge and greater mutual understanding of the issues. The investment involved in these centres is considerable and each has a three-year contract renewable for a further two years.

Two dedicated research centres began work in 2000. The first is focused on the wider benefits of learning and is directed by Professor John Bynner and Professor Andy Green at the Institute of Education, and Professor Tom Schuller at Birkbeck College, University of London. It is researching the non-economic benefits that learning brings to the individual learner and to society as a whole. The overall programme covers health, ageing, family and parenting, crime, citizenship and participation, and leisure and lifestyle. It is undertaking methodological work on models and measures that have been used to assess the social benefits of learning alongside data analysis on indicators of social cohesion and quality of life. For example, one recent research report (Bynner *et al.*, 2001) noted that when controlled for earlier family circumstances and educational achievement, individuals who improve their basic skills suffer less from poor health and are more likely to be active citizens.

The second centre focuses on the economics of education and is directed by Professor Steve Machin at the London School of Economics. It also involves the Institute for Fiscal Studies and the Institute of Education, bringing together researchers from economics, education and other social sciences. A major strand of this centre's work is on the methodological challenge of developing cost-effectiveness measures of educational interventions. The areas of research include the production and supply of education and skills, the demand for education and skills, and the returns to education and skills. One project looked at participation in post-compulsory education and found that it is unlikely to increase further without marked improvement in examination results or major increases in youth unemployment as a result of an economic recession. Further analysis revealed that while prior attainment strongly determined the level of qualification attained, the type of qualification was more likely to be influenced by family characteristics and regional conditions. Another project is looking at the effects of lifelong learning on future income and employment experiences.

A third centre that began its work in 2001 focuses on information and communication technology (ICT). It is directed by Professor Steve Molyneux at the University of Wolverhampton in association with the Learning Lab, a not-for-profit centre (funded by a number of information technology [IT] and telecom companies). This centre is looking at the impact of levels and type of access to ICT on social and educational inclusion, initially for adult learners.

A fourth centre, the National Research and Development Centre for Adult Literacy and Numeracy, has been established as part of the Adult Basic Skills Strategy to develop the knowledge base on how to improve literacy and numeracy and the impact of this on individuals and the economy. It involves a consortium led by the Institute of Education, University of London, together with other universities including Sheffield. It is funded by the DfES's Adult Basic Skills Strategy Unit.

The Learning and Skills Development Agency, which is independent of the government, has established a National Research Centre for Learning and Skills. This was a response to concerns that further education, adult and community learning are underresearched. The new Learning and Skills Research Centre will help address the gaps in knowledge and strengthen the evidence base.

These centres concentrate funding on an area of interest but not on a small number of institutions, since each involves a team from across institutions and disciplines. They are promoting interdisciplinary work which is needed to address more complex issues. They are also providing the opportunity for policy-makers and ministers to gain more immediate access to ongoing findings. Winch

(2001) warns of the dangers of giving the sponsors what it is they want to hear in order to increase the chances of influencing and being consulted in the future. He notes the opposite extreme of failing to understand and acknowledge views that extend beyond the researcher's own ideals by remaining 'excessively true to oneself' (Winch, 2001, p. 450). It is too early to judge how the researchers in the centres will handle this particular balance in the closer relationship that they develop with the sponsor than tends to occur in traditional research projects.

GREATER INVESTMENT IN LONGITUDINAL STUDIES

The Department's research programme was supporting ten longitudinal studies in 2001–02. Major developments have taken place in three areas, two new cohort studies and collaboration in a longitudinal study of ageing. Plans are under way to launch a major new longitudinal survey of 14–21-year-olds which will bring together in one study previously separate proposals for surveys of young people, young ethnic minorities and potential entrants to higher education. The project is seen as a successor to the current Youth Cohort Survey.

The Millennium Cohort, led by the Economic and Social Research Council (ESRC), is a new longitudinal study to which the DfES is contributing. The main fieldwork commenced in autumn 2000, surveying 20,000 babies born between July 2000 and June 2001. Other government departments and the Office for National Statistics are also co-funding this. The study will provide a vital comparison sample for the evaluation of Sure Start (a major new programme for early intervention).

The DfES is currently contributing to the English Longitudinal Study of Ageing, which is also supported by other government departments. The study covers a broad range of topics, all interrelated and relevant to an understanding of the ageing process. The Office for National Statistics is undertaking the study on behalf of the sponsoring departments.

These longer-term studies provide an opportunity for more proactive research questions to be addressed and for complex issues that may be misinterpreted through shorter-term perspectives to be researched. Again, the sustained focus on a given area should enable researchers to develop their theoretical understanding of these issues alongside generating research findings for shorter-term application. The Department is continuing to provide collaborative funding for other longitudinal studies, including the major birth cohort and household studies.

However, there is a serious shortage of researchers with the appropriate skills and techniques to interrogate these databases which are underdeveloped (Gorard, 2001). In order to improve the use of these databases and invest in future longitudinal studies the capacity of researchers needs to be addressed. The Economic and Social Research Council initiative on capacity building led by Stephen Gorard as part of the major research programme on teaching and learning provides an important opportunity for this to happen. Similarly, the government, and to a lesser extent other funders, invest substantially in international comparative studies such as the Third International Mathematics and Science Study (TIMSS), but more could be done to interrogate these data in a variety of ways that might inform policy and practice.

DEVELOPING A FRAMEWORK FOR RESEARCH: THE NATIONAL EDUCATIONAL RESEARCH FORUM

The remit of the National Educational Research Forum is to provide strategic direction for educational research in England and to raise the quality, profile and impact of educational research. Its key objective is to develop a national framework within which a more coherent, better quality and relevant research programme in education can develop.

Set up by the DfES in response to Hillage *et al.* in September 1999, the chair was appointed by the Secretary of State and members by an independent panel following open advertisement. In 2002 it has 19 members including two teachers and one teacher's organisation representative. It is chaired by Sir Michael Peckham, previously Director of the School of Public Policy at University College, London, a key contributor to the development of the National Health Service research and development strategy. Five subgroups focusing on priorities, funding, capacity, quality and impact consulted literature, unpublished reports and expert witnesses to inform its first consultation document.

The Forum published a consultation document in November 2000 (NERF, 2000) outlining possible components of a strategy. It invited individuals, institutions and organisations from within the UK and overseas to contribute actively and imaginatively with suggestions, analyses and ideas. Over 100 responses to the consultation were received and analysed. Two national consultation conferences were held and meetings took place with specific groups who were underrepresented in the responses, such as parents and employers. The draft strategy was welcomed by funders, many educational and professional organisations, individual teachers and parents and government departments. Researchers, however, were more mixed in their responses.

In the light of comments given through the consultation process, both positive and negative, the Forum redrafted and published its strategy document in September 2001 (NERF, 2001). These proposals received wide-ranging support. The proposals include establishing a priorities group, a dedicated education foresight, setting up a funders' forum, improving research capacity, reviewing research training opportunities and improving the knowledge base and access to it.

DEVELOPING LONGER-TERM PRIORITIES IN EDUCATION

The Forum is establishing an education priorities group to develop a methodology and criteria for setting priorities for research and development in education. This group will advise the National Educational Research Forum on priority issues in education and its output will form part of the information made available to research funders, researchers and other interests. Professor Charles Desforges, a member of the Forum and author of the opening chapter of this book, will chair the priorities group and membership will reflect the range of constituencies in education.

The Forum will establish an Education Observatory to examine current and emergent developments as well as medium and longer-term trends likely to shape the future. The Observatory will assume responsibility for taking forward the Foresight proposals outlined in the strategy document. The outputs of the Observatory will inform the activities of the Education Priorities Group and the Forum.

Education needs a dedicated Observatory/Foresight exercise to enable it to be prepared to shape future changes. Its focus will be the learning society, placing learning at its centre wherever it takes place, be that an institution, the home or a workplace. It will look at the national and international context, and at formal and informal learning. It will consider differences in class, gender and race, and will ensure that differentiation is made between different social groups. It also needs to be focused on the role that research can play in helping us be prepared for the future, and in informing us as to what we need to know. The Forum has synthesised the outcomes of other Foresight exercises such as those that have focused on health care and technology so as to complement rather than duplicate them.

ADVISORY PANELS

The DfES set up research advisory panels following other attempts to widen the participation in research priorities (such as open advertisements in the press). There are three panels addressing early years and schooling, education and skills for 14–19-year-olds and higher education, workforce development and skills. On each panel are leading researchers and research analysts. The purpose of the panels is to advise the department about priority areas for research and discuss the latest research evidence drawing out the implications for future work. Feedback from the meetings held to date suggested that it would be appropriate to extend their role to include identifying priorities and shaping the research programme, helping to develop research specifications through literature reviews and advisory work on methodology, peer reviewing tenders and reports, and undertaking and discussing reviews of evidence in key current topic areas.

IMPROVING ACCESS TO CURRENT EVIDENCE

The Hillage *et al.* report and others (e.g. Edwards, 2000; Pring, 2000) have identified the need for greater accessibility to research. Edwards notes that researchers want their work to be noticed and very few do not even wish to be useful. He also acknowledges that busy people should be able to find 'crisp summaries written in plain English'. Many writers refer to the role of mediators such as local education authority advisory staff or teacher educators in transmitting research findings to practitioners. The government strategy has included a number of initiatives designed to improve the relationship between research, policy and practice, including ensuring research findings are more accessible to more people who might want them in a variety of formats.

CURRENT EDUCATIONAL RESEARCH IN THE UK

Hillage *et al.* noted that educational research and development was insufficiently based on existing knowledge. Policy-makers, practitioners and researchers complained of the lack of access to comprehensive databases of current and published research. Current Educational Research in the UK (CERUK) is a freely available database developed by a partnership between the National Foundation for Educational Research (NFER) and the centre known as EPPI which is responsible for developing systematic reviews (see the chapter by Thomas and Harden). Current Educational Research in the UK links closely with the comprehensive databases of educational research and reviews that are being developed by the EPPI-Centre.

It holds information on educational research projects which are being undertaken in the UK covering pre-school, school, further education (FE), higher education (HE), adult, lifelong and continuing education. It was launched in September 2001 and has been warmly welcomed. The DfES makes it a requirement of their research contracts that details are logged onto the database, and other funders are considering doing the same. It is an attempt to ensure that funders, researchers and users can access what is going on and that related projects can assist one another rather than wasting resources through unintended overlap.

RESEARCH ON THE WEB

The Centre for the Use of Research and Evidence in Education (CUREE) is contracted to summarise research findings on the Standards Site of the DfES web site. They identify research and quality assure it with particular consumers in mind, for example, local education authority staff, teachers, lecturers and parents. Part of the work will be seeking to ensure that these groups are able to feed in their priority areas of research. Research is summarised in three to four pages, giving further sources. Around 25 such summaries will be lodged on the site each year. Comments will be invited via the site and once the site is launched in the autumn, there may be areas that generate sufficient interest to set up discussion fora.

The General Teaching Council (GTC) has adopted a 'pedagogical' model of research dissemination called *Research of the month* which interrogates research on behalf of practitioners. For each topic, a team from the Centre for Using Research and Evidence in Education has reviewed, selected and summarised one or more published research studies. Each topic is presented and structured according to a series of questions that the GTC has designed to bring out the messages for teachers and teaching. Findings are illustrated by high-quality case studies. The review criteria for selecting studies cover the readability and relevance of research as well as its ethical integrity and methodological quality.

THE IMPACT OF RESEARCH ON POLICY AND PRACTICE

The subgroup of the Forum (NERF, 2000) that addressed impact, distinguished clearly between dissemination and impact. Most existing activity could better be described as dissemination than impact, and assumed rather than planned. There are a number of research studies that have had a clear impact on policy and in the longer term may be expected to influence practice. However, there are areas that are not well served by good-quality research evidence, where research is inconclusive or in which the research evidence is not easily accessible. These factors may contribute to policies for which underlying research cannot easily be linked. There are other studies such as the work on pupil mobility (Dobson and Henthorne, 1999) which provide rich data but where the issues are highly complex and policy implications are conflicting, making it more difficult to ensure appropriate action is taken. There is much progress to be made in developing the willingness and capacity of policy-makers to use evidence. Both Edwards (2000) and Mortimore and Mortimore (1999) review educational research that has influenced policy and/or practice, and that which has had limited impact. Some examples are provided here for illustrative purposes of research that has informed policy over the last few years.

THE IMPACT OF RESEARCH ON PRIMARY TO SECONDARY SCHOOL TRANSFER AND TEACHING AND LEARNING FOR 11–14-YEAR-OLDS

The review of research and practice on transition and transfer (Galton, Gray and Rudduck, 1999) noted the poor progress made by pupils in Years 7 and 8 (aged 11–13 years) and the drop in motivation that appears to contribute to this. The research evidence has informed policy and practice at national, local education authority and school levels. Nationally, the DfES introduced common transfer forms to ensure all schools receive minimum basic information to enable them to build on pupils' previous standards. The Qualifications and Curriculum Authority developed 'bridging units' which are pieces of work that pupils begin in Year 6 in the primary school and complete in their new school in Year 7, and more recently a wider range of transition units has been developed by the DfES to encourage smoother transfer. The second stage of the Galton, Gray and Rudduck research is an intervention programme in which local education authorities and schools that have volunteered to do so are introducing specific strategies, and outcomes are being carefully monitored.

The main impact of the transition and transfer study was that it informed the National Key Stage 3 Strategy for 11–14-year-olds. Together with international evidence on the middle years of schooling, it informed the teacher development programme. Evidence from studies and reviews of the effectiveness of approaches incorporating thinking skills (McGuinness, 1999) and assessment for learning (Black and Wiliam, 1998; Wiliam and Lee, 2001, often referred to as formative assessment) which demonstrated raised standards, increased motivation, pupil engagement and management of their own learning, further informed this strategy. In autumn 2000, the strategy was introduced as a pilot, targeted at those teaching 11–14-year-olds and included subject training, literacy and numeracy across the curriculum, assessment for learning and thinking skills. The strategy is being independently evaluated by a consortium of researchers from the universities of Bath, London and Melbourne.

Further support for this work was provided through revisions to the National Curriculum in 2000 including thinking skills in the general requirements, published schemes of work and development of resources. Thinking skills and assessment for learning were also prioritised in the guidelines for applicants for Best Practice Research Scholarships and encouraged in the Beacon School policy as a means of schools in receipt of extra resourcing working on these skills with teachers in other schools. The schools in the University of Newcastle school-based research consortium funded by the Teacher Training Agency worked on development of thinking skills with encouraging results (see, for example, McGrane, 2000).

Other areas in which research evidence has had an impact on policy, and in some cases practice, include that on the evaluation of the national literacy and numeracy strategies, school governors, the provision of study support, the evaluation of the Beacon School policy, citizenship and the strategy for continuing professional development of teachers.

What have we learned from these examples about the characteristics of research that has informed policy? Evidence appears to be used earlier in the policy-making process when there is a perceived need to tackle a real problem, where this problem can be clarified with customers and when policy-makers are supported in identifying the appropriate questions. There needs to be evidence which has some clear messages and is summarised and accessible. Timing enables evidence to be used when it is needed, if necessary by giving the emerging findings to date with whatever warnings are necessary that further analysis may change the picture. Not all areas of policy can be informed by evidence if the evidence is not available or exists but is inconclusive.

QUALITY ASSURANCE

The two main methods of quality-assuring research are through peer review of publications and the RAE. Both provide mechanisms that involve peer review but also potentially act as barriers to research influencing policy and practice mainly by requiring a reporting style which is less accessible to practitioners or policy-makers.

The RAE is the main mechanism by which research quality is assessed and funding allocated. Researchers submit a selection of their 'best' publications (in terms of international, academic excellence) to an education subject panel. In the Hillage *et al.* review concerns were raised that researchers find this process conflicts with the demand to disseminate research in ways that might impact on policy and practice. Prior to the 2001 RAE, a task force report recommended to the chair of the education panel that a quarter of the members should be users of research, in particular, teachers. This recommendation was partly implemented, although only one of the four users was a teacher. A second recommendation was that greater emphasis be placed on the impact of research on policy and practice. The criteria were revised to recognise curriculum, teaching and assessment material where justified by the underlying research. The criteria also suggested that the quality of research will often be demonstrated through its influence on other researchers, policy-makers and practitioners. These changes are significant in providing the basis for high-quality, relevant and practical research to be credited.

Journals operate publication policies through peer review. It is the main mechanism for assessing the quality of research and given the focus of the research assessment exercise on published papers in academic journals, of subsequent funding allocations. The quality and consistency of peer review has been debated for many years internationally and in every discipline. The National Educational Research Forum has hosted two education journal editors' conferences and included colleagues from Scotland and Wales. Lively debate took place on the role of editors, the quality of manuscripts submitted, issues relating to peer review and the impact of the RAE on publishing.

CONCLUSION

Returning to Blunkett's ESRC speech quoted in the introduction to this chapter, are government decisions informed by evidence? In a pamphlet by Jake Chapman (2002) about the importance of using systems analysis in policy-making, he suggests that the civil service is judged by failure. It is this he states, that leads to the inevitable distortion of information at every level because no one wishes to communicate bad news or to expose themselves to blame. The modernising government agenda has begun to challenge this culture. Changing cultures is slow and hard, and there are few incentives to complicate the task of policy-making further by grappling with unclear messages from research. However, developments in electronic communication, media and, at a much earlier stage of development, the use of systematic reviews make it possible for the evidence base or lack of it to be challenged. As Winch (2001) has noted, the public and political perception of education is that it is of practical relevance and will therefore be judged on its ability to say something relevant. Researchers have a moral obligation, he claims, to ensure that they do not drop their standards of research to meet these requirements.

The developments described in this chapter are aimed at ensuring that the evidence is both available and accessible. Further progress will need to be made on improving the access to currently available 'best' evidence through systematic reviewing and ensuring this is supported and recognised. The capacity of policy-makers to access and use research involves developing a greater demand for, understanding of and opportunities to participate in research.

This involves culture changes at every level which are beginning to occur but have further to go. Policy-makers need to 'value' the role of evidence. Teachers and parents need to look beyond their own schools for evidence and expect policy-makers to be informed by it. Funders need to plan for dissemination and impact requirements of research funding. Researchers need to be rewarded for appropriate achievements relating to informing policy and practice in assessments of research.

REFERENCES

Atkinson, E. (2000) In defence of ideas, or why 'What Works' is not enough, *British Journal of Sociology of Education*, Vol. 21, pp. 317–30.

Black, P. and Wiliam, D. (1998) *Inside the Black Box: Raising Standards through Classroom Assessment*, London: King's College.

Blunkett, D. (2000) *Influence or Irrelevance: Can Social Science Improve Government?* Secretary of State's ESRC Lecture, 2 February, London: DfEE.

Bynner, J., McIntosh, S., Vignoles, A., Dearden, L., Reed, H. and Van Reenen, J. (2001) *Improving Adult Basic Skills: Benefits to the Individual and to Society*, London: DfEE.

Chapman, J. (2002) *System Failure: Why Governments Must Learn to Think Differently*, London: DEMOS.

Davies, H., Nutley, S. and Smith, P. (eds) (2000) *What Works: Evidence-Based Policy and Practice in Public Services*, Bristol: Policy Press.

Dobson, J. and Henthorne, K. (1999) *Pupil Mobility in Schools*, London: DfEE.

Edwards, T. (2000) *Some Reasonable Expectations of Educational Research*, UCET Research Paper No 2, London: Universities Council for the Education for Teachers.

Furlong, J. (1998) Educational research: meeting the challenge, inaugural lecture, University of Bristol.

Furlong, J. and White, P. (2002) *Educational Research Capacity in Wales*, Cardiff: School of Social Sciences, Cardiff University.

Galton, M., Gray, J. and Rudduck, J. (1999) *The Impact of School Transitions and Transfers on Pupil Progress and Attainment*, London: DfEE.

Goldstein, H. (2000) 'Excellence in research on schools' – a commentary, at www.ioe.ac.uk/hgoldstn

Gorard, S. (2001) *A Changing Climate for Educational Research? The Role of Research Capability Building*, Occasional Paper Series, Paper 45, Cardiff: Cardiff University/ESRC.

Gray, J. (1998) The contribution of educational research to the cause of school improvement, professorial lecture, Institute of Education, University of London, 29 April.

Hargreaves, D. (1994) *The Mosaic of Learning: Schools and Teachers for the Next Century*, London: DEMOS.

Hargreaves, D. (1996) Teaching as a research-based profession: possibilities and prospects, The Teacher Training Agency Annual Lecture 1996.

Hillage, J., Pearson, R., Anderson, A. and Tamkin, P. (1998) *Excellence in Research on Schools*, London: DfEE.

Kirkwood, M. (2002) Educational research in Scotland: policy context and key issues, *Research Intelligence*, Vol. 79, pp. 33–40.

McGrane, J. (2000) *It's All in the Mind: Teachers*, London: DfEE.

McGuinness, C. (1999) *From Thinking Skills to Thinking Classrooms: A Review and Evaluation of Approaches for Developing Pupils' Thinking*, London: DfEE.

Mortimore, P. and Mortimore, J. (1999) Does educational research influence policy or practice? in Abbott, I. (ed.) *The Future of Education Research*, London: Falmer.

National Educational Research Forum (NERF) (2000) *The Impact of Educational Research on Policy and Practice*, Subgroup report, London: NERF; and at www.nerf-uk.org

National Educational Research Forum (NERF) (2001) *A Research and Development Strategy for Education: Developing Quality and Diversity*, London: NERF; and at www.nerf-uk.org

Nutley, S. and Webb, J. (2002) Evidence and the policy process, in Davies, H., Nutley, S. and Smith, P. (eds) *What Works: Evidence-Based Policy and Practice in Public Services*. Bristol: Policy Press.

Pring, R. (2000) *Philosophy of Educational Research*, London and New York: Continuum.

Rudduck, J. and McIntyre, D. (eds) (1998) *Challenges for Educational Research*, London: Paul Chapman Publishing.

Shavelson, R. and Towne, L. (2001) *Scientific Inquiry in Education*, report of the National Research Council, Washington: National Academy Press.

Swann, J. and Pratt, J. (1999) *Improving Education: Realist Approaches to Method and Research*, London and New York: Cassell.

Tooley, J. and Darby, D. (1998) *Educational Research: A Critique*, London: OFSTED, HMSO.

Wiliam, D. and Lee, C. (2001) Teachers developing assessment for learning: impact on student achievement, paper presented to the annual BERA conference, University of Leeds, September.

Winch, C. (2001) Accountability and relevance in educational research, *Journal of Philosophy of Education*, Vol. 35, pp. 443–59.

3

Systematic Reviews: How are they Different from What We Already Do?

PHILIP DAVIES

INTRODUCTION

Systematic reviews of existing research literature are increasingly being used in social science and in public policy-making. The sheer number of existing studies in most substantive areas of social science and public policy, coupled with the rapid growth of access to knowledge and information as a result of information technology, make it almost impossible for social scientists, public policy analysts, and people who use social and political science, to keep abreast of the research literature in any one area. Eddy, Hasselbad and Shachter (1992) have estimated that in the area of health care the average physician would have to read 19 journal articles a day, 365 days of the year, just to keep up to date with the existing evidence in the medical literature. Whilst comparable estimates have not been made in the field of education, it would almost certainly be of a magnitude that is beyond the available time and energies of teachers, educational managers and educational researchers. Moreover, given the limitations of a human's information processing abilities, the complexity of modern professional life almost certainly exceeds the capacity of the *unaided* human mind (Eddy, Hasselbad and Shachter, 1992). Systematic reviews provide one such aid.

The problems of information overload are compounded by the fact that not all research and information is of equal value. Variations in the quality of primary studies, reporting practices, standards of journal editing and publication criteria mean that the existing research literature is of variable quality. Non-uniform practices in indexing research reports also means that studies of differing quality and focus may be identified and retrieved by electronic searching and information processing mechanisms. Consequently, seemingly similar studies may be of varying quality, focus and relevance to users of social science research. Some way of differentiating between good and bad studies, as well as relevant and irrelevant work, is required. Systematic review methodology can provide such a mechanism for differentiating the available research evidence.

A further problem with harnessing the existing research evidence is that single studies usually illuminate only one part of a policy or practice issue. Moreover, such studies are by their nature sample specific, time specific and context specific, which makes it difficult to establish the generalisability and transferability of their findings. A related criticism is that educational research fails the policy-making and broader educational community by the non-cumulative nature of its findings (Hargreaves, 1996; 1997; Hillage *et al.*, 1998; Tooley and Darby, 1998). Systematic reviews provide a more cumulative view of existing research by 'attempt[ing] to discover the consistencies and account[ing] for the variability in similar-appearing studies' (Cooper and Hedges, 1994, p. 4). In turn, this implies that 'seeking generalisations also involves seeking the limits and modifiers of generalisations' (ibid., p. 4) and, thereby, identifying the contextual specificity of available research and evidence.

This is the case for having, and doing, systematic reviews of research evidence. This chapter asks the question: how does this differ from what we already do? It may be that for many researchers and users of evidence, the answer to this question is 'very little, if anything'. The fact that systematic review methodology has been around for at least three decades (or by some accounts three centuries (Chalmers and Tröhler, 2000)), and that there are many educational researchers who are very familiar with the principles and procedures of research synthesis, means that systematic reviews may offer the research and research-user communities very little that is different from what is already common practice. For those less familiar with systematic review methodology, this chapter seeks to identify what it can offer the educational and wider social scientific research community.

TYPES OF RESEARCH SYNTHESIS

Narrative reviews

Research synthesis is the collective term for the family of methods for summarising, integrating and, where possible, accumulating the findings of different studies on a topic or research question. The simplest form of research synthesis is the traditional qualitative literature review, often referred to as the *narrative review*. In its simplest form, the narrative review attempts to identify what has been written on a subject or topic, using which methodologies, on what samples or populations and with what findings. Narrative reviews may provide an overview and summary of research on a topic, and identify the range and diversity of the available literature, much of which will be inconclusive. Narrative reviews are also undertaken in order to find a gap which new research might attempt to fill.

A major limitation of narrative reviews is that they are almost always *selective* in that they do not involve a *systematic, rigorous and exhaustive* search of *all* the relevant literature using electronic and print media as well as hand-searching and ways of identifying the 'grey' literature. The latter is very important given the accumulating evidence (Dickersin, 1997; Rosenthal, 1979;

Smith 1980; Sterling, 1959; Sterling, Rosenbaum and Weinkam, 1995) of publication bias favouring studies with positive outcomes. Narrative literature reviews are also often *opportunistic* in that they review only literature and evidence that is readily available to the researcher (the file-drawer phenomenon). Some narrative reviews may discard studies that use methodologies in which the researcher has little or no interest. Alternatively, they may include studies that use different methodologies and which do not lend themselves to meaningful comparison or aggregation. Narrative reviews often provide few details of the procedures by which the reviewed literature has been identified and appraised. It is also often unclear how the conclusions of narrative reviews follow from the evidence presented. This lack of transparency makes it difficult to determine the selection bias and publication bias of narrative reviews, and runs the risk of overestimating (or in some cases underestimating) the effectiveness of interventions in ways that are hard to identify.

Systematic reviews are different from narrative reviews in that they attempt to deal with all of these limitations. The problems of selection bias and publication bias are dealt with by systematic reviews identifying and critically appraising *all* of the available research literature, published and unpublished. This involves detailed hand-searching of journals, textbooks and conference proceedings, as well as exhaustive electronic searching of the existing research literature. Systematic reviews are also different in that they make explicit the search procedures for identifying the available literature, and the procedures by which this literature is critically appraised and interpreted. This affords a degree of transparency by which other researchers, readers and users of systematic reviews can determine what evidence has been reviewed, how it has been critically appraised, and how it has been interpreted and presented. This, in turn, allows for other interpretations of the evidence to be generated, and for additional studies of comparable quality to be added to the review, if and when they become available. In these ways, an interactive and cumulative body of sound evidence can be developed.

Vote-counting reviews

A type of research synthesis that attempts to be cumulative is the *vote-counting review*. This attempts to accumulate the results of a collection of relevant studies by counting 'how many results are statistically significant in one direction, how many are neutral (i.e. "no effect"), and how many are statistically significant in the other direction' (Cook *et al.*, 1992, p. 4). The category that has the most counts, or votes, is taken to represent the modal or typical finding, thereby indicating the most effective means of intervention.

An obvious problem with vote-counting reviews is that they do not take into account the fact that some studies are methodologically superior to others and, consequently, deserve special weighting. Systematic reviews are different from vote-counting reviews in that they differentiate between studies with greater and lesser size, power and precision. Weights are given:

to reflect the amount of information that each trial contains. In practice the weights are often the inverse of the variance (the square of the standard error) of the treatment effect, which related closely to sample size. The precision (confidence interval) and statistical significance of the overall estimate are also calculated. It is also possible to weight additionally by study quality, although this is not generally recommended.

(Deeks, Altman and Bradburn, 2001, p. 286)

Another problem with vote-counting reviews, as Cook, Altman and Bradburn (1992, p. 4) point out, is that they fail to indicate 'the possibility that a treatment might have different consequences under different conditions'. Crude counting of studies in terms of the direction of outcomes does not take into account that 'person and setting factors are especially likely to moderate causal relationships and help explain why a treatment has the effects it does' (ibid., p. 22). Systematic reviews attempt to incorporate such contextual factors by interpreting the findings of studies and identifying their implications for policy and practice. The importance of going beyond crude quantification was recognised by Donald T. Campbell (after whom the Campbell Collaboration is named), who suggested that: '[There is] the mistaken belief that quantitative measures replace qualitative knowledge. Instead, qualitative knowing is absolutely essential as a prerequisite for quantification in any science. Without competence at the qualitative level, one's computer printout is misleading or meaningless' (Campbell, 1984, p. 141). Later in the same paper Campbell advises that: 'To rule out plausible rival hypotheses we need situation-specific wisdom. The lack of this knowledge (whether it be called ethnography, or programme history, or gossip) makes us incompetent estimators of programme impacts, turning out conclusions that are not only wrong, but are often wrong in socially destructive ways' (ibid., p. 142).

Meta-analysis

Meta-analysis is a type of systematic review that aggregates the findings of comparable studies and 'combines the individual study treatment effects into a "pooled" treatment effect for all studies combined, and/or for specific subgroups of studies or patients, and makes statistical inferences' (Morton, 1999, p. 3). The statistical basis of meta-analysis can be traced back to seventeenth-century astronomy, which suggested 'that combinations of data might be better than attempts to choose amongst them' (Egger, Davey Smith and O'Rourke, 2001, p. 8). More recently, the term 'meta-analysis' has been commonly attributed to Gene Glass (1976) who used the term to refer to 'the statistical analysis of a large collection of analysis results from individual studies for the purpose of integrating the findings'. In the two decades or more since Glass's original meta-analytic work on psychotherapy (Smith, Glass and Miller, 1980) and class size (Glass *et al.*, 1982; Smith and Glass, 1980), meta-analysis has developed considerably in terms of the range and sophistication of data-pooling and statistical analysis of independent studies (see Kulik and Kulik, 1989; Cook *et al.*, 1992; Cooper and Hedges, 1994; and Egger, Davey Smith and Altman, 2001 for more detailed accounts of these developments).

Meta-analysis differs from traditional narrative reviews of evidence by combining the results of single studies and measuring the likely effects of intervention across studies, based on large aggregate samples. Meta-analysis is perhaps best known for combining the results of randomised controlled trials, though as Egger, Davey Smith and Schneider (2001, p. 211) point out, they are also commonly undertaken on non-randomised data from studies that use case-control, cross-sectional and cohort designs. Non-randomised studies, however, are much more susceptible to the influence of confounding factors and bias and 'may produce estimates of association that deviate from the underlying effect in ways that may systematically differ from chance' (Egger, Davey Smith and O'Rourke 2001, p. 9). Combining non-randomised studies will therefore 'provide spuriously precise, but biased, estimates of association' (ibid., p. 9).

Meta-analysis of randomised controlled trials, on the other hand, assumes that each individual trial provides an unbiased estimate of the effects of an experimental intervention, and that any variability of results between studies can be attributed to random variation. Consequently, by combining the results of randomised controlled trials an overall effect of the intervention can be estimated that is unbiased and has measurable precision.

Meta-analysis of randomised controlled trial data, however, has its own limitations. Like other types of research synthesis it requires focused questions to be asked about the intervention(s) under investigation, the population (or subgroups) studied and the outcomes that are being assessed. Given that each of these variables may be different across individual studies, this presents a challenge for the meta-analyst to ensure that there is real consistency between primary studies on all three dimensions. The heterogeneity of samples, research questions asked and outcomes measured raises the 'apples and pears' question of comparability of different primary studies (Slavin, 1984). Random-effects models are used where meta-analysts believe that the primary studies are 'different from one another in ways too complex to capture by a few simple study characteristics' (Cooper and Hedges, 1994, p. 526). Where there is greater homogeneity between primary studies fixed-effects models of meta-analysis may be used. For further discussion of random-effects and fixed-effects models of meta-analysis see Hedges (1994), Raudenbusch (1994) and Deeks, Altman and Bradburn (2001).

Meta-analysis is also limited by the degree of systematic and comprehensive searching that is undertaken for relevant and appropriate primary studies. Extensive, if not exhaustive, searches are required of databases, textbooks, journals, conference proceedings, dissertation abstracts and research in progress, using electronic and hand-searching methods. The need to search unpublished sources (including research in progress) is crucial given the problems of positive (and in some cases negative) publication bias in journals and other print sources.

Meta-analysis is also limited by the independence, data quality and adequacy of statistical reporting in primary studies. The independence of primary studies refers to the possibility that one study may be reported more than once in the research literature, and that different subgroups from a single study may be reported on in different papers. This can lead to the results of individual studies being included more than once in a meta-analysis, and a problem of double-counting effect size. Good meta-analysts will ensure that this is not done, but the reader should be aware of this potential problem.

The quality of data reporting also presents difficulties for meta-analyses. The failure to report follow-up data in a way that is consistent with baseline data is one problem. Another problem occurs where studies do not report, or account for, participants lost to follow up at different data collection points. The problem may be very significant where there is a high lost-to-follow-up rate, and reporting of this is minimal, of those participants who drop out of the primary study. These may be the very people in whom the study (or meta-analysis) is interested, such as non-attenders in school truancy studies, problem drinkers in studies of alcoholism treatment or recidivists in criminological intervention studies. Missing data on moderator and mediating variables also present problems and limitations for meta-analysis (Cooper and Hedges, 1994).

The adequacy of statistical reporting in primary studies is also variable. Different studies use different descriptive and inferential statistics. Some use only means and standard deviations; others use chi-squares, odds ratio and confidence intervals. Measures of dispersion are sometimes not included in research reports with measures of central tendency, which limits the statistical and practical usefulness of the findings. The use of different types of statistical manipulation, such as logarithmic transformations of data, is also very variable and may not be reported in any great detail. The validity and reliability of tests and outcome measures may also be variable and not reported. As Cook *et al.* (1992) point out, there are several ways in which problems of inadequate statistical reporting can be handled by meta-analysts. These include the use of external sources to establish the validity and reliability of instruments used in primary studies, contacting the primary investigator(s) to obtain additional data or clarification of procedures used, and reporting deficiencies of primary data in the meta-analysis, thereby distinguishing between good and poor data.

All these problem need to be confronted and resolved by meta-analysts in order to provide unbiased estimates of the overall likely effects of an intervention and greater precision than that given by narrative or vote-counting reviews.

Best evidence synthesis

Slavin (1984; 1986) has criticised meta-analysis for not always being selective enough in terms of the methodological quality of studies that are included in reviews. Slavin characterises meta-analysis as using 'exhaustive inclusion followed by statistical tests' and of 'including all studies that meet broad standards in terms of independent and dependent variables, avoiding any judgement of quality' (Slavin, 1986, p. 6). This is done, says Slavin, in order to avoid the reviewer's own subjective biases entering decisions about which studies are 'good' and which are 'bad'.

In contrast to this, Slavin suggests 'best evidence synthesis', whereby 'reviewers apply consistent, well justified, and clearly stated a priori inclusion criteria' (ibid., p. 6) of studies to be reviewed. Slavin suggests some guiding principles for choosing a priori criteria, including that primary studies should be germane to the issue at hand, should be based on a study design that minimises bias and should have external validity. By germane, Slavin means that:

> a meta-analysis focusing on school achievement as a dependent measure must explicitly describe what is meant by school achievement and must only include studies that measured what is commonly understood by school achievement on individual assessments, not swimming, tennis, block stacking, time-on-task, task completion rate, group productivity, attitudes, or other measures perhaps related to but not identical with student academic achievement.
>
> (Slavin, 1986, p. 6)

By study design that minimises bias Slavin acknowledges that where 'the independent variable is strongly correlated with academic ability, motivation, and many other factors that go into a decision to, for example, promote or retain a student ... random assignment to experimental or control groups is essential' (ibid., p. 7). In other contexts, however, where the independent variable is less correlated with dependent variables, says Slavin, 'then random assignment, though still desirable, may be less essential' (ibid., p. 7).

By external validity, Slavin calls for outcome variables that have some 'real life' educational significance rather that 'extremely brief laboratory studies or other highly artificial experiments' (ibid., p. 7). This underlines Slavin's concern about the use of diverse measures of educational activities and outcomes, many of which are only remotely related to what is commonly understood by school achievement.

Slavin's 'best evidence syntheses' have been criticised by meta-analysts such as Kulik and Kulik (1989) on the grounds that they 'usually cover relatively few studies', and that they involve 'analyst biases' (Kulik and Kulik, 1989, p. 255). This tension between the statistical benefits of exhaustive inclusion and a large number of primary studies on the one hand, and high-quality reviews of fewer studies using more selective methodological criteria of inclusion and exclusion, is a recurrent theme in systematic review methodology.

In the decade and a half since Slavin's proposal for best evidence synthesis, many of the quality criteria that he called for – i.e. explicit a priori criteria, exhaustive literature searches of published and unpublished studies, listings of included and excluded studies with the reasons for doing so and the study characteristics, transparency of reviewers' procedures and conclusions – have become common practice in systematic reviews and meta-analyses. Also, statistical procedures have been developed to test for the heterogeneity and homogeneity of primary studies (Cooper and Hedges, 1994; Deeks, Altman and Bradburn, 2001), thereby accommodating the problem of combining unlike studies in inappropriate ways (the 'apples and pears' problem). These quality control procedures are central requirements of the systematic reviews that appear in the Cochrane Library of health care interventions, and in the developing Campbell Collaboration's Library of interventions in education, criminal justice and social work.

More recently Slavin and Fashola have presented a review of 'proven and promising programs for America's schools', which uses a rather more pragmatic notion of best evidence synthesis. They noted that:

> Ideally, programs emphasised in this book would be those that present rigorous evaluation evidence in comparison and control groups showing significant and lasting impacts on the achievement of students placed at risk, have active dissemination programs that have implemented the program in many schools serving at-risk students, and have evidence of effectiveness in dissemination sites, ideally from studies conducted by third parties. To require all of these conditions would limit this review to very few programs. To include a much broader range of programs, we had to compromise on one or more criteria.
>
> (Slavin and Fashola, 1998, p. 10)

Some studies are included in this review even though Slavin and Fashola had reservations about some aspects of the primary studies in question. They note, for instance, that the comparison groups used in Mehan et al.'s (1996) AVID project may be susceptible to bias, yet they conclude that 'the college enrollment rates for AVID are impressive, and the program has a good track record in serving students throughout the United States, and for these reasons is worthy of consideration by other schools serving many students places at risk' (Slavin and Fashola, 1998, p. 87). The inclusion of an excellent study such as the AVID project in a major (though not necessarily systematic) review of programmes for American schools may not meet with the approval of some meta-analysts. This study, however, provides valuable evidence not only of what seems to work in terms of promoting the college enrolment of low achieving students with good academic potential, but also good qualitative evidence from case studies, interviews with students and teachers, and ethnographic research, of *why* and *how* the AVID programme succeeds, and has limitations. The synthesis of good qualitative research is less developed than that of controlled experiments, but is attracting considerable attention from researchers interested in evidence-based policy and practice in education and other areas of public services.

Meta-ethnography and synthesis of qualitative research

Meta-ethnography attempts to summarise and synthesise the findings of qualitative studies, especially ethnographies and interpretive studies. It is embedded in the interpretive paradigm of social scientific research and claims to 'be interpretive rather than aggregative' (Noblit and Hare, 1988, p. 11). Noblit and Hare define the interpretive paradigm as:

> research that is termed ethnographic, interactive, qualitative, naturalistic, herma-neutic, or phenomenological. All these types of research are interpretive in that they seek an explanation for social or cultural events based upon the perspectives and experiences of the people being studied. In this way, all interpretive research is 'grounded' in the everyday lives of people.
>
> (Noblit and Hare, 1988, p. 12)

Like meta-analysis, meta-ethnography 'seeks to go beyond single accounts' (Noblit and Hare, 1988, p. 13), but instead of doing so by aggregating samples and identifying consistencies and variability between different studies, it does this by 'constructing interpretations, not analyses' and by revealing 'the analogies between the accounts' (ibid.). Meta-ethnography, say Noblit and Hare, 'reduces the accounts while preserving the sense of the account through the selection of key metaphors and organizers' (ibid.). In an attempt to clarify this, Noblit and Hare suggest that 'when we talk about the key metaphors of a study, we are referring to what others may call themes, perspectives, organizers, and/or con-cepts revealed by qualitative studies' (ibid., p. 14). To this extent, meta-ethnography would appear to have more in common with narrative reviews than with vote-counting systematic reviews, meta-analyses or best evidence synthesis.

Meta-ethnography has some of the same problems as meta-analysis and other types of research synthesis, such as establishing criteria for which studies to include and exclude in a meta-ethnographic review. This is possibly even more difficult with qualitative research in that there seems to be even greater diversity than with quantitative studies in terms of the questions being asked and the theoretical perspectives from which these questions are generated. In other words, the heterogeneity of primary studies may be greater with quali-tative research than is the case with quantitative primary studies.

From an interpretive perspective, meta-ethnography also has a problem of balancing summary statements of qualitative studies with their contextual speci-ficity. Notwithstanding the point made by Noblit and Hare that meta-ethnography is 'interpretive rather than aggregative', there have been attempts by qualitative researchers and meta-ethnographers to 'venture towards achieving more general conclusions from the ethnographic specifics of the separate cases' (Wax, 1979, p. 1). These attempts at aggregation, however, have 'avoided a full exploration of context and did not enable an explanatory synthesis' (Noblit and Hare, 1988, p. 21). Instead, the authors of these attempts at aggregation of qualitative studies complain that they ignore the 'meaning in context' and the ethnographic uniqueness' that is so central to ethnographic and qualitative inquiry.

From the more positivistic perspective of meta-analysis, meta-ethnography is seen as being limited by its inability to provide statistical accumulation of findings, its inability to allow prediction or to specify any degree of confidence about qualitative findings, and by its inability to allow for the statistical control of bias. The apparent lack of any systematic way for meta-ethnography and other types of synthesis of qualitative research to test for, and control, the heterogeneity/homogeneity of different studies, also concerns meta-analysts and those more disposed to quantitative approaches to research synthesis. These concerns and limitations, however, are somewhat cross-paradigmatic and seem to miss the point of what ethnographies and other qualitative studies are trying to achieve (Davies, 2000).

Work is currently under way in the UK to determine quality criteria for qualitative research, and to develop a framework for the critical appraisal of qualitative research studies (Cabinet Office, 2003). Procedures for undertaking systematic reviews of different types of evidence have been developed (EPPI-Centre, 2001), and methods for synthesising qualitative research are being developed (Oakley, Gough and Harden, 2002).

RAPID EVIDENCE ASSESSMENTS

One of the frequent criticisms of systematic reviews is that they take a long time to complete (between six months and one year), and that users of reviews require evidence more rapidly. Establishing an evidence base in any subject does take time, and building up a body of sound evidence is a lengthy process. The rewards for doing so, in terms of having ready access to valid, reliable and relevant review evidence, can take years, and possibly decades, rather than months. In the meantime, it is reasonable for users of research evidence to have some idea of what the existing evidence is telling us, and what gaps remain in the research on some topic or question.

To this end, rapid evidence assessments are being developed in education and other areas of public policy. Rapid evidence assessments are appraisals of existing evidence that sit somewhere between the equivalent of health technology assessments (HTAs) and fully developed systematic reviews in the field of health care. Health technology assessments are descriptive rather than analytical abstracts of health-care interventions that have not been critically appraised and fully evaluated according to systematic review procedures. Nonetheless, they include 'evidence of clinical outcomes relative to no treatment and/or the best existing treatment for the condition in question, including undesirable side-effects and, (for chronic conditions) effects of stopping treatment' (NHS Executive, 1999). In addition, HTAs include estimates of the impact on quality and length of life, estimates of the average health improvement per treatment initiated, and net National Health Service (NHS) costs associated with this health gain. Information is also usually available on other (non-NHS) costs and savings caused by the intervention, any significant differences between patients and subgroups of the population, and the expected total impact on NHS resources (including personnel resources). Health technology assessments typically take between eight and twelve weeks to assemble.

Whilst education and other areas of policy and practice are clearly different from health care, there are parallels that are worth developing in terms of generating structured descriptive appraisals of what works, how, for whom, with what potential negative effects, and at what costs and benefits. Rapid evidence assessments will collate descriptive abstracts of the available evidence in education and other areas of public policy, and will provide an overview of what that evidence is telling us and what is missing from it. They will consist of fairly comprehensive electronic searches of appropriate databases, and some searching of print materials, but not the exhaustive database searching, hand-searching of journals and textbooks or searches of the grey literature that go into systematic reviews. The evidence that goes into rapid evidence assessments will be critically appraised and studies of different quality will be sifted.

It is anticipated that rapid evidence assessment will be completed and available in less than eight to twelve weeks, though this will depend on the topic under investigation, the available evidence and the available resources to review, appraise and summarise the evidence. Rapid evidence assessments will carry a caveat that their conclusions may be subject to revision once the more systematic and comprehensive review of the evidence has been completed. This is consistent with the important principle that systematic reviews are only as good as their most recent updating and revision allows.

SYSTEMATIC REVIEWS AND EDUCATION

Systematic reviews have a distinguished record in educational research. Indeed, it is in educational research that systematic reviews had their origins (Glass and Smith, 1979; Glass et al. 1982; Smith and Glass, 1980) and have been developed extensively over the past two decades (Hedges and Stock, 1983; Kulik and Kulik, 1989; Lipsey and Wilson, 1993). Kulik and Kulik (1989) have reviewed some 150 meta-analyses of educational interventions, and Lipsey and Wilson (1993) have reviewed 302 meta-analyses of psychological, educational and behavioural interventions, two-thirds of which were in education. These systematic reviews covered a wide range of substantive topics, subject areas, methods of teaching and learning, types of school and class organisation, different students and learners, stages of education, and measures of educational outcome and achievement (Davies, Holmes and Woolf, 2000).

The Campbell Collaboration (http://www.campbellcollaboration.org), prepares, maintains and disseminates systematic reviews of the effectiveness of interventions in education, as well as in crime and justice, and in social welfare. Many educational research groups around the world contribute to the Campbell Collaboration's Education Sub-Group, including (in the UK) the Department for Education and Skills (DfES) Centre for Evidence-Informed Policy and Practice at the University of London, Institute of Education. In the field of medical and professional education, there is a growing interest in systematic reviews. Organisations such as Best Evidence Medical Education (BEME) and Association of Medical Education in Europe (AMEE) are leading the way in terms of providing and disseminating high-quality reviews of medical and professional education.

A number of problems remain in developing and using systematic reviews in education. As has already been noted, research synthesis methods are less developed for non-experimental studies than for experimental and quasi-experimental research. This is a problem for education given the prominence of qualitative and non-experimental research in this area, though the contribution of experimental and quasi-experimental research in education is also considerable (Lipsey and Wilson, 1993; Petrosino *et al.*, 2002). The work currently under way for determining the quality of qualitative research (Cabinet Office, 2003), and for synthesising qualitative research evidence (Oakley, Gough and Harden, 2002) and other types of evidence (EPPI-Centre, 2001), will make the synthesis of a broad range of educational research more viable.

Systematic reviews in education also need to be helpful and meaningful to users. This requires them to address questions that are specific enough to be answerable, yet broad enough to be of use to teachers, policy-makers, planners, managers and school governors, as well as parents, teachers and those who use educational services. They must also be expressed in ways that are intelligible to users, which may require translating findings from statistical and analytical terms (e.g. standard deviation units, odds ratio and measures of statistical significance) into measures that have 'real-life' significance (e.g. the number of students who will benefit from an educational intervention). Systematic reviews also need to be accessible to users via media that are valid, reliable and quality assured. The development of web sites, databases and electronic libraries such as those of the Campbell Collaboration, the DfES EPPI-Centre and the Economic and Social Research Council's Evidence Network are making each of these requirements a reality.

Systematic reviews, then, are not necessarily different from what already takes place in educational research, policy and practice. What is different is that there is a growing recognition of the potential of systematic reviews for educational research, policy and practice, and that they must be *systematic*, critically appraised, valid, reliable, transparent, regularly updated and accessible to a wide range of users in ways that are intelligible and useful.

REFERENCES

Campbell, D.T. (1984) Can we be scientific in applied social science, in Conner, R.F., Altman, D.G. and Jackson, C. (eds) *Evaluation Studies, Review Annual, Vol 9*, Beverly Hills, CA: Sage. Reprinted as Legacies of logical positivism and beyond, in Campbell, D.T. and Russo, M.J., *Social Experimentation*, Thousand Oaks, CA: Sage.

Cabinet Office (2003) The quality of qualitative research, research project commissioned by the Strategy Unit, Cabinet Office, being carried out by the National Centre for Social Research, London, Cabinet Office.

Chalmers, I. and Tröhler, U. (2000) Helping physicians to keep abreast of the medical literature: medical and philosophical commentaries, 1773–1795, *Annals of Internal Medicine*, Vol. 133, pp. 238–43.

Cook, T.D., Cooper, H., Cordray, D.S., Hartmann, H., Light, R.J., Louis, T.A. and Mosteller, F. (1992) *Meta-Analysis for Explanation*, New York: Russell Sage Foundation.

Cooper, H. and Hedges, L.V. (eds) (1994) *The Handbook of Research Synthesis*, New York: Russell Sage Foundation.

Davies, P.T. (2000) Qualitative research methods in evidence-based policy and practice, in Davies, H.T.O., Nutley, S.M. and Smith, P.C. (eds) *Evidence and Public Policy*, Bristol: Policy Press (forthcoming).

Davies, P.T., Holmes, E. and Wolf, F. (2000) An organisational framework for preparing and maintaining systematic reviews in education, paper presented at the Inaugural Meeting of the Campbell Collaboration, Philadelphia, PA, 25–26 February.

Deeks, J.J., Altman, D.G. and Bradburn, M.J. (2001) Statistical methods for examining heterogeneity and combining results from several studies in meta-analysis, in Egger, M., Davey Smith, G. and Altman, D.G. (eds) *Systematic Reviews in Health Care: Meta-Analysis in Context*, London: BMJ Publishing Group.

Dickersin, K. (1997) How important is publication bias? A synthesis of available data, *AIDS Education Prevention*, Vol. 9, pp. 15–21.

Eddy, D.M., Hasselbad, V. and Shachter R.D. (1992) *Meta-Analysis By The Confidence Profile Method: The Statistical Synthesis of Evidence*, Boston, London: Academic Press.

Egger, M., Davey Smith, G. and Altman, D.G. (eds) (2001) *Systematic Reviews in Health Care: Meta-Analysis in Context*, London: BMJ Publishing Group.

Egger, M., Davey Smith, G. and O'Rourke, K. (2001) Rationale, potentials, and promise of systematic reviews, in Egger, M., Davey Smith, G. and Altman, D.G. (eds) *Systematic Reviews in Health Care: Meta-Analysis in Context*, London: BMJ Publishing Group.

Egger, M., Davey Smith, G. and Schneider, M. (2001) Systematic reviews of observational studies, in Egger, M., Davey Smith, G. and Altman, D.G. (eds) *Systematic Reviews in Health Care: Meta-Analysis in Context*, London: BMJ Publishing Group.

EPPI-Centre (2001) *Review Group Manual, Version 1.1*, London: Institute of Education.

Glass, G.V. (1976) Primary, secondary and meta-analysis of research, *Educational Researcher*, Vol. 5, pp. 3–8.

Glass, G.V. and Smith, M.L. (1979) Meta-analysis of research on class size and achievement, *Educational Evaluation and Policy Analysis*, Vol. 1, pp. 2–16.

Glass, G.V., Cahen, L.S., Smith, M.L. and Filby, N.N. (1982) *School Class Size: Research and Policy*, Beverly Hills, CA: Sage.

Hargreaves, D.H. (1996) *Teaching as a Research-Based Profession: Possibilities and Prospects*, Teacher Training Agency Annual Lecture, London: TTA.

Hargreaves, D.H. (1997) In defence of research for evidence-based teaching: a rejoinder to Martyn Hammersley, *British Educational Research Journal*, Vol. 23, No. 4, pp. 405–19.

Hedges, L.V. (1994) Fixed effects models, in Cooper, H. and Hedges, L.V. (eds) *The Handbook of Research Synthesis*, New York: Russell Sage Foundation.

Hedges, L.V. and Stock, W. (1983) The effects of class size: an examination of rival hypotheses, *American Educational Research Journal*, Vol. 20, pp. 63–85.

Hillage, J., Pearson, R., Anderson, A. and Tamkin, P. (1998) *Excellence in Research on Schools: Research Report RR74*, Sudbury: DfEE Publications.

Kulik, J.A. and Kulik, C-L. C. (1989) Meta-analysis in education, *International Journal of Educational Research*, Vol. 13, pp. 221–340.

Lipsey, M.W. and Wilson, D.B. (1993) The efficacy of psychological, educational and behavioural treatment: confirmation from meta-analysis, *American Psychologist*, Vol. 48, No. 12, pp. 1181–209.

Mehan, H., Villanueva, T., Hubbard, L. and Lintz, A. (1996) *Constructing School Success: The Consequences of Untracking Low-Achieving Students*, Cambridge: Cambridge University Press.

Morton, S. (1999) Systematic reviews and meta-analysis, workshop materials on Evidence-Based Health Care, University of California, San Diego, La Jolla, CA Extended Studies and Public Programs.

NHS Executive (1999) *Faster Access to Modern Treatment: How NICE Appraisal Will Work*, Leeds: National Health Service Executive.

Noblit, G.W. and Hare, R.D. (1988) *Meta-Ethnography: Synthesizing Qualitative Studies*, Newbury Park, CA: Sage.

Oakley, A., Gough, D. and Harden, A. (2002) (personal communication) Quality standards for systematic synthesis of qualitative research, research project, EPPI-Centre, Institute of Education, University of London.

Petrosino, A.J., Boruch, R., Rounding, C., McDonald, S. and Chalmers, I. (2002) *A Social, Psychchological, Educational & Criminological Trials Register (SPECTR)*, Philadelphia, PA: Campbell Collaboration (http://campbell.gse.upenn.edu).

Raudenbusch, S.W. (1994) Random effects models, in Cooper, H. and Hedges, L.V. (eds) *The Handbook of Research Synthesis*, New York: Russell Sage Foundation.

Rosenthal, R. (1979) The 'file drawer problem' and tolerance for null results, *Psychological Bulletin*, Vol. 86, pp. 638–41.

Slavin, R.E. (1984) Meta-analysis in education: how has it been used?, *Educational Researcher*, Vol. 13, pp. 6–15.

Slavin, R.E. (1986) Best evidence synthesis: an alternative to meta-analysis and traditional reviews, *Educational Researcher*, Vol. 15, pp. 5–11.

Slavin, R.E. and Fashola, O.S. (1998) *Show Me the Evidence! Proven and Promising Programs for American Schools*, Thousand Oaks, CA: Corwin Press.

Smith, M.L. (1980) Publication bias and meta-analysis, *Evaluation Education*, Vol. 4, pp. 22–4.

Smith, M.L. and Glass, G.V. (1980) Meta-analysis of research on class size and its relationship to attitudes and instruction, *American Educational Research Journal*, Vol. 17, pp. 419–33.

Smith, M.L., Glass, G.V. and Miller, T.I. (1980) *The Benefits of Psychotherapy*, Baltimore, MD: Johns Hopkins University Press.

Sterling, T.D. (1959) Publication decisions and their possible effects on inferences drawn from tests of significance – or vice versa, *Journal of the American Statistical Association*, Vol. 54, pp. 30–4.

Sterling, T.D., Rosenbaum, W.L. and Weinkam, J.J. (1995) Publication decisions revisited: the effect of the outcome of statisitical tests on the decision to publish and vice versa, *American Statistician*, Vol. 49, pp. 108–12.

Tooley, J, and Darby, D. (1998) *Educational Research: An Ofsted Critique*, London: OFSTED.

Wax, M. (1979) *Desegregated Schools: An Intimate Portrait Based on Five Ethnographic Studies*, Washington, DC: National Council of Education.

4

Practical Systems for Systematic Reviews of Research to Inform Policy and Practice in Education

JAMES THOMAS AND ANGELA HARDEN

There is a growing interest amongst those working in the field of education for finding ways of bridging the gap between research and policy and practice more effectively. Like other areas of public policy, this interest has gained momentum under the guise of 'evidence-informed' or 'evidence-based' policy and practice. As part of this, in 1999 the then Department for Education and Employment in England (now the Department for Education and Skills) provided resources for a programme of research and training to support evidence-informed policy and practice in education. This initiative is being co-ordinated by the Evidence for Policy and Practice Information and Co-ordinating Centre (the EPPI-Centre) at the Social Science Research Unit (SSRU) which is based at the Institute of Education, University of London. The EPPI-Centre is a centralised resource for people who wish to undertake and/or use the results of systematic reviews of research. Within education, the EPPI-Centre is currently supporting review groups to carry out systematic reviews in many different areas including: assessment; continuing professional development; early years; English; gender; inclusive education; leadership and management; modern foreign languages; post-compulsory education; and thinking skills.

This programme of work at the EPPI-Centre represents the first major UK resource for systematic review work exclusively within the field of education. It has built on programmes of systematic review work on 'social interventions' at the EPPI-Centre, SSRU and elsewhere (e.g. MacDonald, 1997; Oakley and Fullerton, 1996; Oliver and Peersman, 2001) and on the pioneering work of the Cochrane Collaboration[1] and other systematic review work within health care (e.g. Maynard and Chalmers, 1997; NHS Centre for Reviews and Dissemination, 2001). It is exploring ways of working collaboratively with the emerging international Campbell Collaboration, a sister organisation to the Cochrane Collaboration, set up to prepare, maintain and promote the accessibility of systematic reviews on the effects of social and educational practices (Davies and Boruch, 2001; Elbourne, Oakley and Gough, 2001).

This chapter aims to describe the practical systems the EPPI-Centre has set up for conducting systematic reviews in education and to reflect on our experiences of using these systems to support education review groups. It begins, however, by setting out the principles that underpin these systems.

UNDERLYING PRINCIPLES OF PRACTICAL SYSTEMS FOR SYSTEMATIC REVIEWS IN EDUCATION

The research, policy and practice relationship

We use the term 'evidence-informed policy and practice' to refer to the collective set of activities and methods which aim to get high-quality research evidence used for making decisions about policy and practice. The use of 'evidence-*informed*' rather than 'evidence-*based*' is a deliberate choice which reflects our view of a dynamic model of the relationship between research and policy and practice. Within this relationship we see the role of research as 'illuminative' rather than 'definitive'; and the role of the policy-maker or practitioner as one of translator or interpreter of research in a specific context for a particular purpose (Levačić and Glatter, 2001). This view also reflects the reality that research evidence will only be one of a number of resources drawn upon for making decisions (e.g. Davies, 1999; Oakley, 2000; Oliver and Peersman, 2001; Sackett *et al.*, 1996).

The central theme of the EPPI-Centre's work is that much research can have practical application, but at present the potential that this research has to inform policy and practice is not being realised. One of the main aims of the EPPI-Centre, therefore, is to promote the use of research evidence both in the classroom and in the formulation of future policy.

The need for research synthesis

Although much primary research in education addresses issues which concern particular policy and practice questions, selecting from this research to inform a particular decision can be problematic and time-consuming given the sheer quantity of literature from which to choose. Additionally, individual research studies can produce atypical, inconclusive or simply incorrect results and it is not always clear when this is the case. A reasonable solution would seem to be to have summaries or *syntheses* of the research evidence in a particular area readily accessible for practitioners and policy-makers to refer to as and when they are needed. Research syntheses facilitate the use of the full range of available knowledge. Summarising existing research captures another theme of the centre's work: that of building upon existing knowledge (see Figure 4.1). Education research has been criticised as being rather fragmented and not cumulative (DETYA, 2000; Hargreaves, 1996; http://www.nekia.org/pdf/harvey-speech.pdf; Rein, 1976). As well as enabling research to be accessible to a

Figure 4.1 Building upon existing knowledge

wider audience, the EPPI-Centre promotes the summarising of existing knowledge as an important first step before undertaking any new research. Knowing the extent of existing research helps to avoid fragmentation and duplication of effort and to identify research gaps.

The need for systematic research synthesis

Summaries of research have always been produced in the form of literature reviews. Traditionally, these introduce a topic, summarise the main issues and provide some illustrative examples. The type of reviews which the EPPI-Centre promotes are known as *systematic reviews*. These reviews differ from traditional literature reviews in a number of ways. When conducting a system atic review, reviewers aim to answer a specific question rather then summarising a topic area; they attempt to locate as much of all the existing relevant research as is possible; they assess all studies for their methodological quality as well as relevance; and they synthesise the findings of individual studies bringing their results together. The methods used to conduct these steps are documented to make them transparent for readers of the review. This last point enables readers to judge for themselves whether all the relevant studies have been found, whether less reliable studies have been treated appropriately and whether review authors have taken steps to reduce distortions or inaccuracies in their work. These issues, and the different stages in a systematic review are discussed in more detail in this chapter.

Diversity in systematic reviews

An important principle of the practical systems developed at the EPPI-Centre is to facilitate the production of different types of systematic reviews which can answer a range of relevant policy and practice questions. Within the topic of professional development of educational leaders for example, there will be a range of policy and practice questions to be addressed. These might be about what educational leaders need for professional development, the relative impact of different professional development activities or strategies, or about the barriers to implementing a professional development programme. These different questions are likely to be answered by different types of research. For example, a question about the effectiveness of a particular strategy requires research which evaluates that strategy in terms of whether positive or negative changes have occurred in relevant outcomes, whereas the question about need will require surveys of education leaders using structured questionnaires and/or in-depth interviews. Depending on the question, different methods for synthesising research findings in a systematic way are needed.

There has been a long tradition of synthesising systematically the findings of primary research on the effectiveness of interventions within education and the social sciences more generally (Oakley, 2000). Rosenthal (1991) traces early developments of statistical meta-analysis back to the 1940s (a technique for synthesising quantitative measures of the relationship between variables). The same author suggests that from the 1970s interest in the potential of the technique began to grow rapidly, following the publications of Glass and colleagues demonstrating the effectiveness of psychotherapy using statistical meta-analytic techniques (e.g. Glass, 1976). There is now a growing body of literature on methods for conducting this type of research synthesis in the social sciences and there are many examples of reviews using these techniques within education (e.g. Cooper and Hedges, 1994; Lipsey and Wilson, 1993).

In contrast, there has been relatively little attention to synthesis using non-statistical techniques which might be applicable to 'qualitative' research. This is an important gap since although this type of research is not best suited to answering questions about which educational methods lead to the best outcomes, it does answer a different set of questions which may be important for informing policy and practice. Davies (1999; 2000) outlines the following issues which are better addressed by 'qualitative' research: questions about the processes by which educational activities are undertaken; the meanings which education has for different people; and the consequences of education on sense of self and identity. A small amount of guidance on synthesising this type of research does exist (e.g. a guide to 'meta-ethnography' by Noblit and Hare, 1988) and examples of these kinds of syntheses are beginning to emerge in areas such as nursing research (e.g. Paterson et al., 2001) and in research on education for health promotion (e.g. Harden, Oakley and Oliver, 2001; Oliver et al., 2001). Thus, an important part of the work of the EPPI-Centre will be in trying to move forward the methods for the systematic synthesis of diverse types of research (Gough and Elbourne, 2002; Oakley and Oliver, 2001).

User involvement and collaborative working

The description of a teaching profession which sees no relevance in research and of an academic community writing articles largely for its own consumption (Hargreaves, 1996) is also an important influence on the work of the Centre. In order to ensure that the reviews do not suffer from the kind of dislocation described by Hargreaves, 'user' involvement is an important principle in systematic reviewing at the EPPI-Centre. Teachers are just one user community. A broad range of groups has a vested interest in education and, consequently, in what kind of educational research is undertaken and how research findings are shared and put to use. Other user communities that need to influence the work of the initiative include education managers and policy-makers in local and central government, users of education services (e.g. students, parents), education researchers and employers. Engaging a wide range of user communities to work collaboratively on a systematic review has the potential to produce better and more relevant research in the future.

Experiences from the health sector suggest that users can be involved in all stages of a systematic review (Oliver, 1997). Examples include identifying review topics, refining review questions, identifying salient outcomes, conducting reviews, editing final reviews and disseminating review findings. Working in collaboration with user communities rather than seeing their involvement as an 'add-on' appears to be critical for success.

A SYSTEM FOR FACILITATING EVIDENCE-INFORMED POLICY AND PRACTICE THROUGH SYSTEMATIC REVIEWS

There are two main components of the overarching structure at the EPPI-Centre for the promotion of systematic reviews in education (1) review groups whose members carry out and update one or more systematic reviews and (2) a co-ordinating research unit (the EPPI-Centre) that registers and facilitates the work of review groups and co-ordinates methodological and other develop mental work. In this section we describe, first, how review groups and the EPPI-Centre work together to produce systematic reviews and further develop the initiative, and then outline the process, methods and tools that review groups use to conduct systematic reviews. Throughout we will try to illustrate how the principles outlined above are put into practice.

A system for collaborative working amongst review groups and the EPPI-Centre

Like the Cochrane Collaboration, conducting systematic reviews in the EPPI-Centre initiative is done by groups of people called review groups. These are organised around different topic areas in education and members need to share a long-term commitment to the substantive issues within this topic area and to systematic reviewing as a means of obtaining reliable evidence. There is a formal registration process to become a review group which consists of a call for applications and a peer reviewed selection procedure. The call for applications follows a prior consultation process and a priority setting exercise which involves the key user groups outlined above.

Review group members need to be involved in the tasks of producing systematic reviews (e.g. determining review questions, searching and collecting relevant studies, extracting data from studies, writing reports and publications) and also in managing and sustaining the group in the longer term (e.g. co-ordinate the work of the group, raise funds, recruit new members, raise the profile of the group, co-ordinate and provide relevant training and peer refereeing of the group's work). Another key role for review groups is in reflecting on systematic review methods and the initiative as a whole to provide direction for future developments.

Each group has one or more individuals to take responsibility for overseeing the day-to-day work of the group as a whole (review group co-ordinators). The work of newly registered groups is largely linked to completing a first review. As a group develops and begins to produce more reviews, review group co-ordinators need to co-ordinate the production of subsequent reviews, ensuring that review protocols and completed reviews pass through a peer-refereeing system, providing training for undertaking reviews and assuring quality in the reviews of their group. The work for any one review can therefore be seen as a subset of the review group's activity as a whole. Not all members are necessarily involved in any one review, with some members taking responsibility for producing each individual review and others acting as supporters providing comments and advice on different stages of the review.

To maximise the relevance of systematic reviews that they produce, it is important that the review group has structures in place for the involvement of different kinds of research 'users' to allow different perspectives to inform and shape the review. The importance of user involvement is embedded in the requirements for registration as an EPPI-Centre review group. As part of the registration process, prospective review groups must indicate their plans for establishing and sustaining user involvement throughout the group's work, show that their membership will represent a wide variety of educational and research disciplines and interests, and show that they will have at least one current 'front-line' educational practitioner as an active review group member. In addition they must describe the processes that will be used to ensure that the perspectives of all the different groups have been taken into account.

As the co-ordinating centre, the EPPI-Centre and its team members provide a number of key support mechanisms to help review groups. A brief list of these is given in Figure 4.2.

It is important to emphasise that although a key role for the EPPI-Centre is to provide support for review groups, there is a 'two-way' process of learning

Access to the latest versions of EPPI-Centre tools to assist with the preparation of systematic reviews

Assurance of review quality

On-line software for review management and synthesis

Training in systematic review methods

Printed and on-line educational materials

Contact with experienced reviewers

Access to a specialised register of educational research

Supported participation in working groups

Dissemination of review

For more details see the *EPPI-Centre Review Groups Manual* (version 1.1) available on-line at http://eppi.ioe.ac.uk

Figure 4.2   Support available for review groups through the EPPI-Centre

and development. The systems described in this chapter are very much 'work in progress' and the experiences of using these for the first review groups in the initiative is being reflected on continually by those involved to identify strengths and weaknesses for further development. It is not just the systems that are being developed either; the initiative is very much about building capacity for systematic reviewing and collaborative working and dialogue amongst researchers and users of educational research. There are two main ways that the EPPI-Centre and review groups work together which illustrates this two-way process of learning and development. The first is review group workshops held at the EPPI-Centre at key stages of the review process facilitating the sharing of experiences across groups. The second is 'one-to-one' work between members of the EPPI-Centre team and review groups. This complements the cross-review group workshops and allows for more in-depth exploration of systematic review methods within the context of specific reviews.

A system for conducting systematic reviews

As we highlighted earlier, the EPPI-Centre initiative grew out of a desire to learn from the vast body of existing research in a manageable and practical way, building upon other initiatives and methodologies. This section outlines the system for conducting systematic reviews which is under development at the EPPI-Centre. In keeping with its mission as a centre to promote evidence-informed decision-making, the principles which underlie the system are based on pragmatic reasoning founded on research evidence and experience, rather than on any preconceived notion of the 'right' way of doing things.

In the same way that most primary research follows explicit methodologies in order to answer a particular question, systematic reviewing is a particular type of research requiring methodologies and systems to ensure that it gives reliable results and fulfils the principles outlined earlier. For example, some-one setting out to conduct primary research examining the effect of school climate on pupil behaviour will have a precise research question in mind, a specific population in which they are interested, methods for collecting data and a way of analysing the data in order to answer their question. Systematic review methodology consists of a set of steps with similar purposes, although they are adapted to meet the needs of a piece of secondary research.

One of the final stages of any piece of research is an examination of the data which have been collected and a decision about their ability to answer the ini-tial research question. The data upon which the results of a systematic review are based are found in primary research: the integrity of the primary research in a systematic review is therefore of key importance. All the steps and methods described below are designed to ensure that these data are as reliable and com-prehensive as possible. As well as aiding reliability, being systematic and explicit gives greater transparency and accountability than would otherwise be the case. At each stage of the review it should be clear which data have been found and which decisions have been taken. Accountability is particularly important in secondary research since this research builds upon the work of other people. They should be able to see clearly the way in which their work has been used and have enough information to understand the way in which their work has contributed to the review.

Figure 4.3 gives an overview of the discrete stages[2] involved in an EPPI-Centre systematic review in conjunction with EPPI-Centre tools and procedures.

Writing the protocol

The first stage in the process is writing a protocol. This can appear to be a dis-traction which delays the start of the 'real work', but time spent working on a protocol will be paid back in increased efficiency and clarity of purpose for the rest of the review. Systematic reviewing is usually a team effort, perhaps involving people working in different parts of the country and sometimes in different parts of the world. The activity of writing a protocol enables the team to develop a common understanding of the phenomenon being explored and a shared appreciation of the theory which underpins the review question. This is particularly important when 'specialist users' are involved in a review. They are likely to have a different perspective compared with researchers and

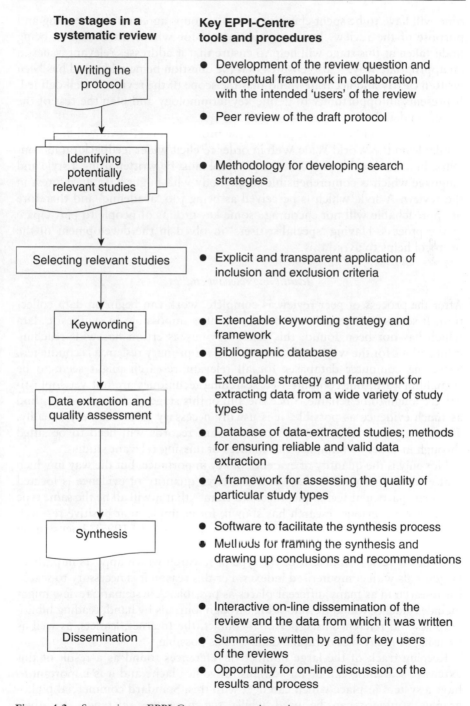

Figure 4.3   Stages in an EPPI-Centre systematic review

time will have to be spent checking that all groups agree on the meaning and purpose of the review. Involving the people for whom the review is being undertaken at this stage will help to ensure that it addresses relevant issues in an appropriate way. It also ensures that the question being addressed has been written clearly and accurately and that the scope of the review is well defined. It presents an opportunity to define key terminology and plan the rest of the review in detail.

As part of the EPPI-Centre process, the protocol is peer-reviewed and made available on the World Wide Web in order to elicit wider feedback on its contents. In order for this to work, the protocol must be written using a style and language which is comprehensible to anybody who might have an interest in the review. A style which is perceived as being too 'academic' and therefore unapproachable will not encourage some key groups of people to participate in the process. Having 'specialist users' involved in the development of the protocol helps to avoid this.

Identifying relevant studies

After the process of peer review is complete, work can begin on data collection. It seems unnecessary to state it, but it is impossible to synthesise data which has not been found; this fairly obvious assertion has wide-reaching implications for the way in which searching for primary research is conducted. Searching computer databases for all relevant research might seem to be straightforward, but computerised searching techniques are not yet sophisticated enough to be reliable. Since the aim of this stage of the review is to find as much evidence as possible, it is usually necessary to search very broadly. This means that large numbers of irrelevant records will need to be sifted through in order to minimise the chances of missing relevant studies.

Not only is the quantity of evidence of key importance, but the way in which that evidence is found is also vital. If a large quantity of evidence is located using one particular technique, there is a chance that it will all be the same type of evidence; previous research has shown, for example, that positive research results are more likely to be published (Dickersin *et al.*, 1997). Focusing on journal articles indexed in bibliographic databases risks skewing the conclusions of the review in favour of the type of research which appears in particular journals with computerised indexes. For this reason it is necessary to search for research in as many different places as possible. A systematic review might include evidence found from looking through journals by hand, reading bibliographies and reference lists, personal contact, the Internet, leaflets, as well as by using as many bibliographic databases as possible.

Keeping track of the large number of references found as a result of this extensive searching can be an administrative headache and it is important to have a system in place which can deal with this. Standard commercial bibliographic software can be used whilst screening the references for their relevance to the review question, but it is usually necessary to combine this with an efficient coding and filing system. The transparency of the review process is also aided by having a system which can demonstrate when and where references were found, and why and whether they were judged to be relevant to the review question.

After the large number of references has been sifted for relevance to the review question, the task of obtaining full reports for all the relevant research begins. Just as it is impossible to be sure that all potentially relevant evidence was located at the searching stage, so it is important to recognise that it may not be possible to obtain every article or report located in the search. Being transparent and open about what it was possible to do within set time constraints will show future users of the review where gaps in the evidence might be found.

Once the individual research reports have been obtained, the next set of tasks involve identifying the findings of each study and deciding which studies can be considered to have provided reliable findings. A coding and classification system is used at this point to categorise different types of research and to examine their quality. The classification system is presented as having three stages here but, for reviews with small numbers of studies, these stages can be condensed.

Keywording

First the reports are classified according to a 'keywording' system. The act of classifying research broadly using a standard system continues the process of identifying evidence to synthesise in a systematic and transparent way. The EPPI-Centre has a core keywording strategy which classifies research according to, for example, study type, topic focus, educational setting, population focus and type of intervention (where appropriate). This allows a broad map of the research to be drawn up allowing the review to focus on a particular subset of studies if the map is large. The research, which is classified according to this system, is entered into a electronic database and is available on-line for other people to use. Usually, a review will have a set of keywords in addition to the EPPI-Centre core strategy. These are used to focus the description of the range of research around the review question. Terms specific to a review can also be present at the next stage: data extraction and quality assessment.

Data extraction and quality assessment

This stage of the review moves on from describing research activity to looking at the kinds of research in detail and, in particular, at their findings. The EPPI-Centre has developed a tool for extracting data from primary research and to enable a reviewer to assess the methodological quality of the study according to certain criteria. It consists of a number of detailed questions which are selected depending on the research design of the study being examined.

Its broad areas include aims and type of study; study development, participation and dissemination; sampling, recruitment and description of the study participants; collection and analysis of data; quality of the study.

Data extraction and quality assessment is a time-consuming procedure and since the results of this form the data upon which the synthesis will be based, it is crucial that it is done as reliably and accurately as possible. It is at this point that judgements are made as to the quality of the research, so accuracy is equally important for reasons of accountability and fairness. To this end, at least two reviewers are always used to examine every piece of research. EPPI-Centre software enables people working on remote sites to enter their results onto a database and provides the reviewers with a report detailing areas of disagreement. Where definitions are unclear and consensus is lacking, discrepancies between reviewers' answers prompts discussion to clarify concepts and helps to ensure that data extraction across studies is done in a consistent way. The software also enables new sets of data extraction guidelines to be combined with existing guidelines. Having the ability to build on existing guidelines without losing the data extractions which have already been entered enables continual development of the guidelines to take place as well as facilitating the use of review-specific guidelines.

In addition to describing the research and its findings in detail, the data extraction process examines the methodology used to conduct the research. These data are used to examine the quality of the research. Based on existing consensus on critical appraisal within the context of research synthesis (e.g. Sackett et al., 1996; Slavin, 1986), the EPPI-Centre has two core principles for assessing the quality of research: that the research design is appropriate to the question being addressed and that the research design has been correctly applied in practice. For example, if a study sought to demonstrate that a particular programme had reduced a school's exclusion rate, but the evidence used to demonstrate the programme's effect was simply composed of asking people what might have happened if the programme had not been in place, one might conclude that the design of the study was incapable of answering the question. Similarly, if the report of a well-designed study stated that a significant amount of data had been lost, then the results of that study might be considered to be unreliable.

The issue of dealing with studies which might not be completely reliable is handled in different ways. Sometimes studies are required to meet a certain number of criteria in order for their findings to contribute to the conclusions of the review. In other cases the results of quality assessment are laid out for the readers to judge for themselves. Whichever method is applied, this is another important principle in the systematic review process: clear criteria for judging the quality of research must be used, and it should be possible for alternative syntheses to be produced using different criteria. Although it is possible that different conclusions might be reached if different criteria resulted in different studies being included, this is part of the transparency of the process and should be considered to be a methodological strength.

Previous research has shown that the use of different criteria for judging the methodological quality of studies does indeed lead to different conclusions (e.g. Peersman *et al.*, 1999).

Synthesising findings and drawing recommendations

The results of the data extraction and quality assessment are stored on a database called EPIC. Whilst data extraction and quality assessment are carried out on individual studies, the synthesis stage involves looking across studies and their findings in order to answer the review question. Synthesis involves displaying and analysing study findings according to a 'conceptual framework' usually outlined in the review protocol and driven by the review question(s). This framework might cover the way in which certain phenomena might relate to one another at a conceptual level or the way in which particular interactions work according to specific theoretical models. For example, for a review on the impact of strategies for the professional development of teachers, the synthesis could be constructed to examine how impact might vary according to different models of how professional development is thought to bring about benefit (e.g. collaborative strategies versus teachers working in isolation). When conducting a synthesis, the data contained in EPIC can be used in a number of ways and subgroups of studies can be analysed in isolation to others in the review. Whilst not a substitute for thought(!) or a clear rationale and framework for the synthesis, this enhances both the speed and range of the analysis, facilitating a review of greater depth and subtlety than might otherwise be possible in the time available.

There are two main ways to combine studies in a systematic review: quantitatively whereby the results of several studies are statistically pooled (e.g. statistical meta-analysis), or qualitatively where the results are summarised and integrated using words (e.g. narrative synthesis). There are merits and shortcomings associated with each, and they are not necessarily mutually exclusive (see Cooper and Hedges, 1994; Slavin, 1986). While narrative synthesis is appropriate for most types of research, for others it may also be possible to use statistical meta-analysis. Using the conceptual framework for the review and whichever method of synthesis is appropriate, the conclusions and recommendations are written in the light of the evidence found in the reliable studies contained in the synthesis. Recommendations are usually of two types: recommendations for policy and practice and recommendations for research.

Communicating review findings

The next stage is to draft the report of the review. The report is then sent out to peer referees who are asked to provide comments on its suitability for publication in the EPPI-Centre's Research Evidence in Education Library (REEL) (see below). Peer referees are asked to comment on the extent of user involvement in the review and its relevance to different user groups, whether the methods used in the review were appropriate, the clarity with which review methods and findings are reported and whether or not the authors acknowledge strengths and weaknesses of the review.

In addition to traditional printed media, the review is published on-line on REEL, accessible via the EPPI-Centre web site. The Research Evidence in Education Library presents the review report alongside the bibliographic database and its associated data extractions. It also includes a non-technical summary of the review and shorter summaries written by different types of users outlining their perspectives on the review and its findings.

Issues of transparency and accountability are aided by having the opportunity to view on-line reviews together with the data upon which they are based. Many users of reviews will not need to refer to the individual data extractions. However, where people have questions about the processes used in the review (the way conclusions regarding the quality of individual studies have been reached, for example), the availability of the 'raw data' on which the review is based may do much to explain why decisions have been made in a particular way. The systematic process does not prevent the conclusions and recommendations being influenced by the perspective of the individuals conducting the review, but it should ensure that these perspectives are made explicit and open to scrutiny. The Research Evidence in Education Library promotes a dialogue between readers of the reviews and review groups by enabling visitors to leave feedback. This feedback is published alongside the review, together with a response by the review group.

Updating the review

Keeping the data used in the production of a review in one place makes the production of updates to the review much less labour intensive. New searches must be run to find studies which were conducted or published after the initial searches, but the guidelines, framework for the synthesis and most data extractions are already in place. If the update is to be conducted by different reviewers, then their task will be aided by having the data for the review stored in a systematic and easily accessible way.

CONCLUSIONS

This chapter has described a major new initiative in the field of education, which is part of a larger move towards bridging the gaps between research, policy and practice within this field. In particular, we have illustrated the major elements in the EPPI-Centre systems for conducting systematic reviews. These systems combine the major advantages of ensuring rigour and transparency, the flexibility of being applicable to all forms of research question, including synthesis of qualitative interpretative data, and meaningful user involvement. The utility of these systems is demonstrated in the first systematic reviews addressing a range of research questions by EPPI-Centre review groups. These reviews provide a synthesis of reliable evidence for practical purposes.

The first EPPI-Centre reviews in education and their accompanying tools and databases are available on-line at http://eppi.ioe.ac.uk/reel/

NOTES

1. An international network committed to collating, critically appraising, synthesising and disseminating evidence on the effectiveness of health-care interventions.
2. In practice some stages overlap.

REFERENCES

Cooper, H. and Hedges, L. (1994) *The Handbook of Research Synthesis*, New York: Russell Sage Foundation.

Davies, P. (1999) Qualitative research methods in evidence-based policy and practice, in Davies, H. Nutley, S. and Smith, P. (eds) *What Works? Evidence-based Policy and Practice in Public Services*, Bristol: Policy Press.

Davies, P. (2000) The relevance of systematic reviews to educational policy and practice, *Oxford Review of Education*, Vol. 26, pp. 365–78.

Davies, P. and Boruch, R. (2001) The Campbell Collaboration. *British Medical Journal*, Vol. 323, pp. 294–5.

Department of Education, Training and Youth Affairs (DETYA) (2000) *The Impact of Educational Research*, Canberra: Department of Education, Training and Youth Affairs.

Dickersin, K., Chan, S., Chalmers, T. and Sacks, H. Jr (1987) Publication bias and clinical trials, *Controlled Clinical Trials*, Vol. 8, pp. 343–53.

Elbourne, D., Oakley, A. and Gough, D. (2001) Collaboration with the Campbell Collaboration (letter), *British Medical Journal*, Vol. 323, p. 1252.

Glass, G. (1976) Primary, secondary and meta-analysis of research, *Educational Research*, Vol. 5, pp. 3–8.

Gough, D. and Elbourne, D. (2002) Systematic research synthesis to inform policy, practice and democratic debate, *Social Policy and Society*, Vol. 1, pp. 225–36.

Harden, A., Oakley, A. and Oliver, S. (2001) Peer-delivered health promotion for young people: a systematic review of different study designs, *Health Education Journal*, Vol. 60, pp. 1–15.

Hargreaves, D. (1996) *Teaching as a Research-based Profession: Possibilities and Prospects*, Teacher Training Agency Annual Lecture, London: TTA.

Lovačić, R. and Glatter, R. (2001) Really good ideas? Developing evidence-informed policy and practice in educational leadership and management, *Educational Management and Administration*, Vol. 29, pp. 5–25.

Lipsey, M. and Wilson, D. (1993) The efficacy of psychological, educational and behavioural treatment: confirmation from meta-analysis, *American Psychologist*, Vol. 48, pp. 1181–209.

MacDonald, G. (1997) Social work: beyond control? in Maynard, A. and Chalmers, I. (eds) *Non-Random Reflections on Health Services Research*, London: BMJ Publishing Group.

Maynard, A. and Chalmers, I. (1997) *Non-Random Reflections on Health Services Research*, London: BMJ Publishing Group.

NHS Centre for Reviews and Dissemination (2001) *Undertaking Systematic Reviews of Research on Effectiveness: CRD's Guidance for Those Carrying Out or*

Commissioning Reviews (2nd Edition), York: NHS Centre for Reviews and Dissemination, University of York.

Noblit, G. and Hare, R. (1988) *Meta-Ethnography: Synthesizing Qualitative Studies*, London: Sage.

Oakley, A. (2000) *Experiments in Knowing: Gender and Method in the Social Sciences*, Cambridge: Polity Press.

Oakley, A. and Fullerton, D. (1996) The lamp-post of research: support or illumination? in Oakley, A. and Roberts, H. (eds) *Evaluating Social Interventions*, Ilford: Barnardos.

Oakley, A. and Oliver, S. (2001) Looking to the future: policies and opportunities for better health, in Oliver, S. and Peersman, G. (eds) *Using Research for Effective Health Promotion*, Buckingham: Open University Press.

Oliver, S. (1997) Exploring lay perspective on questions of effectiveness, in Maynard, A. and Chalmers, I. (eds) *Non-Random Reflections on Health Services Research*, London: BMJ Publishing Group.

Oliver, S. and Peersman, G. (2001) *Using Research for Effective Health Promotion*, Buckingham: Open University Press.

Oliver, S., Oakley, L., Lumley, J. and Waters, E. (2001) Smoking cessation programmes in pregnancy: systematically addressing development, implementation, women's concerns and effectiveness, *Health Education Journal*, Vol. 60, pp. 362–70.

Paterson, B., Thorne, S., Canam, C. and Jillings, C. (2001) *Meta-study of Qualitative Health Research: A Practical Guide to Meta-analysis and Meta-synthesis*, London: Sage.

Peersman, G., Harden, A., Oliver, S. and Oakley, A. (1999) Effectiveness reviews in health promotion: different methods, different recommendations, *Health Education Journal*, Vol. 58, pp. 192–202.

Rein, M. (1976) *Social Science and Public Policy*, Harmondsworth: Penguin Books.

Rosenthal, R. (1991) *Meta-analytic Procedures for Social Research*, London: Sage.

Sackett, D., Rosenberg, J., Muir Gray, R., Haynes, B. and Richardson, W. (1996) Evidence based medicine: what it is and what it isn't, *British Medical Journal*, Vol. 312, pp. 71–2.

Slavin, R.E. (1986) Best-evidence synthesis: an alternative to meta-analytical and traditional reviews, *Educational Researcher*, Vol. 9, pp. 5–11.

5

Developing Evidence-Informed Policy and Practice in Educational Leadership and Management: A Way Forward[1]

ROSALIND LEVAČIĆ AND RON GLATTER

INTRODUCTION

In the light of the current promotion of evidence-informed policy and practice (EIPP), we examine its potential in relation to educational leadership and management. We begin by considering what may be meant by the term and some of the issues to which it gives rise. We then look at some factors promoting and inhibiting the development of EIPP. Finally, and most importantly, we suggest a way forward for developing EIPP in educational leadership and management, including some ideas about the possible role of the British Educational Leadership, Management and Administration Society (BELMAS) in supporting an EIPP agenda.

Our general stance is that we see considerable potential in this approach, which is why in this chapter we go beyond a conceptual discussion to develop a set of proposals. Evidence-informed policy and practice is concerned, among other things, with the culture of the research community and the relationships of its members with policy-makers and practitioners (matters which have been central to BELMAS in the 30 years of its existence). It requires the creation of structures and practices that promote effective interaction between the three communities. This is not a simple task. Hence, we seek in what follows to be realistic and to take account of the context within which each community operates and the pressures to which it is subject.

EIPP IN CONTEXT

In order to assess the problems and possibilities of EIPP we need to be clearer as to what the term might mean. The word 'evidence' defines the term more narrowly than if 'knowledge' or 'research' were used instead. However, in public debate these three words tend to be used interchangeably. For instance, David Blunkett, the former Secretary of State for Education, in a lecture to an Economic and Social Research Council (ESRC) seminar affirmed his belief 'that having ready access to the *lessons learnt from high quality research* (emphasis added) can and must vastly improve the quality and sensitivity of the complex and often constrained decisions we, as politicians, have to make' (DfEE, 2000a). He stated that 'good, well-founded *evidence* (emphasis added) for key issues is needed' and proclaimed that the 'new Centre for Management and Policy Studies in the Cabinet Office is promoting practical strategies for *knowledge-based policy-making*' (emphasis added). At the same time, he endeavoured to appeal to the whole research community by also calling for 'blue-skies research which thinks the unthinkable'. This speech indicates well why we need to disentangle the term 'evidence-informed policy and practice' from the broader but clearly related issue of the value of research – in all its variety – to society. Evidence-informed policy and practice cannot be the only justification for social research nor can all social research fit into an EIPP framework.

Evidence-informed policy and practice presents the challenging aim that 'decision-making at every level can be done in the knowledge of the best possible evidence' (Sebba, 1999, p. 6). This contrasts with alternative sources of 'knowledge' upon which policy-making can be based. Davies (1999), for example, lists these as political ideology, conventional wisdom, folklore, wishful thinking and public-opinion formers using selective, unsystematic and biased research. Thus what counts as 'evidence' is crucial in defining EIPP and in staking it out as a terrain for particular researchers and their associated research methodologies. Hence EIPP is bound to be contested territory. Defined too narrowly it will have very little currency amongst educational researchers; defined too broadly it will collapse under the inability to agree on what counts as 'evidence'.

The recent shift in terminology from 'evidence-*based*' to 'evidence-*informed* policy and practice' seems important, for at least two reasons. The first relates to the conjectural and changing nature of knowledge (and hence evidence) and the fact that 'the relationship between knowledge production and knowledge use is problematical' (Pratt and Swann, 1999, p. 5). As Boyd (1998) argues, it may be simplistic to assume that the main contribution of research to policy is problem-solving by straightforwardly providing 'data for decisions' or clear evidence on 'what works'. Its more significant functions may be to illuminate and formulate problems and define alternatives.

The second reason for the importance of the shift concerns the nature of professionalism and policy-making. Central to both is the exercise of judgement and this requires appropriate 'space': 'The judgements that shape professional work involve applying the knowledge base to unique and particular circumstances' (Luntley, 2000, p. 8). In the same way '[p]olicy-makers translate evidence in the context of the policy process taking into account resource and political implications' (Sebba, 1999, p. 4).

Evidence-informed policy and practice thus consist of a set of interrelated processes involving various stakeholders by which research issues are selected, evidence on these collected, validated and communicated, and then used or ignored in decision-making by two key players – policy-makers and practitioners, though lay and client audiences may also have roles. Evidence-informed policy and practice corresponds closely to the 'knowledge chain' that consists of knowledge systems, knowledge creation, dissemination, absorption and application in decision-making and practice. Actual 'knowledge chains' involve the interaction of experts, intermediaries, managers and decision-makers, using data, information, and knowledge exchanged through a variety of media (ESRC, 1999).

A model of EIPP may help in distinguishing the key processes, their relationship to each other and the main stakeholders. This enables us to focus on the major components of EIPP and to locate problems and possibilities in relation to these. A model of EIPP applicable to education or other areas of social policy is depicted in Figure 5.1. Since EIPP is seen as an interconnected sequence of processes, where one breaks into the cycle is not particularly significant.

Research

Research is all the activities that generate research findings and conclusions. We need to distinguish two types of research that can inform practice: 'public-domain' research and 'private-domain' research.

- Public-domain research consists of investigations that aim to contribute to the accumulation of openly accessible knowledge. It is mainly undertaken by 'professional' researchers in universities and research institutes, although practitioners also contribute through part-time postgraduate study and subsequent active research.
- Private-domain research refers to institutionally based research undertaken mainly by practitioners into their own practice or that of groups of colleagues or their educational institution. It is intended for informing practice. Clearly action research is included within this category, though it also embraces other forms of research, for example institutional research into student and parental perceptions, such as the Scottish Office Education Department's school ethos indicators (SOED, 1992a; 1992b) and value-added analysis of student level test and examination data. The research is undertaken by practitioners or alternatively by consultants employed by them, such as providers of statistical analysis of institutional value added pupil performance data.

There is a tendency in the current debate on EIPP to associate it with public-domain research, as for example in discussions on forming a Campbell Collaboration for organising and disseminating peer reviews of public-domain research in education (Boruch, Petrosino and Chalmers, 1999). An important

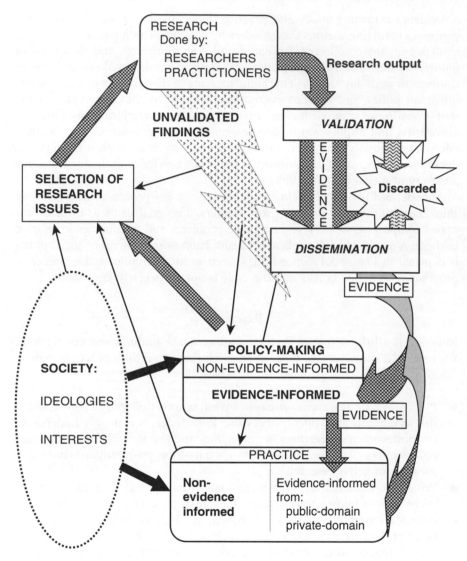

Figure 5.1 EIPP model

issue is whether the promotion of EIPP as referring to public-domain research will further promote the professionalisation of research with the attendant marginalisation of practitioner research (Anderson and Herr, 1999).

Validation

A key process in EIPP is the validation of research. This is the determination of what is good quality research and hence what findings and conclusions count as evidence. The different research paradigms are distinguished by the kinds of criteria they use to determine good-quality research, an important element of which is what counts as valid evidence. A crucial issue for EIPP in educational management is which research paradigms to include. Currently the most influential model of EIPP comes from health care, in particular the Cochrane Collaboration (www.cochrane.org) which organises, conducts and disseminates systematic reviews of research on health care interventions (Chalmers, Sackett and Silagy, 1997). Here the criteria for validating evidence are those required for valid evidence of causality derived from randomised controlled trials. Clearly, the issue for education – even more so for educational leadership and management – is how to develop and implement agreed criteria for validated evidence not only for non-randomised controlled trials (RCT) research using statistical analysis of observational data but also for qualitative research.

Validation criteria affect what research is undertaken and how it is conducted, as well as the peer evaluation of published research findings. One of the main planks of EIPP is improved validation through systematic reviews of the literature on given issues and the dissemination of syntheses of validated findings in ways appropriate for the particular stakeholders. The DfES funded Evidence for Policy and Practice Information Co-ordinating Centre (EPPI-Centre) in Education is (in 2002) supporting systematic reviews of ten issues in education (see www.ioe.ac.uk).

The EIPP model in action means that some research findings are not validated by the criteria employed by the EIPP community: the research is in effect designated as not of sufficiently high quality. Figure 5.1 depicts unvalidated research as being discarded. Such non-validation is clearly controversial, so 'unvalidated' research gets disseminated outside the EIPP system by members of the research community or the media who are sympathetic to the 'unvalidated' research. Hence 'unvalidated' research can influence policy and practice.

The validation process for private-domain research is much less public. However, its validation criteria are normally derived from public-domain research methods, even though they may be less formal and rigorous. Greater exposure of practitioners to EIPP relating to public-domain research is likely to feedback into the criteria used for judging the quality of institutional evidence that is used to inform practice.

Dissemination

The dissemination of validated research findings within and beyond the research community is the next crucial stage of EIPP. An important element of EIPP is the advocacy of far more replicatory research and of research that is cumulative as it builds on previous work. Peer organisation of systematic literature reviews enables evidence to be efficiently accumulated and disseminated, so that it can more readily be built upon. In education (as in other social sciences) placing greater emphasis on replicatory research and systematic review requires a change in what is valued by the research community (Apple, 1999). Funding bodies and academic journals tend to place much more value on 'original' research: research replicating previous studies is rare and that which reanalyses data from previous studies even rarer, particularly in qualitative research.

If evidence is to influence policy and practice it must be effectively disseminated to these audiences. This requires communicating findings at different levels of sophistication depending on the users' prior knowledge and available time. To influence these audiences, findings need to be communicated briefly in non-technical language, but still retaining the correct interpretation of the evidence. This can be particularly difficult when evidence is equivocal or applies to particular circumstances but not others. At the dissemination stage of EIPP some evidence is lost through poor communication and only part of it is actually received by policy-makers and practitioners. This is depicted in Figure 5.1 as a leakage of validated evidence into the discarded category.

Policy-making and practice

The next stage in the EIPP cycle is the influence of validated evidence on policy-making and practice. It is safe to assume that only a fraction of the validated evidence disseminated actually succeeds in influencing policy and practice. The EIPP model treats policy-making and practice as distinct spheres of activity. Policy-makers and practitioners seek to influence each other and both communities may use recourse to 'evidence' as part of these efforts. There is a substantial research literature on how policy is made and implemented (e.g. Ham and Hill, 1993; Weiss, 1991) and on professional practice which can help us to understand how evidence may or may not influence policy and practice (Eraut, 1994). Reports from the USA (National Research Council, 1999) and Australia (Selby Smith, 1999), concerned with the influence of education research on policy and practice, both reinforce the view discussed above, that it is more appropriate to aspire to evidence-informed rather than evidence-based policy and practice.

> It is seldom the case that a specific social problem is solved by a decision to use the results of a research study ... Knowledge use is more likely to be a process of 'enlightenment' that is gradual, indirect and interactive, characterized by incremental changes that aggregate over time to become significant structural and substantive changes. (National Research Council, 1999, p. 44)

Selby Smith (1999) in a study of the impact of vocational education and training research on decision-making makes a similar point, noting that the influence mainly occurs via affecting the climate of opinion. Both these reports stress the importance of building and maintaining linkages between the research community and policy-makers and practitioners, if policy and practice in education is to be more securely founded on a sound research base.

The EIPP model categorises policy-making as either evidence-informed or non-evidence-informed, though as the discussion above indicates, there is no rigid divide between the two. For the purposes of the EIPP model, successfully disseminated validated evidence influences policy-making and hence practice via the effects of evidence-informed policies on practice.

The EIPP model also divides educational practice by teachers and educational managers into evidence-informed and non-evidence-informed, recognising the opaque boundary between the two. As with policy-making, the mission of EIPP is to increase the proportion of practice that is evidence-informed. The distinction between public- and private-domain research and the relatively low profile of practitioners in public-domain research have important implications for the respective power of researcher and practitioner communities.

In the top-down public-domain version of the EIPP model (the more common one) 'validated evidence' is produced by the research community, using practitioners (and their clients) as the subjects of research. The issue then is how to get practitioners to take on board evidence so that it influences their practice. Eraut (1994) distinguishes between public propositional knowledge and personal knowledge: 'In general, many differences can be found between the personal knowledge of working professionals which informs their judgement or becomes embedded in their performance and the public knowledge base of their professions as represented by publications and training courses.'

Eraut subdivides personal knowledge into personal propositional knowledge – that which the individual can articulate – and tacit personal knowledge – that which individuals use in their practice without being fully conscious of it or being able to articulate it. He claims that 'a significant proportion of the learning associated with any change in practice takes place in the context of its use' (ibid., p. 33). Practitioners can only use public propositional knowledge in their work when they have internalised it so that it becomes part of their personal knowledge. It follows from this that if researcher generated and validated evidence is to influence practice, making it accessible to practitioners is not sufficient. They must be motivated to use it in their practice and be able to learn how to use it in their work contexts.

The practitioner-as-researcher has two potential roles in EIPP. One is undertaking public-domain research, for which practitioners do not generally have the time and resources available to professional researchers. The practitioner is much more dominant in the other role, that of generating and using private-domain research in order to inform practice. The problem is for practitioners to have sufficient incentives, resources and capacity for informing practice with private-domain research evidence.

Unvalidated findings are depicted in the EIPP model in Figure 5.1 as influences on policy and practice that lie outside the EIPP system. Practitioners, like policy-makers, are influenced by 'non-validated evidence', due often as much to the absence of validated evidence than to ignoring extant evidence.

For example, in making resource allocation decisions headteachers and governors (as well as the current government) are predisposed to believe in the effectiveness of teaching assistants. However, we currently have no UK evidence that teaching assistants produce measurable increases in pupils' learning. Preliminary analysis of data from a study of 9000 Key Stage 1 children in 220 schools indicated that the adult:child ratio has no effect on literacy or maths attainment (Blatchford *et al.*, 2002). The Tennessee STAR experiment also found that teaching assistants had no effect on pupils' attainment in maths and English language (Finn and Achilles, 1999).

Selection of research issues

The determination of issues selected for research is the outcome of competition for scarce research resources. Evidence-informed policy and practice is embedded in what for want of a better label we term 'plural society' – that amalgam of interests and ideologies that vie for influence over the structures for and forms of political decision-making in society. The goals that EIPP addresses are, of course, determined politically and reflect particular interests and values that have been successful in influencing these goals. What issues are currently dominating policy and practice agendas will influence not only what existing research is validated and disseminated to policy-makers and practitioners but also what new research is undertaken. An attempt is made in Figure 5.1 to depict the pervasive influence of interests and ideologies on all stages of the EIPP cycle.

In the current UK policy context, primacy is famously accorded to the pragmatic, rather than the ideological or idealistic, through the dictum 'what works is what counts'. Yet any assessment of 'what works' must be informed by some criteria, with particular relative weights attached to them, and these criteria and their weightings will inevitably be derived from a set of values. So the extent of pragmatism may be smaller than is claimed, and the values underpinning 'pragmatic' policy are a legitimate and important subject for research.

Another feature of contemporary governance, at least in England, is its centralised character: 'Increasingly, the direction of change in educational thinking and practice is top-down' (Davies, 1999, p. 108; see also Glatter, 1999). Policy-making is also accorded an aura of certainty and finality. As the former Secretary of State for Education and Employment perceived the position 'We know what works and how to spread it' (Blunkett, 2000a, p. 2). In a television interview, Tony Blair expressed his frustration that 'when I'm sitting as Prime Minister trying to get something done ... you can have a really good idea and drive it through from the top' (Blair, 1999), but its journey could be blighted on the way down by layers of bureaucracy and the risk-averse nature of the public sector. The Prime Minister's views on the shortcomings of the public sector have been much debated. Of greater interest to the present discussion is the notion of the 'really good idea' originating from the centre. How do central policies arise? One view, which may or may not be an accurate account, is that:

> National policy-making is inevitably a process of bricolage: a matter of borrowing and copying bits and pieces of ideas from elsewhere, drawing upon and amending locally tried and tested approaches, cannibalising theories, research, trends and fashions and not infrequently flailing around for anything at all that looks as though it might work.

(Ball, 1998, p. 126)

A government which promotes EIPP, by putting new funding into research to support it and diverting existing research funding towards EIPP, is exerting more control over research than a government which maintains policy-making as a 'knowledge-free zone'. Hence, one of the important criticisms of EIPP is that it promotes government control of research to the detriment of the longer-term benefits of society from research (Hammersley, 2000), which are broader and more intangible than the instrumental goals which are given priority by EIPP. Since policy goals are contested in a plural society, educational research is not a purely instrumental activity, and the intellectual foundations of policy-makers' goals should come under scrutiny (White, 2000). Such analysis can be an important engine of social advance: 'Criticism (specifically that which is constructive) is crucial to any endeavour designed to develop knowledge and improve practice' (Pratt and Swann, 1999, p. 8).

A crucial issue for EIPP is whether it is founded on the values of research objectivity and rationality, in conformity to which researchers strive to ensure that their validation of evidence is not affected by personal political beliefs or interests. An alternative value perspective is that the purpose of social research is to form part of the ammunition in the competition of ideas through which differing political interests vie for influence and power. (Lindblom [1987] makes this distinction.) From this perspective researchers interpret evidence through their political values and justify this as serving higher ends.

The fundamental argument for EIPP is that it leads to better achievement of the intended goals of practice and policy, through the use by policy-makers and policy-implementers of 'validated' research evidence in their decision-making. If the research evidence used to inform policy and practice is biased, then research will lose its claim to assist in determining the best means for achieving particular social goals and instead will function only as material for legitimating policies and practices based solely on interests and ideologies. In this event its currency will diminish further over time. An interesting example of the misuse of research evidence in order to legitimate policy is given by Allington and Woodside-Jiron (1999). They argue (with evidence) that certain educational researchers provided a misleading review of '30 years of research: what we know about how children learn to read' which was highly influential in Texas and California in mandating a literacy curriculum that placed great emphasis on phonics. In this example both researchers and policy-makers were in alliance, the former to further careers and the latter to legitimate policies founded on opinion and tradition concerning 'back-to-basics' in teaching.

It is our view that researchers should not become polemicists and that EIPP should strive for 'political unbiasedness' in the validation of evidence. This seems to be the consensus view among those advocating EIPP, a stance which separates it from those who see social research as inherently non-objective and necessarily linked to an ideology. Though in advocating a 'disinterested' stance, one must still recognise that EIPP serves the interests of those researchers whose methods it utilises.

When policies have such widespread effects, as is likely in a relatively centralised governance structure, it is important that they are well founded and are indeed based on 'really good ideas'. This suggests that EIPP is at least as necessary to the stage of policy development as it is to that of policy implementation, evaluation and practitioner use. The contribution of research to problem formulation and the definition of alternatives, mentioned above, is relevant here.

FACTORS PROMOTING AND INHIBITING EIPP

The current policy climate in the UK appears more supportive to research than that under the previous government. The so-called 'Third Way' to policy-making emphasises a pragmatic approach to improving learning outcomes, founded on applying evidence of 'what works' not on ideology. The government's expenditure on educational research has increased and it has claimed to be taking steps to ensure that policy-makers are well informed about the current state of knowledge in their areas (DfEE, 1999a). It has also established a number of research centres (Wicks, 2000).

Policy statements on research (DfEE, 1999a; DfEE, 2000a) have indicated support for a breadth of research activity, including not just the evaluation of policy initiatives and systematic reviews on the one hand and 'blue skies' research on the other, but also research which 'gives a coherent picture of how society works: the main forces at work, and those which can be influenced by government' (DfEE, 2000a, p. 1). This suggests a view of EIPP which goes beyond a technicist approach, and which is not restricted to a current policy agenda. While attacking some research for being too inward looking and piecemeal, Blunkett's speech to the ESRC also conceded that government needed to eschew anti-intellectualism and learn to interpret and apply evidence.

In addition, both new and older government agencies, such as the Teacher Training Agency and the National College for School Leadership (NCSL), as well as statutory bodies such as the General Teaching Council, have developed a significant research dimension and have growing capability in research.

Examples related to leadership and management

Achieving the stated aspirations may take some time. The explicit use of evidence in policy formation still appears rare. For example, in relation to the far-reaching and controversial proposals on the performance management of teachers, the claim was made that 'In designing our proposals, we have taken account of experience in private and public sectors, and of research findings' (DfEE, 1999b, para. 54). There was no discussion of which findings were drawn on or how these related to the specific proposals. This was a noteworthy omission in an area in which the research findings are equivocal to say the least (for example, IPD, 1999; Marsden and French, 1998). Perhaps in an age in which, as Scott (1999, p. 322) argues, 'electoral politics seem to be more dominant than ever', it is naive to expect that high-profile policies mandated from the centre will always be founded on a thorough review of all the evidence or subject to independently evaluated pilots. A researcher respondent to the DfEE-commissioned review of educational research relating to schools considered that 'Policy-makers introduce initiatives which are not allowed to fail' (Hillage et al., 1998, p. 42).

The use of research evidence needs to be extended in another area even closer to leadership and management – that of the definition of standards for assessing individuals' fitness for leadership positions and for recruitment to them. The development of professional standards in education has been a feature of recent years, deriving from the competency movement in vocational education and training in the UK (Raggatt and Williams, 1999) and it appears likely to become more widespread (DfEE, 2000b). Standards were developed by the Teacher Training Agency for headteachers (TTA, 1997) as well as for other categories of school staff, but despite the wealth of research into head-teachers over the past 20 years (Hall and Southworth, 1997) there is no evidence that it had any influence on the construction of the standards. The standards formed the basis for the assessment of candidates for the National Professional Qualification for Headship (NPQH) during its first three years of operation (1997–2000).

More recently, a different approach to the specification of headship has begun to be taken. As part of the development of the national Leadership Programme for Serving Headteachers, the management consultancy Hay McBer conducted 'behavioural event interviews' (BEIs) with 40 headteachers in which the subjects described their actions and feelings in specific school improvement situations. The data were subjected to thematic and statistical analysis to produce 15 characteristics of headship which were considered to be related to 'superior performance'. The resulting framework was termed 'Models of Excellence' and underlay the design and delivery of the programme, which has been running since 1998 and has been taken by many hundreds of headteachers. The research was extended to cover more head-teachers and some deputy heads in order to inform the development of the new version of NPQH, which is to become a mandatory qualification for headship. The government also commissioned Hay McBer to conduct research into effective teaching in connection with their plans for teacher performance management referred to earlier (Hay McBer, 2000).

The development of the 'Models of Excellence' was therefore ostensibly a research-based approach, in contrast to the process which underlay the construction of the National Standards for Headship. However, the research has not to our knowledge been published and we are not aware of any plans to publish it, although brief summaries were eventually produced by the consultants (see, for example, Forde, Lees and Hobby, 2000). Furthermore, this research does not test whether the characteristics of the models of excellence are associated with value-added pupil attainment. This is highly relevant to the issue of validation, which we raised in our discussion of Figure 5.1. We would suggest that an EIPP approach requires such models and the research on which they are based to be subjected to rigorous processes of validation, particularly where the models are intended to underpin large-scale programmes of professional development or the implementation of national staff management policies.

Rather than ignore EIPP, a government may attempt to use it spuriously by attempting to legitimate a policy by appealing to misleading and unvalidated evidence. An example of this is the current policy of promoting specialist schools. Any school that meets the required standard will now be able to become specialist. It is claimed in the recent White Paper, *Schools: Achieving Success* (DfES, 2001, pp. 39–40) that the policy is based upon evidence:

> Specialist schools are a key part of our proposals for a more diverse system because of their proven success, as demonstrated by research by Professor David Jesson which shows specialist schools adding more value to their pupils' achievements.

A box highlights the summary results of Jesson's research (Jesson, 2001) which was funded and published by the Technology Colleges Trust, which assists and promotes specialist schools. Two of the key findings reproduced are:

- the 391 specialist schools operating in the summer of 2000 (excluding selective schools) averaged 53 per cent of their pupils attaining five GCSEs at grades A* to C compared to 43 per cent in other non-selective schools in England though attainment of the specialist school pupils at age 11 had been similar to that at other schools
- specialist schools add more value between 11 and 16 and also between 14 and 16 than other schools.

However, Jesson's statistical analysis was conducted with school level prior attainment and later achievement data (i.e. predicting schools' average key stage KS3 and GCSE results from their average KS2 results). A study conducted with aggregate level data is, as is well known in the statistics literature, subject to aggregation bias and can produce a correlation in the opposite direction to that from the pupil level data, which should be used in order to obtain valid value added measures of pupil performance (as pointed out by

Schagen and Goldstein, 2002). The Jesson research did not mention that on average the percentage of students eligible for free school meals (FSM) was higher in non-specialist schools than specialist schools and did not allow for the negative impact this variable has on both school level and student level attainment. An analysis of GCSE results for 2001 at pupil level (Levačić, 2002) (which controlled for pupil level KS2 scores, pupil gender, age, and school characteristics including FSM percentage and average KS2 score) showed that on average being a student at a specialist school was associated with one and a half more GCSE grades. We cannot say from this association whether there is any causal relationship between schools becoming specialist and being more effective, since schools were selected into specialist status. There has been a dearth of valid evidence on the relative performance of specialist schools: thus the policy has been based on hope, ideology and intuition rather than on sound evidence.

It may reasonably be argued that embedding an EIPP approach will inevitably take time, and that the examples discussed above contain indications of increasing attention being given to evidence and research. However, the increasingly centralist and political nature of educational policy-making discussed earlier may well be a significant inhibiting factor. The political imperative determined by the electoral cycle to have quick results means there is often inadequate time for piloting interventions and responding to evaluations of pilots before full-scale implementation takes place. Thus ministers can find themselves subsequently defending positions they have taken up without an adequate evidential base. Politicians may consider themselves unable to admit to an error because of the political consequences of loss of legitimacy and credibility: they have a 'sunk investment' in what looked originally like 'really good ideas' but in fact turn out on investigation to be poor ones. The equivalent phenomenon in the business world has been termed 'strategic entrapment' (Proctor, 1993) in which decision-makers persist with an ineffective course of action to justify the resources they previously invested in that strategy.

The Research Assessment Exercise

Both promoting and inhibiting factors are also to be found in a key aspect of the framework surrounding educational research, the Research Assessment Exercise (RAE). The criteria for assessment used by the Education Panel for the 2001 exercise referred to 'the educational significance of the research and its relevance for the academic community, policy-makers and practitioners' (HEFC(E), 1999 para. 3.59.15). Such significance could be included in claims by institutions relating to the two key criteria, the quality of published output and the vitality of a department's research culture. The new recognition given to 'educational significance' could be seen as a response (arguably a limited and provisional one in the context of the exercise as a whole) to the criticisms of the RAE as a significant restraining influence on the development of more policy and practitioner focused research in education (Hillage et al., 1998;

Tooley, 1998). The new emphasis on 'users' might also in part have been a reaction to the growing professionalisation of research which, Scott (1999, p. 318) has argued, 'has tended to exclude "amateur" researchers whose main involvement is as policy-makers or practitioners'.

On the other hand the criteria still gave prominence to originality as a characteristic of quality and they did not provide explicit encouragement for researchers to engage in replicatory studies or to devote energy to disseminating the results of their work to practitioners and policy-makers and developing long-term linkages with them. At the time of writing we do not know whether there will be another RAE and, if there is one, what approach it will adopt to the issues raised here.

Research and researchers

Other inhibiting factors are intrinsic to the process of research, even when the research is designed to yield evidence for policy or practice. We have already suggested that research may not be able to provide 'data for decisions' in a straightforward, problem-solving sense. In addition, it may take a considerable time for studies to yield validated findings. This was the case in relation to studies of the impact of competition and parental choice in which the authors were engaged during the 1990s. In (hopefully rare) cases, the evidence may not arrive until the topic of the research has ceased to be of interest or relevance to user groups. The growing rapidity of change within both society and the educational process exacerbates this tension while at the same time reinforcing the need for EIPP to offer guidance in a turbulent world. Leithwood describes the dilemma succinctly: 'It is the unique demands placed on leadership of changing policy contexts that creates some of the greatest challenges for those engaged in leadership research. This is the case because the pace of policy change often far outstrips the pace of research about its consequences and implications for leadership' (Leithwood, 2001, p. 230). Researchers and other stakeholders should address how the problem may at least be mitigated.

Finally, the research process, even when conceived of (as we conceive of it here) in terms of disinterested enquiry, is likely to have a sceptical character (Bridges, 1999; Merton, 1973) since it is founded on questioning. This can often present an uncomfortable and unwelcome challenge to practitioners or policy-makers who are understandably committed to initiatives in which they have a personal investment.

It is important that this account does not leave the impression that all the constraints upon the development of EIPP lie outside the research community: with politicians, officials, practitioners, the RAE and the research process. As the Institute of Employment Studies report persuasively argued, there are many ways in which researchers can and should adapt their methods and practices to speak more convincingly and helpfully to user audiences, not least in the area of accessibility: 'The burgeoning forest of academic research and papers appears to be increasingly impenetrable to an academic audience, let alone the wider education community' (Hillage *et al.*, 1998, p. 52). The development and maintenance of long-term research-policy-practice partnerships is a key element in the Strategic Education Research Programme proposed by the US National Research Council (1999) and is also fostered by the ESRC's Teaching and Learning Research Programme. The community of scholars and researchers in educational leadership and management in the UK has from its origins been strongly committed to a close linkage between theory, research and practice for improving education, a commitment that is reflected in the membership mix of BELMAS. In the next section, we will outline some ways in which an EIPP approach might sustain and enhance this linkage.

A WAY FORWARD

In this section we focus on how EIPP could be taken forward with respect to educational leadership and management, within the aegis of BELMAS as an organisation dedicated to promoting the symbiosis of research and practice. Hence we focus more on practice than on policy. There are four main processes within the EIPP cycle depicted in Figure 5.1 which need to be addressed in thinking about a way forward:

- practitioner interaction with research
- the validation process
- the dissemination of validated research
- the selection and conduct of research.

These processes are interrelated. We need to be clear about what kinds of evidence practitioners need for informing their practice before we proceed to organising better validation and dissemination processes. In turn the availability of accessible and validated evidence will stimulate practitioners' use of it to inform their practice.

Practitioner interaction with research evidence

A first step is to develop a clear idea of the needs of practitioners with respect to informing their practice with 'validated' evidence from the public domain. A key question is 'what aspects of educational research supporting EIPP are appropriate for educational leadership and management as a "field of inquiry"'? Is it to be limited to research which is about leadership and management or widened to include research evidence on educational practices which head teachers and other leaders/managers of student learning, as well as policy-makers, need to know in order to make evidence-informed decisions? We would argue for the latter interpretation because this is the evidence base educational leaders need to have at their finger tips in order to take informed decisions about what educational practices to adopt or modify in their own contexts.

How broadly the topics are defined clearly determines how wide the net is cast for research which is to be included in the validation process. In particular, are the topics to be confined to those which come within the classification of 'interventions' – that is, concern the manipulation of particular variables or processes which have intended and unintended educational consequences? The discussions about a proposed Campbell Collaboration to undertake and disseminate reviews of educational research have been couched in terms of educational interventions (Boruch, Petrosino and Chalmers, 1999; Oakley, 1999). Limiting the research evidence included to educational interventions would make the enterprise more manageable but would exclude more wide-ranging research that is concerned with educational practices in natural settings which do not involve 'interventions'. In the light of evidence that social science research currently influences policy and practice mainly indirectly via creating a climate of opinion, we need to include within EIPP for educational management and leadership research which goes beyond the technical 'what works' variety, provided that it is evidentially based.

Topics and practices that are currently at a stage where systematic reviews for practitioners could be extended or developed include: the effects on student learning and other outcomes of:

- class size
- setting, banding and grouping by ability or gender
- peer group tutoring
- gender differences
- specific strategies/programmes for teaching literacy and numeracy
- organisation of the school day/year
- using target-setting for improving students' educational outcomes
- use of homework at different ages
- specific uses of ICT to enhance learning.

Important topics in the field of leadership and management practices are:

- teacher performance management and performance-related pay
- models of excellence for headship
- teacher appraisal
- monitoring teaching and learning
- involving parents in pupils'/students' learning.

A crucial issue for BELMAS is its role in promoting a culture in which educational leaders and managers use validated research evidence, from both public- and private-domains, to inform their practice. According to Davies (1999, p. 111): 'The problem is not so much that teachers do not undertake research or that they are often excluded from determining the research agenda (both of which may be true), but that there is often not a culture of teachers using research to inform their everyday school practice'. The problematic nature of the research–practice interface has long been recognised: it is also contentious because it concerns power relations between practitioners and academic researchers, as experts and gatekeepers of public-domain research. The relationship is made more complex and contentious when politicians impose on teachers educational practices/interventions, which the former claim are founded on research evidence, even though this evidence is still highly disputed amongst the research community.

The Teacher Training Agency is working to promote practitioner involvement in research, both as active researchers and users of research findings. In a survey of 302 headteachers and deputies in 1997 (TTA, 2000) 96 per cent said that they considered research findings in their work. The second most frequently cited area of research (after learning) was management and leadership, though there was a tendency to reference less recent research. Following on from this survey, the TTA has been developing a number of approaches to making teaching an evidence-based profession (TTA, 2001). These include small-scale grants to enable teachers to conduct research or interest colleagues in the findings of their research degrees, school-based research consortia, specific research projects involving teachers, dissemination and teacher–researcher links. The TTA has also set up a National Teacher Research Panel in order to provide a channel for teacher involvement at national level in informing and influencing educational research.

BELMAS members who work in higher education can assist in the development of a practitioner culture of EIPP in a number of ways. A key role is as providers of postgraduate courses in educational management and leadership. To evaluate evidence teachers need to know about relevant research methodologies. Such knowledge is better developed conducting research relevant to their own practice. Most postgraduate courses include research methods and research projects. However, the research is usually conducted in relative isolation, is inevitably small scale and lacks an integrative framework within which research evidence can build cumulatively. We need a way of linking academic–researcher peer group efforts to review and disseminate research on key topics with practitioner research undertaken under the auspices of different higher education (HE) institutions and in many different educational settings. If validated evidence were more easily available to practitioners and if they could relatively easily check summary evidence in reviews against original studies, practitioners would be in a better position to select projects for their own research which are relevant to their practice and/or can add cumulatively to public-domain evidence.

The validation process

The specialist role for academic researchers is in the validation process for public-domain research, in particular mobilising resources for the conduct of systematic reviews. A focus on the importance of reviewing existing research requires a change in what the research community values as 'good research practice'. Much greater value needs to be given to research synthesis, conducting a thorough survey of existing research before embarking on a new study, and doing replicatory and cumulative studies, as well as to dissemination to professional audiences. A peer group conducting a systematic review of a specific topic needs to start by agreeing criteria for (1) quality of research method which a study must meet to be included in the review, and (2) categorising and judging the evidence produced in each study. After conducting an initial review or set of related reviews the peer group needs to keep the database of research surveys up to date.

In considering areas suitable for review and meta-analysis, we need to recognise and build upon previous attempts to provide syntheses of existing research. For example, in the field of educational leadership and management several noteworthy reviews have been published in recent years. The ESRC commissioned Wallace and Weindling to produce an analytical review of research that had been funded by the council relating to reforms in school management. The result was a booklet highlighting key findings and messages for practitioners (Wallace and Weindling, 1997) as well as a discussion of the exercise and its implications for future research aimed at an academic audience (Wallace and Weindling, 1999). Hall and Southworth (1997) published a valuable review and synthesis of research on school headship in Britain since the 1970s. Taking a more international (and quantitative) perspective, Hallinger and Heck (1998; 1999) systematically reviewed a wide range of studies in addressing the key question: 'Can leadership enhance school effectiveness?' Such existing overviews and the methods underpinning them should provide a useful basis for developing new reviews and syntheses of the research literature.

A notable development is the School Leadership Review Group, organised by SCRELM (Standing Committee for Research in Educational Leadership and Management) under the auspices of the EPPI-Centre at the Institute of Education (see Chapter 4 for information about the EPPI-Centre). The review group aims to undertake systematic reviews into research on school leadership and details about its first review, carried out in 2001–02, are presented in the next chapter of this book.

A research review group needs to agree validation criteria and implement these agreements. A crucial and contentious issue, already raised in the discussion of the EIPP model, is what is to count as validated evidence and hence which kinds of research evidence can be diffused within the EIPP cycle. Not all forms of educational research are appropriate for EIPP: for a start, only empirical research is relevant for 'what works in practice', though such research needs to theoretically informed. A further restriction is that not all empirical research produces data, findings and conclusions that can be validated using peer-agreed conventions. Another criterion that would impose a further restriction is that the research selected for validation for EIPP, and the validation process itself, should be 'disinterested' – that is, not deliberately biased by the social beliefs and personal interests of the researcher.

In attempting to delineate the types of educational research that could be validated for EIPP, the typology of educational inquiry proposed by Constas (1998) is helpful. He distinguishes three dimensions that characterise a method of social inquiry. These are the methodological, political and representational dimensions.

The *methodological dimension* is the criteria by which evidence to support propositions is amassed. The methodological domain is 'normative' if there are agreed rules for assessing evidence, in particular the criteria of internal and external validity and reliability/replicability. The alternative methodological domain is 'idiosyncratic', when evidence is personal and situational: each project uses its own data preferences.

The *political dimension* is subdivided into 'centred' and 'decentred'. A research approach is centred when it eliminates or ignores power relations that affect the investigation or treats them as variables to be analysed in a detached way. In contrast, decentred research sets out to challenge established power relations.

The *representational dimension* concerns the ways in which research findings are presented. The traditional academic stance, which Constas calls bounded, is described as depersonalised, distanced and objective. Forms of presentation which break these rules, for example evocative narratives, are termed unbounded. Constas then distinguishes seven research typologies according to which combination of centred/decentred, normative/idiosyncratic, bounded/unbounded they involve.

Evidence-informed policy and practice falls into the centred-normative category. We have previously argued that it should be disinterested and not polemical (hence centred) and that it should have agreed rules for validation (normative). This restriction would exclude research which promotes specific ideological perspectives, whatever their political orientation. Whether or not the presentation of evidence for educational management should have agreed rules and conventions is problematic. If peer groups are set up to review research topics and disseminate reviews, they are likely to develop rules for presentation. Different forms of presentation, in particular different forms of language and pictorial representation, will be deemed appropriate for different purposes and audiences, as is now the case in journals aimed at academic, mixed or professional audiences. An important challenge for implementing the validation process for EIPP in educational leadership and management is reaching widespread agreement on normative rules for the methodological dimension and implementing these. This will need to be done by review groups set up to prepare reviews of evidence on specific topics, such as, the effect of educational leadership on organisational performance or what are the qualities of 'effective'/'excellent' educational leadership?

Because of the nature of the issues of importance in educational leadership and management, the research included in validation for EIPP cannot be restricted to random controlled trials of educational interventions. Nor should they be excluded. It will be distracting to devote energies to debating the superiority or otherwise of random controlled experiments in educational research. Instead, we should accept and value the continuum of research designs relevant for investigating educational practices, rather than pigeon holing them as discrete and separate. This continuum of research designs is depicted in Figure 5.2. First, educational practices can be subdivided into those that can be regarded as 'interventions' – deliberate manipulation of structures, systems, financial rewards or other variables, which are intended to bring about a discrete change in practice. This could be undertaken as a random controlled experiment, where subjects are randomly assigned to intervention and non-intervention states. Alternatively, the intervention may take the form of a natural experiment (no random assignment), where a particular change takes place in some natural settings and not in others. This enables researchers to gather data on settings where the intervention does and does not take place. By gathering a wide range of data from the selected intervention and non-intervention settings and applying statistical techniques used in observational studies, the threats to internal validity from non-random assignment can be considerably reduced (Meyer, 1995).

Moving further along the continuum, there are interventions that are universally applied to an education system (such as local management of schools, national curricular changes, performance management of teachers) so that there are no control groups which are not experiencing the intervention. Unfortunately for EIPP research, much educational intervention has been of this type.

A great deal of empirical educational research is not concerned with assessing the impact of educational interventions. This is classified in Figure 5.2 as non-intervention research: this collects observational data from natural settings. In some research designs settings can be deliberately selected to exhibit contrasts or similarities (e.g. research on different leadership styles or on differential school effectiveness). Or the settings may be selected to be representative so as to enhance generalisability. Alternatively, there may be no particular pattern or intent in the selection of settings for research.

Whether the data collected are quantitative or qualitative is not necessarily determined by the type of research design. Although random controlled trials (RCTs) generate quantitative data in order to investigate effects sizes, the research design can be enhanced by collecting qualitative data to assist in understanding reasons for differences in effects sizes between settings and participants. Although qualitative research designs are usually associated with research in natural settings, quantitative data are also gathered from non-intervention natural settings (e.g. data on pupil attainment and pupil background and school variables in school effectiveness research designs).

The normative criteria for the methodological domain are essentially the same for quanitative and qualitative data, so long as the qualitative research designs are normative and not idiosyncratic. These are shown in Figure 5.3. For instance, Guba and Lincoln (1981) proposed a set of rules for 'meeting tests of rigour' to ensure that the trustworthiness of the information and

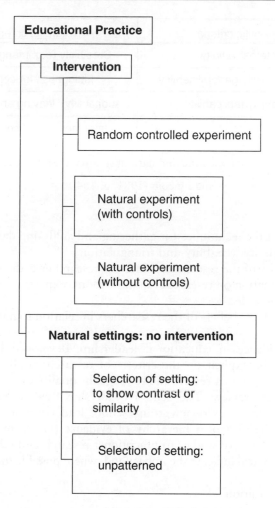

Figure 5.2   The continuum of research designs for educational settings

interpretations drawn from naturalistic inquiry match those of scientific inquiry. The scientific criteria (used for evaluating evidence from random controlled trials as well as from statistical tests of observational quantitative data) for validity are matched by corresponding naturalistic criteria.

Miles and Huberman (1984) proposed 12 tactics for testing or confirming findings in qualitative research.[2] Patton (1990) in the last chapter of his book, *Qualitative Evaluation and Research Methods*, also addressed the issue of enhancing the quality and credibility of qualitative analysis, listing three major considerations:

Scientific criteria	Naturalist criteria
Internal validity	Credibility (e.g. triangulation)
External validity/generalisability	Fittingness for context
Reliability/replicability	Auditability: leaving an audit trail
Objectivity	Data: factual and confirmable

Figure 5.3 Mapping of scientific and naturalist criteria for research validity

Source: derived from Guba and Lincoin (1981, p. 104).

- the rigour of the techniques for gathering and analysing data, attending to issues of validity, reliablity and triangulation
- the credibility of the researcher: since the researcher is the research instrument, information on researcher qualifications, experience and perspective should be provided
- the philosophical beliefs of the researchers in relation to naturalist inquiry.

Reviews of evidence in educational leadership, developed by peer review groups, should be explicit on the criteria of research validity used to select research for inclusion in a review and to judge the quality of evidence presented in the subsequent review. The School Leadership Review group has stated that (www.eppi.ioe.ac.uk/reviewgroups/school_leadership-home): within the framework of the idea of a hierarchy of evidence (i.e. from RCTs through well-designed qualitative studies to practitioner research and school based data collection) review will indicate the impact and, where possible the effects size on:

- school organisation
- leadership and management performance
- teacher performance
- student learning and behaviour
- educational outcomes.

The development of agreed and commonly applied criteria in the validation process for EIPP should have spillover benefits in improving the quality of research undertaken, in the research methods learnt in educational management courses and in the consequent ability of practitioners to evaluate research evidence critically and undertake their own research contributions.

Dissemination

The visible outcome of successful establishment of a structure for EIPP would be easy access for practitioners to evidence on the effects of specific educational practices. One of the major constraints on practitioners informing their practice with evidence is lack of time to become informed. Hence quick, cheap and ready access is required, which accommodates differences in the extent to which uses wish to become acquainted with the breadth and depth of the evidence. The Internet is particularly suited to providing access to evidence for informing practice, which meets these criteria. Practitioners should be able to access a web site on which they would find high-quality research surveys of the evidence on the effects of specified educational practices. The surveys should be accessible at three levels:

- a bullet point summary
- a survey article
- original high-quality studies included in the survey.

Too often texts making evidence-based claims of 'what works' are insufficiently referenced to the sources of evidence and, even if these are provided, it takes time and effort to acquire the sources. Busy professionals do not have the time to pursue original sources, so that it is too easy to proselytise for a particular practice on the grounds that there is evidence that it works when the evidence may well be equivocal or context specific. It also useful if the methodological perspective of the review is classified as, for example, in the *Review of Reviews* report to the ESRC's Teaching and Learning Steering Committee (ESRC, 1999), which classifies listed reviews as 'technical', 'interpretative' and 'mixed'. While both the ESRC and the NFER have supported on-line databases of research studies, they do not focus on reviews of the type advocated here.

Selection of research studies: evaluation of pilots

The earlier discussion noted the problem from a policy-making perspective that research evidence is not sufficiently relevant or timely with respect to current policy interventions. In particular, the time frame of policy-makers and practitioners is shorter-term than that of researchers. In contrast, from a research perspective valid evidence on the impact of educational interventions on learning and other outcomes takes time to emerge, collect, analyse fully and present. Overcoming this dichotomy requires building up and sustaining long-term linkages between researchers, policy-makers and practitioners, so that the EIPP cycle can be made more effective through continual interaction between research and policy/practice. It also requires accommodation by both parties. Policy-makers would need to acknowledge the dangers of mandating large-scale national implementation of major policy innovations which have not had independently evaluated trials. The research community would need to recognise the time pressures involved in policy change, develop better and faster methods for the evaluation of pilots, value this form of research activity more highly and accept that all the requirements of rigorous research may not be achievable within the time frames available. Indicative results may need to be regarded as acceptable when the alternative is no evaluation at all. A change in the culture of both parties would be needed. Researchers would need to be prepared to risk producing findings and conclusions which are liable to later revision, while politicians would need to be more open about the tentative nature of proposed policy solutions and less prone to entrapment in sunk policy investments. Other features of such a learning culture would be open, unhindered publication and a preparedness by policy-makers and practitioners to modify course in the light of the results.

CONCLUSIONS

If we look to other models of EIPP, such as the Cochrane Collaboration and the proposed Campbell Collaboration for education, we can see that they are very focused in organising the validation stage of the EIPP cycle. Clearly this is an essential part of EIPP and without it we cannot expect practitioners and policy-makers to base decisions on 'the best available evidence'. It is also the part of the EIPP cycle for which 'professional' researchers have particular responsibility. However, it is only part of EIPP and its development has to link in closely to the interests and aspirations of the other stakeholders, in particular practitioners and policy-makers. More broadly, the 'new model for educational research' proposed by the National Research Council (1999) emphasises interactions among researchers, practitioners and policy makers in a programme of research, synthesis and implementation which concentrates on a limited number of important topics.

Evidence-informed policy and practice will only fulfil its potential in education if it is not misused by its stakeholders. Researchers may be tempted to progress their careers by promoting insufficiently validated research (which can happen with well-intentioned media efforts to disseminate research), while policy-makers in search of legitimation for their policies may be too ready to seize selectively on insufficiently validated evidence.

To develop EIPP in educational leadership and management we need to work towards the creation of a web site on which users can find high-quality reviews of evidence on the effects of specific educational practices and interventions which are accessible at different levels. Progress has already been made in setting up the School Leadership Review group.

The cultures of academic researchers and HE teachers, practitioner and policy-making communities need to promote EIPP as the professional norm. This can be encouraged though professional development programmes, organised in HE, by the NCSL and other agencies, and placing greater emphasis on teachers undertaking research which provides evidence for informing decision-making and evaluating practice.

NOTES

1. This chapter is a revised and updated version of our 2001 paper, 'Really good ideas? Developing evidence-informed policy and practice in educational leadership and management', *Educational Leadership and Management*, Vol. 29, No. 1, pp. 5–25.

2. Checking for representativeness; checking for researcher effects; triangulation; weighting the evidence; examining contrasts and comparisions; checking the meaning of outliers; using extreme cases; ruling out spurious relationships; replicating a finding; checking out rivals explanations; looking for negative evidence; getting feedback from informants (Miles and Huberman, 1984, p. 231)

REFERENCES

Allington, R.L. and Woodside-Jiron, H. (1999) The politics of literacy teaching: how 'research' shaped educational policy, *Educational Researcher*, Vol. 28, No. 8, pp. 4–13.

Anderson, G.L. and Herr, K. (1999) The new paradigm wars: is there room for rigorous practitioner knowledge in schools and universities, *Educational Researcher*, Vol. 28, No. 5, pp. 12–21.

Apple, M. (1999) What counts as legitimate knowledge? The social production and use of reviews, *Review of Educational Research*, Vol. 69, No. 4, pp. 343–6.

Ball, S. (1998) Big policies/small world: an introduction to international perspectives in education policy, *Comparative Education*, Vol. 34, No. 2, pp. 119–30.

Blair, T. (1999) *Question Time*, BBC1, 7 July.

Blatchford, P., Goldstein, H., Martin, C. and Browne, W. (2002) A study of the class size effects in English school reception year classes, *British Educational Research Journal* (in press).

Blunkett, D. (2000) quoted in, *Education Journal*, January.

Boruch, R.F., Petrosino, A.J. and Chalmers, I. (1999) The Campbell Collaboration: a proposal for a systematic, multi-national, and continuous review of evidence, presented at meeting on Research Synthesis and Public Policy, University College London, July.

Boyd, W.L. (1998) Paradoxes of educational policy and productivity, Annual Meeting of the American Educational Research Association, San Diego, CA, April.

Bridges, D. (1999) Educational research: pursuit of truth or fancy?, *British Educational Research Journal*, Vol. 25, No. 5, pp. 597–616.

Chalmers, I., Sackett, D. and Silagy, C. (1997) The Cochrane Collaboration, in Maynard, A. and Chalmers, I. (eds) *Non-random Reflections on Health Services Research*, London, British Medical Journal Publishing Group, pp. 213–49.

Constas, M.A. (1998) Deciphering post-modern educational research, *Educational Researcher*, Vol. 27, No. 9, pp. 36–42.

Davies, P. (1999) What is evidence-based education?, *British Journal of Educational Studies*, Vol. 47, pp. 108–21.

Department for Education and Employment (DfEE) (1999a) *Developing DfEE's Research Strategy: A Prospectus*, London: DfEE.

Department for Education and Employment (DfEE) (1999b) *Teachers – Meeting the Challenge of Change: Technical Consultation Document on Pay and Performance Management*, London: DfEE.

Department for Education and Employment (DfEE) (2000a) Blunkett rejects anti-intellectualism and welcomes sound ideas, *DfEE News*, No. 43/2000, pp. 1–3.

Department for Education and Employment (DfEE) (2000b) *Professional Development: Support for Teaching and Learning*, London: DfEE.

Department for Education and Employment (DfEE) (2001) *Schools: Building on Success: Raising Standards, Promoting Diversity and Achieving Results* (Green Paper), London: DfEE.

Department for Education and Skills (DfES) (2001) Schools: Achieving Success (White paper), London: DfEE.

Economic and Social Research Council (ESRC) (1999) *Review of Reviews: a report to the Steering Committee of the Teaching and Learning Research Programme*, www.ex.ac.uk/ESRC_TLRP

Eraut, M. (1994) *Developing Professional Knowledge and Competence*, London: Sage.

Finn, J.D. and Achilles, C.M. (1999) Tennessee's class size study: findings, implications, misconceptions, *Educational Evaluation and Policy Analysis*, Vol. 21, No. 2, pp. 97–109.

Glatter, R. (1999) From struggling to juggling: towards redefinition of the field of educational leadership and management, *Educational Management and Administration*, Vol. 27, No. 3, pp. 253–66.

Guba, E.G. and Lincoln, Y.S. (1981) *Effective Evaluation*, San Francisco: Jossey-Bass.

Hall, V. and Southworth, G. (1997) Headship, *School Leadership and Management*, Vol. 17, No. 2, pp. 151–70.

Hallinger, P. and Heck, R. (1998) Exploring the principal's contribution to school effectiveness: 1980–1995, *School Effectiveness and School Improvement*, Vol. 9, No. 2, pp. 157–91.

Hallinger, P. and Heck, R. (1999) Can leadership enhance school effectiveness? in Bush, T., Bell, L., Bolam, R., Glatter, R. and Ribbins, P. (eds) *Educational Management: redefining theory, policy and practice*, London: Paul Chapman Publishing.

Ham, C. and Hill, M. (1993) *The Policy Process in the Modern Capitalist State*, Sussex: Wheatsheaf Books.

Hammersley, M. (2000) Diversity or control in educational research, Conference on Diversity or Control in Educational Research, City University, January.

Hay McBer (2000), *Research into Teacher Effectiveness: A Model of Teacher Effectiveness*, report by Hay McBer to the Department for Education and Employment, June, www.dfee.gov.uk/teaching reforms/mcber

HEFC(E) (1999) *Research Assessment Exercise 2001: Assessment Panel's criteria and working methods*, London: HEFC(E).

Hillage, J., Pearson, R., Anderson, A. and Tamkin, P. (1998) *Excellence in Research on Schools*, London: DfEE.

Institute of Personnel and Development (IPD) (1999) *Performance Pay Trends in the UK*, London: IPD.

Jesson, D. (2001) *Educational Outcomes and Value Added Analysis of Specialist Schools for the Year 2000*, London: Technology Colleges Trust, www.tctrust.org.uk

Leithwood, K. (2001), School leadership in the context of accountability policies, *International Journal of Leadership in Education*, Vol. 4, No. 3, pp. 217–35.

Levačić, R. (2002) 'The effectiveness of specialist schools in England: rhetoric and reality' British Educational Research Association Annual Conference, University of Exeter.

Lindblom, C. (1987) Who needs what social science research for policy making?, in Shadish, W.R. and Reichart, C.S. (eds) *Evaluation Studies Review Annual*, Berkeley, CA: Sage.

Luntley, M. (2000) *Performance, Pay and Professionals*, Ringwood, Hants: Philosophy of Education Society of Great Britain (Business and Medical Books Centre).

Marsden, D. and French, S. (1998) *What a Performance: Performance-Related Pay in the Public Sector*, London: Centre for Economic Performance, London School of Economics.

Merton, R.K. (1973) *The Sociology of Science: Theoretical and Empirical Investigations*, Chicago, IL: Chicago University Press.

Meyer, B.D. (1995) Natural and quasi-natural experiments in economics, *Journal of Business and Economic Statistics*, Vol. 13, No. 2, pp. 151–61.

Miles, M.B. and Huberman, A.M. (1984) *Qualitative Data Analysis*, London: Sage.

National Research Council (1999) *Improving Student Learning: A Strategic Plan for Education Research and its Utilization*, Washington, DC: National Academy Press.

Oakley, A. (1999) An infrastructure for assessing social and educational interventions: the same or different, presented at meeting on Research Synthesis and Public Policy, UCL, July.

Patton, M.Q. (1990) *Qualitative Evaluation and Research Methods*, London: Sage.

Pratt, J. and Swann, J. (1999), The crisis of method, in Swann, J. and Pratt, J. (eds) *Improving Education: Realist Approaches to Method and Research*, London: Cassell.

Proctor, J. (1993) Strategic windows and entrapment, *Management Decision*, Vol. 31, No. 5, pp. 55–9.

Raggatt, P. and Williams, S. (1999) *Governments, Markets and Vocational Qualifications: An Anatomy of Policy*, London: The Falmer Press.

Schagen, I. and Goldstein, H. (2002) Do specialist schools add value? Some Methodological problems, *Research Intelligence*, Vol. 80, August, pp. 12–15.

Scott, P. (1999) The research-policy gap, *Journal of Education Policy*, Vol. 14, No. 3, pp. 317–37.

Sebba, J. (1999) Developing evidence-informed policy and practice in education, British Educational Research Association Annual Conference, University of Sussex, September.

Selby Smith, C. (1999) The relationship between research and decision-making in education: an empirical investigation, Monash-ACER Centre for the Economics of Education and Training, Working Paper 24.

Scottish Office Education Department (SOED) (1992a) *Using Performance Indicators in Primary School Self-Evaluation*, Edinburgh: SOED.

Scottish Office Education Department (SOED) (1992b) *Using Performance Indicators in Secondary School Self-Evaluation*, Edinburgh: SOED.

Teacher Training Agency (TTA) (1997) *National Standards for Headteachers*, London: TTA.

Teacher Training Agency (TTA) (2000) *Deputy/Headteachers' Views on Accessing and Using Research and Evidence – Results from a Pilot Survey*, www.canteach.gov.uk/research/evidence

Teacher Training Agency (TTA) (2001) *Improving Standards: Research and Evidence-Based Practice*, www.canteach.gov.uk/research/evidence

Tooley, J. with Derby, D. (1998) *Educational Research – a Critique: A Survey of Published Educational Research*, London: Office for Standards in Education.

Wallace, M. and Weindling, D. (1997) *Managing Schools in the Post-Reform Era: Messages of Recent Research*, Cardiff: Cardiff University of Wales for the Economic and Social Research Council.

Wallace, M. and Weindling, D. (1999) Overview of a group of research projects and relevance to school management, in Bush, T., Bell, L., Bolam, R. Glatter, R. and Ribbins, P. (eds) *Educational Management: Redefining theory, policy and practice*, London: Paul Chapman Publishing.

Weiss, C.H. (ed.) (1991) *Organisations for Policy Analysis*, New York: Sage.

White, J. (2000) Editorial Introduction to M. Luntley *Performance Pay and Professionals*, Ringwood, Hants: Philosophy of Education Society of Great Britain (Business and Medical Books Centre) pp. vii–xii.

Wicks, M. (2000) Quality research, *Education Journal*, February.

PART TWO

PART TWO

6

Foul is Fair and Fair is Foul: Conducting a Systematic Review of an Aspect of Educational Leadership and Management

LES BELL, RAY BOLAM AND LEELA CUBILLO

INTRODUCTION

The development of systematic reviews of research in education has been accompanied by a debate about the desirability, nature and purpose of such reviews. For example, the emergence of the systematic reviewing process has been presented as a case of epistemological witchcraft through which the curse of positivist research, 'long thought dead and gone, has popped out of its grave and found ... ready converts' (Stronach and Hustler, 2001, p. 523). It is argued that the search for evidence on which to base practice is linked to positivist assumptions about the nature of knowledge, the existence of universal truth and the possibility of identifying best practice solutions that have universal relevance. The criteria for evaluating the validity of research whose findings may be included in any search for evidence-based practice are, according to Hammersley (2001), derived from a model of research that gives the highest value to studies involving explicit and replicable procedures. These usually include some form of control and allow for statistical generalisation and the random controlled trial (RCT) is regarded as the most significant. At the same time, Hammersley argues, the reviewing process itself must match similar criteria by employing explicit procedures and criteria for the selection and evaluation of studies. Two ingredients that allegedly contribute to the spell to revitalise positivism, therefore, are, first, the extent to which systematic review processes favour one approach to educational research over another and, secondly, the degree to which systematic reviews can be presented as the most appropriate way to explore educational research.

A third ingredient that needs to be added to the systematic review cauldron is one that seems to receive far less attention, the nature of the relationship between research, policy and practice. It is beyond the scope of this chapter to consider it in detail. Suffice to say that this relationship is far from linear and rational. As Davies, Nutley and Smith (2000) point out, it is often founded on custom and practice and is, at best, incremental rather than based on a rigorous review of the evidence. Nevertheless, policy in education and more widely has long been influenced by research; witness, for example, the development strategies employed to cope with urban deprivation based on evidence that links aspects of social class and educational achievement (Bell, 1999a). At times, educational policy has been based on research conclusions drawn from fields other than education, for example, the development of the educational market as a result of findings from research on economic modelling (Bell, 1999b). This government has already taken a clear stance on its use of educational research to formulate policy (DfEE, 2000). The use of systematic reviews to establish 'what works', what forms of social interventions are effective, is a further development in the policy-research-practice relationship (Evans and Benefield, 2001). As Sebba (2000) argues, there was, until recently, no evidence about the cost-effectiveness of educational interventions. This has led Oakley (2000) to ask what was so special about those in education that they do not need to show that their interventions are successful. This question, in itself, is interesting in that it pre-supposes that educational research is significantly concerned with intervention studies. This has given rise to concerns not only about the search for universal solutions to local problems in the relationship between research, policy and practice but to a concern that the thrust to evidence-based policy is an attempt to impose central control on the research agenda (Hammersley, 2001). These concerns are compounded because, as Stronach and Hustler (2001) argue, there may be no substantial evidence to demonstrate the applicability to education of evidence-based policy or practice, the systematic reviews required nor the medical model from which the process derived. Perhaps one way to explore these issues further is to consider an attempt to develop a systematic review in an area in which there is considerable political interest, that of the management and leadership of schools. This chapter reports on such a review and, in doing so, explores a range of issues emanating from the process.

EDUCATIONAL LEADERSHIP AND MANAGEMENT

Educational leadership and management is regarded by policy-makers and practitioners alike as a key factor in ensuring a school's success. One finding of school effectiveness research is that purposeful leadership by the headteacher is crucial to a school's performance (Mortimore et al., 1988; Sammons, Hillman and Mortimore, 1995). Moreover, the belief in the role leadership plays in determining a school's success and growth has latterly prompted the Secretary of State for Education to establish a National College for School Leadership (NCSL). The NCSL is tasked with supporting school leaders and managing their training and professional development. In other words, there is a strongly held belief that school leadership makes a difference.

Although school leadership is now accepted as centrally important, the nature and focus of leaders' actions are either contested or unclear. Scholars and researchers debate the relationship between leadership and management

(Bolam, 1999) and the form or style of leadership (Leithwood and Jantzi, 1999). Research suggests that school leaders concentrate on organisational cultures (Hargreaves, 1994), strategic planning and marketing (Davies and Ellison, 1997). Taken together, the literature shows that leadership and management is diverse in its scope and pluralistic in its emphases. Research in the UK and internationally also shows that the majority of studies into the leadership and management of schools investigates headteachers and principals (Southworth, 1997). There is little research into deputy heads and middle managers. Consequently, there is implicit agreement that not only is leadership determined by organisational role but that, in schools, leadership is predominantly exercised by those in the highest position. This literature also suggests that educational leadership and management constitutes a broad field of research. The literature falls into four fairly distinct types produced by theorists, researchers, policy-makers and practitioners. Research studies are often rooted in sociology, philosophy, history, social psychology, occupational psychology, economics, management studies, education and andragogy. There is also wide variation in methodologies. Quantitative methods are used mainly by US researchers, whereas British research favours qualitative approaches (Bolam, 1999).

However, despite the breadth and variety of research and scholarship, over the last ten years there has been convergence about the focus and priorities of school leaders. A review of developments over a 25-year period, notes that:

> There is now much more clarity and agreement about the core tasks of teaching and schooling and, therefore, about the tasks of school management ... this has come about because of the introduction of such major policy changes as the National Curriculum and assessment and the national inspection system. One does not have to agree with every aspect of these reforms to recognise that they, together with the research and development work on effective schools and improvement, all place increasing emphasis on effective teaching and learning.

> (Bolam, 1997, p. 277)

Such an outlook parallels research in North America which has investigated and promoted instructional leadership (Leithwood and Jantzi, 1999). If there is now greater agreement than previously about the focus of leadership, international research has also moved on from its initial preoccupations. Researchers in the early years of research in this field focused on answering the question: 'Do principals make a difference?' More recently they have transcended the bounds of this question to try to understand 'not only if principals have effects on school outcomes, but more particularly the paths through which such effects are achieved' (Hallinger and Heck, 1998, p. 187).

SETTING UP AND MANAGING THE REVIEW

The review explored in the rest of this chapter is one of first six reviews that began in February 2001 within the framework established by the Evidence for

Policy and Practice Information and Co-ordinating Centre (EPPI-Centre) as outlined in Chapter 4. The idea of a review in the field of educational leadership and management was initiated by the Standing Conference for Research in Educational Leadership and Management (SCRELM) Co-ordinating Committee and, after a successful bid for funding, established an advisory review group with the authors of this chapter taking leading roles. The advisory group was responsible for:

- co-ordinating the review
- decisions about specific review topics
- inviting participation
- allocation of work and review schedules
- contributing to the 'mapping' exercise
- approving the final report.

Reviewers were drawn from SCRELM membership, teachers and representation from one teachers' professional association.

The actual process of conducting this systematic review was approached as a pilot project. It was recognised by those involved that the framework was not fully adapted for use with the types of research that were likely to be identified in this field and that ongoing development of it was necessary. Furthermore, there was uncertainty amongst the reviewers themselves about their understanding of the process to be sure that it could be applied in an unproblematic way. As one of the first systematic reviews in education, emphasis was placed on the process itself, its management, the training of reviewers and user involvement.

THE REVIEW PROCESS

It was intended that the review would focus on the distinctive core processes of educational leadership, that is leadership strategies and methods for improving teaching and learning, for raising standards and school improvement. This involved reviewing available research evidence of all types, emphasising empirical, well-designed studies in primary, secondary and special schools. There were three overall aims for this first review. The first was to embark on a process of mapping the field of educational leadership and management and identify subdivisions within which might be the subject of subsequent specific reviews. This process would build upon a series of seminars that took place in the late 1990s funded by the Economic and Social Research Council (see Bush et al., 1999; *Educational Management and Administration*, 1999).

The second aim was to address the main and subsidiary research questions through systematic review. The questions were:

(main)

- What is the evidence of the impact of school leadership and management on student/pupil outcomes?

(subsidiary)

- What is the impact of various leadership and management strategies on four aspects of student/pupil outcomes: achievement; attitudes; behaviour and recruitment?
- How did the school leadership and management strategies adopted contribute to these outcomes?

The third aim was to learn how to carry out an EPPI-style systematic review, to trial the EPPI methodology and explore its utility, feasibility and viability for this field of scholarship and research.

The review process involved consultation with user groups. This was carried out through the members of the advisory group and user/practitioner (teachers, governors and members of teachers' associations) involvement in the small groups that conducted the individual reviews. The criteria adopted for selection of studies to be reviewed were as follows:

- Time frame: for UK research, it was judged appropriate to consider research since 1988 to the present day. This allowed us to concentrate on leadership in English schools since the 1988 Education Reform Act. For North America and Australian research, the start-date was 1980 since when there has been considerable interest in 'instructional leadership' and school effects.
- Geographical limits: the review was confined to research reported in English. This meant that most of the work reviewed was from the UK, North America, Australia and New Zealand together with some from Scandinavia, Holland, Hong Kong and Singapore. In the event, it was decided to restrict the search largely to research on English schools.
- Population groups: the review focused on school headteachers and their equivalent in other countries. (Subsequent reviews will include other formal leadership roles – deputies, heads of departments, senior leadership teams.)

In order to clarify exactly what the precise meaning of the review question, the relevant terminology was defined:

- *Leadership:* headteachers, deputy heads, assistant head, principals, vice-principals, heads of departments, subject leaders/co-ordinators.
- *School:* primary, elementary, infant, junior, nursery, middle, lower, first, secondary, high, upper, special.

- *Outcomes:* cognitive outcomes as measured by standardised tests. (School effects research very largely restricts itself to these measures and usually with regard to reading and mathematics.)
- *Achievement:* could include both cognitive and non-cognitive outcomes.
- *Attitudes:* pupil self-esteem, attitudes to learning as measured by indices of motivation, and/or affective scales.
- *Behaviour:* rates of exclusion, suspension of pupils from school, attendance, pupil self-reports.

The identification and selection process concentrated on finding those studies that used measures of pupil performance to gauge whether and how school leaders' actions had impacted on pupil outcomes. The approach used and outcomes are described below.

- The initial search of five major databases, BEI, ERIC, ERA, First Search and World Cat, using the various search terms yielded references to over 100,000 papers and books. Replications accounted for the major proportion of these. This was particularly frustrating as they frequently occurred within the same database.
- A second problem was one of semantics. Not only did consideration have to be given to the difference in usage in different countries, it was necessary to be aware of other context-related terminology. For example, the commonly used 'headteacher' in the UK is not often recognised by US-based databases, where the term 'principal' is more likely to be used. Furthermore, a search for 'head' in ERIC yielded several hits for a head-start programme for early years.
- There was also the issue of the selection criteria. It was difficult to limit searches to either the country or to a specific year, particularly at the early stages of the search. The country is not often specified in the title. Dates were even more difficult to specify, as the range of dates varied with the database, and again, were not always specified in the title or abstract.

A second search strategy using a combination of terms reduced the initial number to about 20,000 hits by excluding items not directly related to schools and senior managers in schools. The next stage was the selection of studies for further examination by manually working through some 5,000 titles and abstracts (where these were available) using the criteria in the review questions. This search identified 18 studies. Hand-searching of a number of journals increased the list to 23. Records of the studies were stored on the bibliographic database, End-Note. SCRELM members were invited to recommend studies for investigation. While there was only a limited response to this request, the information provided by those who did respond was very useful in helping to ascertain both significant research and some 'grey literature'. Thirty-six studies were eventually identified and abstracts and full papers sought.

    This list was presented to the advisory group for consideration and was finally reduced to 27 studies. Of the nine that were excluded, three were omitted simply because they were not available for review during the time frame. The others fell into two categories:

- They did not meet the selection criteria exactly.
- The description of the study in the title and/or abstract had not accurately reflected the content of report, which failed to meet the selection criteria.

The process of reviewing was carried out in two stages. First, all documents were subjected to a keywording exercise designed to ensure that they should be included in the review and identify basic data about each item. This was followed by a much more detailed review based on a review guidelines document that poses an extended list of questions designed to elicit data about the item being considered. Everyone participating in the review underwent training on the process. Ten 'triads' of reviewers were established. Six of these included a practitioner as one of its members. Two or three papers were reviewed by each triad and quality was assured through parallel reviews of a selection of studies that were undertaken by the EPPI-Centre team.

THE OUTCOMES OF THE PROCESS

Progress has been made towards achieving each of the aims of the review process. However, the first aim, to map the field, has proved problematic. Bush (1999, p. 3) notes that:

> educational management as a field of study and practice was derived from management principles first applied to industry and commerce, mainly in the United States ... The former infant prodigy has progressed from being dependent upon ideas developed in other settings to become an established discipline with its own theories and some empirical data to test their validity in education. This transition has been accompanied by lively argument about the extent to which education should be regarded as simply another field for the application of general principles of management or be seen as a separate discipline with its own body of knowledge.

His comments about relationships between the field of educational leadership and management research and practice and other fields are important because they suggest that the field may have a 'nested' nature. This is exemplified through the review. *School leadership* is at its heart. However, this is located within the broader field of *educational leadership and management*, which in turn, is related to the wider field of leadership and management research and practice. In other words, while the focus of this map is school leadership and management, awareness of relationships to wider and related areas should be sustained.

Early in the process it was recognised that maps represent a selective view of reality. Inevitably any map presents a simplified picture and one that is designed for a particular purpose – a national roadmap differs from a national railmap, for example, because they have different purposes. Maps are influenced by the standpoint of the cartographer, what is chosen to be included and excluded and the scale and projection used to represent the three dimensional world on a two dimensional surface. Therefore, there are advantages and disadvantages in mapping.

The disadvantages are that the map excludes important features and that it compartmentalises or fragments the field into separate areas that are loosely connected or disconnected. The advantages are that the scope of the field is limited, a sense of territory is defined, features in the landscape are identified and travellers can locate themselves and navigate a course. In mapping the field of school leadership and management research it is not intended to chart the whole field of educational leadership and management, let alone that of leadership and management. Metaphorically, the intention is to produce a map of a country, or a state within a country, but not a map of a continent, let alone the globe or universe.

The review group noted that school leadership research aims critically to inform educational judgements and decisions in order to improve educational action. It follows from this that school leadership is an applied field of knowledge. It is a field distinguished by its subject matter and it is essentially practical rather than theoretical. The field is also composed of a number of overlapping and related parts, including educational administration, educational management, educational policy and educational leadership. The process of mapping the field and any map produced should enable those using the map to develop a sense of:

- what we know (what is or used to be)
- what we do not know
- how we know what we know (its validity, ideology, replicability).

This knowledge should also help us to identify areas for investigation.

Moreover, the mapping process will develop over time and the quality of the maps should improve. Indeed, it should be an objective of the mapping exercise that early efforts are made redundant by later ones. As the review process develops, each review, in turn, will add to our knowledge of what we know and how we know these things and thus, more precise and detailed knowledge about the field of school leadership will be recorded. The first maps should aid discovery and exploration so that more accurate and complete charts can be subsequently developed.

The review group considered a number of possible maps. One provided by Mike Bottery (2001) suggested that we need an initial map for areas of leadership which are, and have been studied, researched and written about and which identify those areas of leadership which *ought* to be studied. Leadership, he sees, as essentially concerned with the following questions:

- What is leadership?
- What is it that makes a leader?
- What do we want leaders to be concerned with?
- What makes leaders more effective in what they do?

- How do these prior questions affect the selection criteria you adopt for new leaders?
- What kinds of education and training do such leaders need?
- How do you go about creating the conditions for such kinds of leaders to flourish?

Janet Ouston (2001) viewed producing a map as a phased process that includes:

- describing the context
- defining the methodology
- examining the indicators of knowledge, skills and personal attributes included in the study, and whether any of these – either singly or in inter-action – relate to 'effective' or 'poor' leadership and management
- identifying the criteria used for 'effective' and 'poor' leadership and management in research (i.e. what are the outcome measures?).

Reviewing research on management development would require additional assessments of the pedagogy and development model used. Initial definitions of subcategories that lie within the different categories of 'context', 'methodo-logy', 'knowledge', 'skills', 'personal attributes', 'outcomes', 'pedagogy' and 'development model' (and possible others) will need to be developed, and will probably be based on existing literature. They should, however, be able to be extended to meet the demands of research under review.

Bush (2001) suggested seven questions to stimulate the mapping exercise:

- How are educational purposes defined, or redefined, by leaders?
- How do leaders develop and implement their vision for the school and how does this relate to school culture?
- What are the main definitions and concepts of school leadership? How do they influence school leadership practice?
- Who are the 'school leaders' and how do they exercise their influence? What are the structures that enable individual and team leadership to flourish?
- What are the main leadership processes and how do they relate to school vision and culture?
- How are aspiring and established leaders prepared for their leadership roles?
- How do leaders evaluate school outcomes and how, if at all, does the evaluation lead to reviews of educational purpose and actions?

Bolam's (2000) framework uses five headings:

- The changing context and its influence on effective leadership performance
- The influence of personal factors on effective leadership performance

- The influence of types of setting on effective leadership performance
- Effective leadership performance in relation to specific tasks and processes
- Training and development for effective educational leadership.

Bolam's framework can be used as the provisional starting point for the mapping exercise. It adopts a contingency perspective on leadership and assumes that the effective performance of individual leaders is affected by a range of factors, most of which can be influenced to enhance performance.

Part of the difficulty in mapping the field of educational leadership and management stemmed from semantic differences and expectations among the key players. One interpretation of mapping the field is to regard it as a process of scanning the keywords identified to describe the studies being reviewed. Another approach is to identify the entire terrain of the field. Thus, the mapping of the field is a complex and difficult process.

The second aim, to address the review questions by carrying out a systematic review of available literature, was achieved in a limited form. The limitations stemmed largely from two factors. First, the reviewers and the review group were not sufficiently familiar with the technicalities of conducting reviews using the framework. This resulted in some inefficiency. Secondly, considerable effort went into involving practitioners which itself resulted in delay. Moreover, there were practical difficulties relating to the timing of the training and the deadline for completing the reviews. As a result, what emerged was a limited review of the literature based on an effective, but not an exhaustive, literature search.

The review process identified seven studies that satisfied the criteria and which, therefore, formed the basis of the draft synthesis report (Bell *et al.*, 2002). The findings from all eight studies point broadly in the same direction although the robustness of their designs varied considerably. In their descriptive study of 57 British primary, secondary and special schools, Bolam *et al.* (1993) concluded that participative approaches to leadership mediated by teacher activity were perceived by their respondents to be effective in contributing to student outcomes. However, it was unclear what impact the various leadership and management strategies actually had on student outcomes because the proxy measures were respondent perceptions.[1]

Four primary school studies were deemed to be designed well. Leithwood and Jantzi's (1999) outcome evaluation study of Canadian elementary schools measured teacher ratings of organisational conditions, student ratings of family culture and engagement and the relationships between leadership, organisational conditions, family educational culture and student engagement. No analysis by gender was presented. They found that family educational culture explained very large proportions of student engagement and that transformational leadership had strong effects on school organisational conditions. The authors cautioned against dismissing as not meaningful the, admittedly small, effects of leadership on student engagement, concluding that future research should focus on the measurement of 'student background' variables. Cheng's

(1994) outcome evaluation study of Hong Kong primary schools found that 'strong' leadership was correlated to organisational characteristics, teacher group performance, teacher individual performance, student performance and principal leadership, with the implication that principals' leadership is important to school performance at the organisational level. The 'negligible' relationship of leadership to principal and school demographic characteristics was taken to suggest that leadership style may not be attributable to the pre-existing demographic factors although, it is important to note, no account of socio-economic status apparently was taken in this study. The overall conclusion was that, although principals' leadership may have direct effects on organisational characteristics and teachers' performance, it is the latter two that may affect students' performance. Thus, the effect of principal leadership on students was mainly indirect. Judgements on student outcomes were based on attitude measures rather than test scores.

Van de Grift and Houtveen's (1999) outcome evaluation investigated the relationship between variables retrospectively, as measured by school leadership questionnaires and tests of Dutch primary school pupils in arithmetic, language and information processing. The otherwise sound methodological quality of the study was diminished because data were collected on three occasions from different samples. In 1989 no significant correlation was found, but the results for 1993 show a weak correlation between leadership and educational achievement in three subjects (arithmetic, language and information processing). They conclude that the findings provided weak evidence that principals did have an effect on their schools and that this increased between 1989 and 1998 but that better evidence is required based on an experimental or quasi-experimental design.

Leitner's (1994) soundly designed outcome evaluation of 27 US elementary schools used measures of principal instructional management, socio-economic status (SES) and student achievement scores in mathematics, language and reading. No significant positive relationship was found between principal instructional management and increased student learning which appeared to be influenced by environmental and organisational characteristics and SES.

Two secondary school studies had robust designs. Wiley's (2001) outcome evaluation study analysed the relationship between faculty, leadership and student achievement in maths in 214 US metropolitan high schools using a self-completion instrument and an independently validated student test. It found evidence of a positive relationship between faculty relations and student achievement in mathematics, especially in lower socio-economic status schools. Transformational leadership had some impact within a weak professional community but greatly impacted within a strong professional community. Thus, the social organisation of teachers and administrators within schools can affect student achievement. Finally, the large-scale, three-year outcome evaluation study by Silins and Mulford (2000) collected data from teachers and principals plus outcome data from Year 10 students in Australian secondary schools. A sophisticated design used model building and path analysis and established that the more transformational and distributed the leadership, the better the student outcomes a backdrop of family influence and support. Such school level factors had a stronger influence on students' academic achievement than students' SES or home background.

A number of reviewers argued that the limited number of items included in the final synthesis did not do justice to the richness of the field. The explanation for the small number of studies included, in part, can be found in the response to the third aim of the project. The third aim, to learn how to carry out an EPPI-style systematic review, to trial the EPPI methodology for systematic reviews and explore its utility, feasibility and viability for this field of scholarship and research, tended to occupy most of the energies of the reviewers. The limitations imposed by the structure of the main review question were designed to enable a systematic literature search within the time constraints. Selection terms to define the review question were identified at an early stage of the review process. While this had seemed a good idea at the time, in reality it was not really helpful because the terms were too specific to be of much use for an initial search. At this stage, the criteria for identifying studies need to be broadly inclusive rather than exclusive.

This view appears to contradict other EPPI review groups who suggest a need for the implementation of 'quality' criteria at an early stage in order to filter low-quality studies early on. While there is a tension between the quality of the study and relevance of the study, there is potentially a danger of relevant work being overlooked by doing this – significant in a field of research where there is such a paucity of literature. In this review, a balance between the two positions was sought. Unless it was very clear that the study would not be appropriate, it was considered for the next stage. Undoubtedly, there were some rather amorphous studies.

There were further limitations to the selection criteria. Time and geographical limits applied to the searches (post-Education Reform Act 1988, UK-based studies) became complex or even unworkable in practice:

- Time limit – while there were very sound reasons for only considering studies after 1988, it was necessary to be more specific in terms of what that delimitation signified. For example, were studies that were actually conducted after that period included or simply those published after 1988? Moreover, it is not always easy to decide when a study was conducted.
- Geographical limits – initially, it was decided to concentrate on UK-based research. Again the delimitations were not always that simple or transparent: international collaboration, comparative studies and the publication of work in international journals makes the task somewhat more complex. In any case, because of the lack of research in this area within the UK, it was finally decided to extend the review to significant research reported in English and has therefore included work conducted in North America and Australia.
- Databases also have an inherent weakness. Search mechanisms are only able to identify studies by the title. Therefore if the specific selection term

is not present in the title, it risks being excluded. However, after examining the references more closely, it was possible to understand how various words and combinations of words were interpreted within that database. In one database, it was more useful to leave out any reference to leadership in the search terms and then search the base manually to identify those that concerned leadership – 'school effectiveness' rather than 'school effectiveness and leadership'. This was important because the database identified hits from the title of the papers, not the content. If a keyword is not present in the title it is omitted from the list. Another issue was our selection criteria. It is not possible at the initial stage to limit either to country or a specific date: the country, because these are often not specified in the title; and the date, because they vary with the databases. A more useful (but still not infallible) mechanism may be one in which the abstracts are taken into consideration, assuming one exists for the study.

Developmental changes in the format of the review guidelines resulted in problems at the data input and analysis stages.

CONCLUSION

The debate about the nature of systematic reviews continued through the review process and remains current. The process has a significant number of advocates. They see it as a useful addition to the range of techniques available to scholars in the field. Others involved in this first review took the view that, as a process, it requires significant modification before it is useful for analysis of educational research. A small group continue to believe that systematic reviews are intended to cast the spell of positivism over the field of educational leadership and management or, at the very least, are part of a process of redefining what counts as valid research into school leadership and management.

A number of reviewers identified ways in which the process might be adapted to be more applicable for educational research generally. One reviewer noted that when asked to establish if the study had a clear statement of purpose, a number of related questions might also be asked. These included:

- Do the authors make explicit why this is their purpose?
- Is there an opportunity for reviewers to identify other purposes that in their professional judgement exist within the field but have not been followed in this paper?
- Will the reviewers be allowed to explain why the authors have focused on this purpose?
- Is the methodology clearly explained?
- Are the criteria used to select the sample literature explicit?
- Is there a conceptual framework for organising the literature?

- Do the authors give recognition to work that is not part of the review but they know exists and is important within the field?
- Do the authors relate the review to current policy and historical contexts?

Similarly, another reviewer commented that the guidance for reviewers conflates facts and values, and suggested it would be better to ask separate questions such as 'What type of literature is used?' and 'Is there enough literature being used?' A further example of the same problem was identified by yet another reviewer who was concerned that reliability and validity are linked together and the review asked to comment on them as one, whereas there may be different comments about each of them.

Although there were a number of suggestions about how the review process could be made more appropriate to the field of educational leadership and management, the question about whether it is possible to adopt it within the field is still outstanding. The issue here is whether the model, with its origins in health care, is appropriate. As one reviewer argued: 'I think that a systematic review of a research topic is valuable, but the present EPPI method is not right. The basic flaw is to start with a RCT (random controlled trial) model and then try to adapt it to education, and educational leadership and management.'

It is evident that this type of review model is not applicable to many of the categories of studies that are likely to be found in the field of educational leadership and management. In particular it specifically excludes conventional reviews that are a significant feature of this field and contribute greatly to the process of synthesising and disseminating research findings. (e.g. Hallinger and Heck, 1999). As another reviewer pointed out some of the changes made to the format of the questions for reviewers were unhelpful: 'In the original description 'assessing educational research' was used. It is interesting to note that this expression has been replaced by the term 'primary studies in educational research'. This would, of course, exclude some of our most significant studies, which happen to be reviews.'

This was typical of a number of comments that criticised the explicit hierarchy of research studies that underpins this approach to systematic reviews. The pre-ordinance of RCTs and a hierarchy that then moved through well-designed quantitative and qualitative studies to practitioner research and school-based data collection was not thought adequately to reflect the nature of much of the research in this field.

One response to this might be to argue that more RCTs should be conducted in this field but this pre-supposes that such studies are both methodologically possible and ethically desirable. There are significant epistemological issues here that derive from the positivist assumptions about the nature of research and the extent to which research in this field can fit into such a framework. These issues were also evident both in the use of terms within review model and the focus of the model itself. One reviewer noted that: 'There is too much concentration on methodology and too little on the substance of the research – the balance is completely wrong – e.g. 90% on methods and 10% on findings. It should be the other way round! It produces such an atomised product that the main points from the paper are lost.'

It was also noted that the questions used to interrogate the studies made a number of assumptions about the types of study that would be found, for example, the focus is on intervention studies. It was difficult to categorise 'intervention type' in many studies in this review because no direct intervention took place. The process assumes that studies are largely based on intervention and that there would be a relationship between both the nature of the intervention and the research design and between the intervention and the participants. This is exemplified by the inclusion of a question about the extent to which interventions are based on needs assessment. However, at the same time, there seems to be some confusion over the use of terminology. As one reviewer pointed out, some sections of the guidelines: 'refer to "evaluation" but the rest use the term "intervention". These are different processes but the questions seem to pre-suppose that they are the same.

Furthermore, it seems that the inclusion of descriptive studies, as an alternative, had not been considered. This meant that studies involving practitioners providing accounts linked to their informed professional judgement that illuminate school improvement were difficult to fit into the review process categories because they were developed from alternative ontological and epistemological foundations.

Several reviewers identified alternative review models that might be more appropriate, including a less exhaustive (and exhausting) approach advocated by Slavin (1995) based on a hierarchy of studies rather than a hierarchy of research designs. It was also noted that Hallinger and Heck provide a powerful argument in favour of more flexible review guidelines:

> Despite the generally positive assessment of the literature, we must also emphasise the limitations of this body of research. Even as a group the studies do not resolve the most important theoretical and practical issues entailed in understanding of the principal's role in contributing to school effectiveness. These concern the means by which principals achieve an impact on school outcomes as well as the interplay with contextual forces that influence the exercise of school leadership.

> (Hallinger and Heck, 1999, p. 186)

In other words, there are more ways to answer the question about educational leadership than 'does it work?'. This is important because one conclusion drawn from the conduct of this review is that it is important in matters related to school leadership and management to recognise the nature of the evidence available. In this way the relationship between the evidence and the use to be made of the outcomes of reviews can be determined. The evidence does not have to be the product of strictly controlled experiments based on a clearly identifiable intervention with outcomes that can be confidently claimed to be the result of such interventions. Most social settings are too complex to allow such a causal connection to be robustly established. It is unlikely that causal relationships in educational leadership and management can be established to the extent that research evidence can be used as a firm basis on which to base policy and practice.

The most that can be expected is that generalisation might be made from relevant studies with a reasonable degree of confidence and the outcomes of reviews may be included in the range of sources that are used to inform policy formulation and its implementation in practice. This is not a council of despair. The evidence base from which policy and practice might be informed can be improved and extended considerably by such reviews and they may become a necessary part of the formulation of policy and the identification of good practice. However, they will not, in themselves, provide a sufficient basis for action. Scope must always remain for the exercise of professional judgement based on an intimate knowledge of the context within which each school is located.

NOTE

1. This chapter is based on the work of the School Leadership and Management Review Group up to the first draft report in May 2002. Subsequent revisions of that report have produced modifications to both the process and the findings as reported in this chapter.

INCLUDED STUDIES

Ainscow, M. and Southworth, G. (1996). 'School improvement: a study of the roles of leaders and external consultants.' *School Effectiveness and School Improvement* 7(3): 229–51.

Barker, B. (2001). 'Do leaders matter?' *Educational Review* 53(1): 65–76.

Bolam, R., A. McMahon, K. Pocklington and D. Weindling (1993). *Effective Management in Schools: A report for the Department for Education via the School Management Task Force Professional Working Party*. London: HMSO.

Caldwell, B.J. (2000). 'Scenarios for leadership and abandonment in the transformation of schools.' *School Effectiveness and School Improvement* 11(4): 475–99.

Cheng, Y.C. (1994). 'Principal's leadership as a critical factor for school performance: evidence from multi-levels of primary schools.' *School Effectiveness and School Improvement* 5(3): 299–317.

Cotton, C. (2001). *The role of the headteacher in school improvement: listening to the voice of practitioners*. British Educational Research Association Annual Conference, Leeds University.

Day, C., Harris, A. and Hadfield, M. (1999). *Leading Schools in Times of Change*. European Conference on Educational Research, Lahti, Finland.

Day, C., Harris, A. and Hadfield, M. (2001). 'Grounding knowledge of schools in stakeholder realities: a multi-perspective study of effective school leaders.' *School Leadership and Management* 21(1): 19–42.

Diggins, P.B. (1997). 'Reflections on leadership characteristics necessary to develop and sustain learning school communities.' *School Leadership and Management* 17(3): 413–25.

Dinham, S., Cairney, T. et al. (1995). 'School climate and leadership: research into three secondary schools.' *Journal of Educational Administration* 33(4): 36–58.

Ferguson, N., Earley, P. et al. (1999). 'New heads, OFSTED inspections and the prospects for school improvement.' *Educational Research* 41(3) Winter.

Hallinger, P. and Heck, R. (1999). Can leadership enhance school effectiveness? in Bush, T., Bell, L. Bolam, R. Glatter R. and Ribbins P. (eds) *Educational Management: Redefining theory, policy and practice.* London: Paul Chapman Publishing.

Hallinger, P. and Heck, R.H. (1998). 'Exploring the principal's contribution to school effectiveness: 1980–1995.' *School Effectiveness and School Improvement* 9(2): 157–91.

Jackson, D.S. (2000). 'The school improvement journey: perspectives on leadership.' *School Leadership and Management* 20(1): 61–78.

Leithwood, K. and Jantzi, D. (1999). 'Transformational school leadership effects: a replication.' *School Effectiveness and School Improvement* 10(4): 451–79.

Leithwood, K. and Jantzi, D. (2000). 'Principal and teacher leadership effects: a replication.' *School Leadership and Management* 20(4): 415–34.

Leitner, D. (1994). 'Do principals affect student outcomes: an organizational perspective.' *School Effectiveness and School Improvement* 5(3): 219–38.

Silins, H.C. (1994). 'The relationship between transformational and transactional leadership and school improvement outcomes.' *School Effectiveness and School Improvement* 5(3): 272–98.

Silins, H.C. and Mulford, W. (2000). 'Leadership for organizational learning in Australian secondary schools.' In Leithwood, K. (ed.) *Understanding Schools as Intelligent Systems.* Greenwich, CT: JAI Press.

Silins, H.C. and W. Mulford (2000). *Towards an Optimistic Future: Schools as Learning Organisations – Effects on Teacher Leadership and Student Outcomes.* AARE-NZARE Conference, Sydney, Australia.

Silins, H.C. and Mulford, W. (in press). 'Leadership and school results'. in Leithwood K. and P. Hallinger (eds) *Second International Handbook of educational Leadership and Administration.* Norwell, MA: Kluwer Academic Publishers.

Silins, H.C. and Mulford, W. (2001) *Reframing Schools: The Case for System, Teacher and Student Learning.* The Learning Conference, Spetses, Greece, 4–8 July.

Silins, H.C., Mulford, W. and Zarins, S. (1999). *Organisational Learning in Australian High Schools: Nature and Practices.* AARE-NZARE Conference, Melbourne, Australia.

Southworth, G. (in press). 'Lessons from successful leadership in small schools.' In Leithwood K. and Hallinger, P. (eds) *Second International Handbook of Educational Leadership and Administration* Norwell, MA: Kluwer Academic Publishers.

Van de Grift, W. and Houtveen, A.A.M. (1999). 'Educational leadership and pupil achievement in primary education.' *School Effectiveness and School Improvement* 10(4): 373–89.

Wiley, S.D. (2001). 'Contextual effects on student achievement: school leadership and professional community.' *Journal of Educational Change* 2: 1–33.

REFERENCES

Bell, L. (1999a) Back to the future, the development of education policy in England, *Journal of Educational Administration*, Vol. 37, Nos 3 and 4, pp. 200–28.

Bell, L. (1999b) Primary schools and the nature of the education market place, in Bush, T., Bell, L., Bolam, R., Glatter, R. and Ribbins, P. (eds) *Educational Management: Redefining theory, policy and practice*, London: Paul Chapman Publishing.

Bell, L., Bolam, R., and Cubillo, L. (2002) *The School Leadership Review Group Draft Final Report*, Leicester: University of Leicester.

Bolam, R. (1997) Management development for headteachers: retrospect and prospect, *Educational Management and Administration*, Vol. 25, No. 3, pp. 265–83.

Bolam, R. (1999) Educational administration, leadership and management: towards a research agenda, in Bush, T., Bell, L., Bolam, R., Glatter, R. and Ribbins, P. (eds) *Educational Management: Redefining theory, policy and practice*, London: Paul Chapman Publishing.

Bolam, R. (2000) Mapping the field, paper presented to the Standing Conference for Research on Educational Leadership and Management Mapping Group, Reading. December.

Bolam, R., McMahon, A., Pocklington, K. and Weindling, D. (1993). *Effective Management in Schools: A report for the Department for Education via the School Management Task Force Professional Working Party*, London: HMSO.

Bottery, M. (2001) Mapping the field of leadership studies: some preliminary thoughts, paper presented to the Standing Conference for Research on Educational Leadership and Management Mapping Group, Reading. December.

Bush, T. (1999) Introduction: setting the scene, in Bush, T., Bell, L., Bolam, R., Glatter, R. and Ribbins, P. (eds) *Educational Management: Redefining theory, policy and practice*, London: Paul Chapman Publishing.

Bush, T. (2001) Mapping the field of educational leadership, paper presented to the Standing Conference for Research on Educational Leadership and Management Mapping Group, Reading. December.

Bush, T., Bell, L., Bolam, R., Glatter, R. and Ribbins, P. (eds) (1999) *Educational Management: Redefining theory, policy and practice*, London: Paul Chapman Publishing.

Cheng, Y.C. (1994) 'Principal's leadership as a critical factor for school performance: evidence from multi-levels of primary schools, *School Effectiveness and School Improvement*, Vol. 5, No. 3, pp. 299–317.

Davies, B. and Ellison, L. (1997) *School Leadership fro the 21st Century: A Competency and Knowledge Approach*, London: Routledge.

Davies, H., Nutley, S. and Smith, P. (eds) (2000) *What works? Evidence-Based Policy and Practice in Public Services*, Bristol: Policy Press.

Department for Education and Employment (DfEE) (2000). Blunkett rejects anti-intellectualism and welcomes sound ideas, *DfEE News*, No. 43/00.

Educational Management and Administration (1999) Vol. 27, No. 3. Special Edition: Redefining Educational Management and Leadership.

Evans, J. and Benefield, P. (2001) Systematic reviews of educational research: does the medical model fit? *British Educational Research Journal*, Vol. 27, No. 5, pp. 527–42.

Hallinger, P. and Heck, R.H. (1998) Exploring the principal's contribution to school effectiveness: 1980–1995, *School Effectiveness and School Improvement*, Vol. 9, No. 2, pp. 157–91.

Hallinger, P. and Heck, R. (1999) Can leadership enhance school effectiveness? in Bush, T., Bell, L., Bolam, R., Glatter R. and Ribbins, P. (eds) *Educational Management: Redefining theory, policy and practice*, London: Paul Chapman Publishing.

Hammersley, M. (2001) On systematic reviews of research literature; a 'narrative response to Evans and Benefield', *British Educational Research Journal*, Vol. 27, No. 5, pp. 543–76.

Hargreaves, D. (1994) *The Mosaic of Learning*, London: Demos.

Leithwood, K. and Jantzi, D. (1999) Transformational school leadership effects: a replication, *School Effectiveness and School Improvement*, Vol. 10, No. 4, pp. 451–79.

Leitner, D. (1994) Do principals affect student outcomes?: an organizational perspective, *School Effectiveness and School Improvement*, Vol. 5, No. 3, pp. 219–238.

Mortimore, P., Sammons, P., Stoll, L., Lewis, D. and Ecob, R. (1988) *School Matters: The Junior Years*, Somerset: Open Books.

Oakley, A. (2000) *Experiments in Knowing: Gender and Method in Social Sciences*, Cambridge: Polity Press.

Ouston, J. (2001) Untitled paper presented to the Standing Conference for Research on Educational Leadership and Management Mapping Group, Reading. December.

Sammons, P., Hillman, J. and Mortimore, P. (1995) *Key Characteristics of Effective Schools: A Review of School Effectiveness Research*, report by the Institute of Education for the Office for Standards in Education.

Sebba J. (2000) Department for Education and Employment (schools research), in Davies, H., Nutley, S. and Smith, P. (eds) *What works? Evidence-Based Policy and Practice in Public Services*, Bristol: Policy Press, pp. 240–4.

Silins, H.C. and Mulford, W. (2000) Towards an Optimistic Future: Schools as Learning Organisations – Effects on Teacher Leadership and Student Outcomes, AARE-NZARE Conference, Sydney, Australia.

Slavin, R.E. (1995) Best evidence synthesis: an intelligent alternative to meta-analysis, *Journal of Clinical Epidemiology*, No. 48, pp. 9–18.

Southworth, G. (1997) Primary headship and leadership, in Crawford, M., Kydd, L. and Riches, C. (eds) *Leadership and teams in Educational Management*, Buckingham: Open University Press.

Stronach, I. and Hustler, D. (2001) 'Editorial: old whine in new battles', *British Educational Research Journal*, Vol. 27, No. 5, pp. 523–6.

Van de Grift, W. and Houtveen, A.A.M. (1999) Educational leadership and pupil achievement in primary education, *School Effectiveness and School Improvement*, Vol. 10, No. 4, pp. 373–89.

Wiley, S.D. (2001) Contextual effects on student achievement: school leadership and professional community, *Journal of Educational Change*, Vol. 2, pp. 1–33.

7

Research and Evidence-Based Practice: Focusing on Practice and Practitioners

PHILIPPA CORDINGLEY

INTRODUCTION

Much of the debate about research and evidence-based practice looks through the research end of the telescope. It addresses questions about how far research can provide reliable information as the basis for practice. The literature also highlights failures to take account of research findings by policy-makers and practitioners. This chapter considers the issues from the other end of the telescope: it looks at the nature of practice and what this means for research and evidence.

The chapter moves from a brief analysis of the nature of knowledge and skills in teaching and learning contexts to look at some of the literature about how such knowledge and skills are developed. It explores the boundaries between the roles and responsibilities of researchers and those of users of research and evidence who put research to work in practice contexts. It also explores whether using research to inform, or as a basis for, practice means engaging *in* research. The chapter concludes with a brief look at the consequences of these issues for research design, conduct, communication and use. In so doing it begins to consider whether we should be exploring the nature of practice-based research alongside research-based practice?

THE NATURE OF TEACHING AND LEARNING

Much has been written elsewhere about teaching and learning, and the focus of this book is upon how research and evidence are deployed within it. But use of knowledge involves learning, and learning is context specific. So, a discussion of research and evidence-based practice must begin with a brief analysis of the context in which the research or evidence is to be made meaningful and put to work. Charles Desforges initiates this process in his examination of evidence-informed policy (EIP) in Chapter 1. However, in that chapter,

Desforges analyses teaching and learning from evidence-informed policy rather than the evidence-informed practice perspective that is adopted here.

Teaching and learning in school classrooms involves huge numbers of variables, which interact quickly and dynamically through multiple, second-by-second judgements by teachers. The teacher's knowledge, plans and understanding are interpreted differently by large numbers of pupils each with different starting points. Pupils' responses also affect each other even if the teacher is teaching in a transmission mode. If teaching is interactive, pupils support and challenge each others' learning through their questions, ideas and knowledge in ways that call for new, well-informed and creative responses from teachers. In this context teachers need an intimate grasp of an idea or strategy in order to deploy it. Their grasp of ideas and skills will need to be complex and multi-layered. To summarise Desforges' introductory remarks about teacher knowledge, and to provide a context for what follows, I suggest that teachers' practical, subject, theoretical knowledge and understanding will need to embrace:

- their subject
- the ways in which learners commonly approach the subject or curriculum area, including common misconceptions
- the ways in which the subject or curriculum area can be explored, explained and brought to life.

All this will need to be understood in the context of specific knowledge about the starting points of particular learners and be operationalised through skills in managing dynamic interactions between them. For a fuller summary of Shulman's (1986) cornerstone taxonomy of teacher knowledge and a representation of it in pictorial form (ibid., p. 67) see the *Effective Teachers of Numeracy* study by Askew *et al.* (1997).

Such complexity means that, in practice, knowledge is hard to achieve and resistant to change; it must be internalised or routinised as many authors have noted (for example, Desforges, 1995) if it is to be put to work to solve genuine learning and teaching problems. Such problems occur in the blink of an eye in interactive classroom settings. If teachers' knowledge is not available to them equally quickly, they will not be able to deploy it at all. Knowing that, for example, using more open-ended questions has the capacity to deepen learning is quite different from knowing how to do it. As Black and Dylan (1998) and many others have noted, asking deeper, open-ended questions that will push thinking forward, requires good knowledge of the subject and of what the particular learners involved already know and can do. More specifically, good subject knowledge is required to form the question – to pose it for example through a relevant, concrete analogy. It is also needed to link the multiple and diverging pupil responses that such questions generate back to the learning target. Good knowledge of pupils' starting points is essential to ensuring that the question is genuinely challenging and within pupils' reach.

Knowledge from academic research, or from more direct evidence from a teacher's own classroom is no less, or more, important than these varied forms of practical knowledge. But such knowledge needs to be integrated with the more practical forms of knowledge, before it can be put to work in classroom settings.

CHANGING ROUTINISED KNOWLEDGE AND STRATEGIES

Whilst the literature about internalised or tacit knowledge is also extensive (see, for example, Ryle, 1949) the literature about changing tacit knowledge is less so. Nonetheless, authors such as Gusky (1986), Hargreaves (1993), Huberman (1985) and Eraut (1994) all explore how tricky developing or enhancing tacit knowledge can be. Teachers, by definition, are unaware of routinised or internalised knowledge. Medwell *et al.* (1998), for example, observed highly effective teachers of literacy and interviewed them after the lesson. The researchers found that the teachers routinely underestimated the complexity of the lesson they had just taught. In particular, they were unaware of the grammatical content of a lesson in which word, sentence and text level teaching had been highly effectively embedded in work on poetry and dismissed the lesson as just a 'poetry lesson' presumably because they had internalised the grammatical content and were focusing upon the poetry. As the researcher put it, the teachers knew their subject in the form it took within the classroom context. If teachers underestimate or are unaware of the concepts underpinning their pedagogic strategies, it will be difficult to relate new approaches to existing ones. To ease this process of taking on board evidence or research findings, teachers need help in making their existing practices and the underpinning knowledge of it explicit, so that they can be compared with new approaches. Case studies and illustration seem to be particularly important in this context, especially via video clips of practices at work, (Cordingley and the National Teacher Research Panel, BERA, 2000a). Such case studies or illustrations represent not a means of 'dumbing down' research but of enabling teachers to assess the implications for change and supporting them as they internalise knowledge in its newly interpreted and integrated form.

The work of Joyce and Showers (1988) neatly underlines the importance of not underestimating the processes needed to ensure that new approaches – in this case, ones derived from consulting research and evidence – are interpreted for a specific context and embedded in practice. They trace connections between:

- in-service interventions
- changes in teachers' abilities to reproduce new strategies out of context or on a one off basis
- embedded change where teachers had full (which they describe as executive) control of a strategy so that they were able to deploy it at will for a sustained period after an intervention.

Teachers in the Joyce and Showers study showed almost no 'executive control of new knowledge' resulting in regular use of strategies from in-service education in classrooms until the teachers involved had had chance to:

- absorb information and theory
- see theory demonstrated
- practiced putting theory to work in classroom contexts
- received feedback based on observation of their practice; together with expert coaching – on a sustained basis.

This need for a series of complex and interactive intervening steps between encountering and using new knowledge by teachers does not seem, according to Israel Rich (1993) to be a phenomenon restricted to new teachers. Both expert teachers and novices, faced with information about a new approach and a desire or pressure to use it, seem to experience very similar development strategies and behaviours.

This short summary and interpretation of the research using and changing tacit knowledge is derived from an analysis of the research on teacher acquisition of and use of knowledge which can be found in a review of the research for the Teacher Training Agency's (TTA) policy of promoting teaching as a research and evidence-informed profession (Cordingley and Bell, 2002).

IMPLICATIONS FOR RESEARCH AND EVIDENCE-INFORMED PRACTICE

This snapshot of the complexity of practitioner knowledge and of the even more complex process of developing such knowledge so that it can be skilfully employed in dynamic interactive settings, not only implies a need for complex and sustained effort in order to develop practitioner knowledge. It also creates a highly context specific environment. It follows that all research, however large scale, brilliantly conceived, executed and communicated, needs to be actively interpreted by users for their own context. This is not to say that policy-makers at school, local, regional or national level cannot intervene in response to large-scale research findings. It suggests, rather, that generic policy interventions can never take the forms of recipes; they will always depend upon skilled teacher interpretation and judgement if they are to have an impact upon day-to-day practice. This, in turn, suggests that neither researchers and Evidence-Informed Policy-makers nor those advocating research and evidence-informed practice can escape from engaging with, and/ or supporting, individual teachers in individual classrooms. Public education systems are, of course, littered with policies and research initiatives that have had little impact upon the education system as a whole. This does not necessarily imply that the only useful unit of analysis, or indeed action, in using research is the individual teacher. The experience of a growing number of national schemes to fund and support teacher use of and/or engagement in research schemes, all suggests that collaborative and cumulative engagement in and with research have a great deal to offer and represent a congenial and fertile means of building a critical mass of teacher interest and skill in using larger scale research. Such initiatives include the TTA Teacher Research Grant scheme (TTA, 2002a), the TTA School-Based Research Consortia (TTA, 2002b), and Best Practice Research Scholarships (BPRS). But, if individual interpretation of research is complex, collaborative interpretation is doubly so. The use of research or research and evidence-informed practice needs, therefore, to be understood as at least as complex and technically demanding an activity as conducting the research in the first place.

WHAT ARE THE IMPLICATIONS FOR RESEARCH ITSELF?

This introduction to the use of research through the practitioners' end of the telescope has, of course, some of its roots in the tradition of teacher research which is well rehearsed in the literature in the work of Stenhouse (1975) and many others after him. There can be no problem in describing teacher research or 'systematic enquiry (by teachers) made public' in the Stenhouse tradition, as 'research-based practice'; such a description would be tautological. But the broad rubric teacher research encompasses a huge range of practice, methods and values. The important question is what counts as teacher research? Battles rage, about whether all 'teacher enquiry' should be called research (Foster, 1999; Gorard, 2001)[1] and also about whether teacher enquiry necessarily involves engaging with evidence from the literature as well as from a teacher's own classroom.

From my perspective the question about what counts as teacher research calls for a careful and differentiated answer. Not all teacher enquiry aims to produce evidence and understanding in a public form that can be tested and reviewed by others. Some teacher enquiry simply seeks to enhance the practice of the enquirer through the use of evidence. The aim is developmental. Analysis for contradictory as well as confirmatory evidence, reviewing what is known already and even writing reports to enable scrutiny, may not figure in the process. This kind of developmental enquiry represents potentially good continuing professional development. But it seems not to represent research per se, not least because it is not made public. If the goal is to inform the practice of others then there is every reason for the work to be made public – to enable testing, replication and interpretation for other contexts. But if the goal is solely to inform the practice of the teacher involved there is no reason why it should be made public. This kind of continuing professional development (CPD) can accurately be described as *evidence*-based or informed practice. The teacher is engaging with systematically acquired evidence about their own teaching and learning. Whether or not it is *research*-informed practice depends upon whether the teacher involved also drew upon research of others.

The previous paragraph argues that although not all teacher enquiry can be sensibly described as research, it can be described as evidence-informed practice. It also suggests it is possible to distinguish between research and/or evidence-informed practice. Can we go further? Is it sensible or possible to conceive of research based or informed practice that does *not* involve teachers in undertaking research? Stenhouse (1975) and others after him (Rudduck, 2001; Elliott, 1991; 1993), assert that engaging with research means engaging in it. Does this also apply to research based or informed practice? I think not. This chapter goes on to explore whether it is necessary to *engage in* research to engage *with* it.

The literature review (Cordingley and Bell, 2002) discussed in setting the context for this chapter, highlights extensive agreement in the research that changes in teacher knowledge calls for:

● activities that reveal teachers' existing internalised skills, practice and knowledge
● experimentation with new approaches and ideas
● sustained testing and adaptation (what David Hargreaves calls tinkering)
● feedback and coaching based on observation.

Once again the literature reinforces the message that engaging with research or research-based practice is a complex and evidence-dependent business. But this list of what is entailed in systematic changes in teacher knowledge and skills does not include quite a number of activities that are commonly accepted as tests of research, such as:

● systematic recording of data to enable subsequent analysis by the teacher or by others
● identification of a research question
● triangulation in order to validate data
● publication to enable scrutiny of the research.

The implication is that using research involves some research processes but not necessarily a complete sequence or cycle. This distinction is not one imposed solely by academic researchers. For example, all the requirements from the list above have been adopted by the National Teacher Research Panel as criteria for research (TTA, 2002).

It is reasonable, then, to argue that in the absence of a full cycle of research activities, teacher enquiry might reasonably be described as 'research and evidence-based practice' but not *necessarily* also as research. Perhaps this argument can usefully be made concrete through an example.

In the TTA/CfBT-funded, North East School-Based Research Consortium, teachers were actively involved in looking at the claims from large-scale published research and choosing teaching strategies suggested by such work to develop and test in their own classrooms. The teachers collected video recordings of their initial and succeeding efforts to use these approaches. They developed diaries recording their own perceptions of these efforts and collected pupil learning logs setting out pupils' perceptions of lessons involving the new strategies. These materials were reviewed by the teachers along with a teacher coach who had previously worked through this cycle. The teachers were engaging with both the research findings of academic researchers and of colleague teacher researchers. They were also all engaging with evidence to support the development of their practice. They quite properly want respect for this very rigorous pedagogical development activity – without having to write it up to enable peer review, without analysing broader patterns and without having their efforts caught up in a tide of theoretical argument or polemic. This is a fine, if personal and idiosyncratic, example of 'teacher enquiry', of 'teacher engagement with research' or 'research-based practice'. Teaching is a deeply challenging and intellectually demanding as well as practical activity. Surely research and evidence-informed teaching is not, and should not be, considered somehow less admirable than conducting research? But is it sensible to call such activity 'engagement *in* research'? How did the teachers involved approach this issue?

Many teachers in the Consortia got involved because they were interested in what thinking skills offered in relation to their teaching and their children. They did not choose to describe themselves as researchers. Some of them became interested in research as a result of their use of video and pupil learning logs. Others were intensely interested in research, perhaps because they were registered on a master's course, or because they had been asked to take on the role of school research co-ordinator. This second group of teachers did describe themselves as engaging *in* research. They coded and analysed video clips, identified patterns across the journals, video clips and pupil learning logs of different teachers, and explored connections with pupil outcomes. They looked for confirmatory and contradictory evidence. They fully expected to participate in all relevant research processes and forms of communication. They did, for example, write to enable peer review. There seems little doubt that the second group were engaging with *and* in research at the same time as illustrating exemplary research and evidence-based practice.

There are two important postscripts. It is worth noting that the final reports from the consortia suggest that those teachers who did engage fully in research in all its modes felt they gained much more from the process than their colleagues (there is no record of whether their colleagues felt the same thing). It is also important to note that the teachers engaging in, as distinct from with, research were also almost certainly crucial catalysts and mediators between research and practice for their colleagues who chose to engage with research but not in it. These final reports suggest that for many teachers to engage *with* research it is necessary for some to engage *in* it – to create stepping stones between the two.

Second, I make no claim that this example is unique. There are similar examples across all four TTA-funded school-based research consortia and, no doubt, across other national and local initiatives such as the DfES Best Practice Research Scholarships, ESRC networks and collaborative, enquiry-orientated initiatives such as Improving the Quality of Education for All.

What I hope this section has illustrated is:

- that research and evidence-based or informed practice may be distinct from each other in minor ways but that both are very similar to teacher engagement *with* research
- the ways in which such work is distinct from teacher engagement *in* research
- that all of these forms of activity have an important part to play in enhancing teachers' professional knowledge and practice
- that whilst individual teachers are engaging *with* research without engaging *in* it, their experience is more meaningful if they are able to work closely with other teachers who *have* engaged in research
- that teacher engagement *in* research quite definitely entails teacher engagement with it and also constitutes research and evidence-informed/based practice
- that both engagement with and in research are highly desirable, and are also perfectly valid forms of research and evidence-based practice.

WHERE IS THE BOUNDARY OF
RESPONSIBILITY BETWEEN RESEARCH
AND PRACTICE IN SUCH EXPERIENCES?

As has been noted, much of the practical exploration of research and evidence-informed practice by practitioners through schemes such as the consortia and the TTA research grants emphasises the requirement of teachers to interpret knowledge from research or from other sources for their own context, and the complex steps involved in changing teachers' knowledge and skills. This emphasis calls into question simple models of research dissemination. Knowledge and understanding from research cannot simply be written up by researchers, read by teachers and, from this basis, instantly shape teacher and learner transactions.

As has been stated earlier in this chapter, research must, at the very least, be communicated in ways that enable and encourage the revelation of existing knowledge or comparisons between research and existing practice. It must also be communicated in ways that enable teachers to test and interpret the implications for their own context. So, for example, the National Teacher Research Panel (Cordingley, 2000a) highlights the importance of:

- case studies that illustrate new approaches and widespread existing practices vividly in practical terms
- sufficient detail of the teaching intervention or knowledge in action to enable teachers to test it out for themselves
- sufficient detail about the starting points of pupils and the communities, phases or subjects involved in research outputs for teachers to see how their own pupils are similar to or different from these involved in studies.

If research and evidence provides such materials, teachers will be able to use research to inform their practice whether or not the examples grow out of samples and methods structured to support generalisation structured. But will they do so? They will not (whether or not researchers believe they should) I would argue, unless the research addresses issues that:

- teachers care deeply about
- teachers have to address anyway.

Nor will teachers work through the complicated and sustained processes needed for embedded changes in practice unless they believe it will enhance learning outcomes for their pupils. They are just as aware as researchers of problems in attributing cause and effect in the context of the number of intervening variables. See for examples the papers by each of the four school-based consortia about credibility of evidence (Cordingley, 2000b). They would also be sceptical of 'killer facts or results' that imply that X or Y strategy will, as sure as eggs are eggs, raise attainment in P and Q. But they do, nonetheless, want to know about outcomes as well as strategies and about connections between the two.

For research and evidence-based or informed practice to make sense then, teachers' perspectives about issues worth researching and their active involvement in the creation of research communication material is essential. This implies a closer and overlapping set of roles and responsibilities between teachers and researchers. There can be no simple cut-off between the creation of knowledge or evidence through research by academic researchers and its use by practitioners. Certainly writing and reading academic research reports does not constitute an adequate bridge between the two. Neither does working on research and evidence-informed practice through the lens of the supply side. Pedagogic research that does not take teachers' needs and realities into account from the start will struggle hard to feature in research-based practice.

I conclude with a final close-up of research-based practice through the other end of the telescope. Encouraging and enabling teachers to base practice on research or to use it to inform practice are, in themselves, teaching and learning problems. Solving the problems inherent in connecting research and practice means that researchers have to use messages from pedagogic research to shape their research outputs as well as the practice of teachers. What is sauce for the goose is definitely sauce for the gander! Research and evidence-based or informed practice calls for dynamic, interactive, whole profession, teacher centred and differentiated research communication. Just as learners do the learning in school classrooms, practitioners, not researchers, do the learning in using research and evidence. So, reflecting ever more deeply on the nature of knowledge (something akin to looking at fuzzy generalisations as curriculum content), on beautifully formed research designs (like schemes of work or handouts) or research reports (the equivalent of classroom presentations) will achieve no more, I would argue, than transmission teaching. The researcher, like the teacher, has important, specialist knowledge and expertise – but the teacher, like the learner, is the person who must act and whose needs must be taken into account at every turn. Fortunately, however, researchers have a very sophisticated group of learners to work with – the teaching profession.

NOTE

1. There are specific problems with these two particular articles that are worth noting for the record, although they are not central to the argument here. Both of these papers focus on a small sample of pilot projects and evaluate them against aims set by the researchers rather than the initiative. One or two points raised by Foster had in fact already been publicly recognised by the TTA as important before he wrote his paper and used it to adjust the scheme as a whole. Others were simply misunderstandings of the role of the summaries and their relationship with the full reports or incorrect assumptions about the academic steering that was a condition of the scheme. Gorard's paper assumes incorrectly that the pilot was established to draw funds away from academic research. It also appears only to work on the evidence as presented by Foster.

REFERENCES

Askew, M., Brown, M., Rhodes, V., William, D. and Johnson, D. (1997) *Effective Teachers of Numeracy: Report of a Study Carried Out for the Teacher Training Agency*, London: King's College, University of London.

Black, P. and Dylan, W. (1998) *Inside the Black Box: Raising Standards through Classroom Assessment*, London: School of Education, King's College.

Cordingley, P. (2000a) *Teacher Perspectives on the Accessibility and Usability of Research Outputs: A Paper Prepared by Philippa Cordingley and the National Teacher Research Panel to the BERA 2000 Conference*, London: TTA.

Cordingley, P. (2000b) *Teacher Perspectives on the Credibility and Usability of Different Kinds of Evidence: Reflections from Across the Four TTA Funded School-Based Research Consortia. A Paper Presented at the BERA 2000 Conference*, London: TTA.

Cordingley, P. and Bell, M. (2002) *Literature and Evidence Search: Teachers' Use of Research and Evidence as They Learn to Teach and Improve their Teaching*, London: TTA.

Desforges, C. (1995) How does experience affect theoretical knowledge for teaching? *Learning and Instruction*, Vol. 5, No. 4, pp. 385–400.

Elliott, J. (1991) *Action Research for Educational Change*, Buckingham: Open University Press.

Elliott, J. (1993) Professional education and the idea of a practical education science, in Elliott, J. (ed.) *Reconstructing Teacher Education*, London: Falmer.

Eraut, M. (1994) The acquisition and use of theory by beginning teachers, in Eraut, M. (ed.) *Developing Professional Knowledge and Competence*, London: Falmer.

Foster, P. (1999) 'Never mind the quality, feel the impact': a methodological assessment of teacher research sponsored by the Teacher Training Agency, *British Journal of Educational Studies*, Vol. 47, No. 4, pp. 380–98.

Gorard, S. (2001) *A Changing Climate for Educational Research? The Role of Research Capability-Building*, Occasional Paper 45, Cardiff: Cardiff University School of Social Science.

Guskey, T.R. (1986) Staff development and the process of teacher change, *Educational Researcher*, Vol. 15, No. 5, pp. 5–12.

Hargreaves, D.H. (1993) A common-sense model of the professional development of teachers, in Elliot, J. (ed.) *Reconstructing Teacher Education: Teacher Development*, London: Falmer.

Huberman, M. (1985) What knowledge is of most worth to teachers? A knowledge-use perspective, *Teaching and Teacher Education*, Vol. 1, No. 3, pp. 251–62.

Joyce, B. and Showers, B. (1988) *Student Achievement through Staff Development*, London: Longman.

Medwell, J., Wray, D., Poulson, L. and Fox, R. (1998) *Effective Teachers of Literacy: A Report of a Research Project Commissioned by the Teacher Training Agency*, Exeter: University of Exeter.

TTA (2002) *National Teacher Research Panel (NTRP) framework*, London: Teacher Training Agency.

TTA (2002a) *Teacher Research Grant Scheme. Summaries 1997–2000*. London: Teacher Training Agency.
http://www.canteach.gov.uk/community/research/grant/

TTA (2002b) Summary of the Consortia: Overview Report, London: Teacher Training Agency.

Rich, I. (1993) Stability and change in teacher expertise, *Teachers and Learning*, Vol. 9, pp. 137–41.

Rudduck, J. (2001) Teachers as researchers: the quiet revolution, address for the DfES and TTA Conference at the Queen Elizabeth II Conference Centre, March.
www.canteach.gov.uk/community/research/conference/jeanruddock/index.htm

Ryle, G. (1949) *The Concept of Mind*, Harmondsworth: Penguin Books.

Shulman, L.S. (1986) Those who understand: knowledge growth in teaching, *Educational Researcher*, Vol. 15, No. 2, pp. 4–14.

Stenhouse, L.A. (1975) *An Introduction to Curriculum Research and Development*, London: Heinemann Educational Books.

8

Practitioner Research in Educational Leadership and Management: Support and Impact

MARIANNE COLEMAN

This chapter is devoted to an examination of the relationship between practitioner research in schools and colleges and the ways in which it can inform the practice of educational leadership and management. In the same way that classroom practice or the teaching of an individual subject may be informed by systematic and critical research and reflection, the management and leadership of schools and colleges can be examined and improved through practitioner research.

The development of practitioner research is often in partnership with a higher education institution (Southworth, 1998) and may also be part of an award-bearing course (Dadds, 1995; Dadds and Hart, 2001; Murray and Lawrence, 2000). Murray and Lawrence (2000 p. 10) describe practitioner-based enquiry (PBE) as: 'a process in which teachers, tutors, lecturers and other education professionals systematically enquire into their own institutional practices in order to produce assessable reports and artefacts which are submitted for academic credits leading to the awarding of degrees, certificates and diplomas of universities, colleges and other professional associations'.

This process of enquiring into and reflecting on their own practice is particularly stressed in relation to practitioner action research (Lomax, 2002). In addition, the process and impact of practitioner research is often associated with school improvement (Halsall, 1998). In a recent discussion on the web site of the National College for School Leadership, Jackson (2001) endorsed the concept of practitioners undertaking research in their institutions via accredited courses leading to development and improvement within the school. The practitioner research that forms the basis for this chapter and from which all the examples are drawn (Middlewood, Coleman and Lumby, 1999) has been carried out for accreditation with a higher education course associated with the idea of institutional improvement. In the research that forms the basis for this chapter, the practitioner researchers were all students for the MBA in educational management offered by the University of Leicester. The ethos of this course encourages professional development and institutional improvement through the investigations undertaken as coursework.

The degree was established in 1992 and is taught in three ways: campus based, school and college based and by distance learning. About half the distance learning students are international and live in over 40 different countries. In the latter part of the 1990s staff who were heavily involved in teaching the course undertook an evaluation to identify the extent to which the aims of the course were being achieved (Middlewood, Coleman and Lumby, 1999). The intention was to investigate the impact on students and their institutions of the work undertaken for the course. In order to do this we, the staff concerned, undertook a survey of those students who were studying through distance learning and who had completed at least two assignments and also conducted interviews with the practitioner researcher and others, particularly senior managers, in a range of schools and colleges. Where possible the schools and colleges were visited, otherwise the interviews took place by telephone. The case study schools and colleges were selected on the basis of replies to the survey from distance learning students, or they were purposively chosen from schools where a number of teachers were studying by the 'school-based' route. In these cases, the course is actually run in a school and the teachers study together and are taught a module each term on a weekly basis by university lecturers. This model of delivery provides great opportunities for teachers to work in a concerted way to bring about change and improvement. However, in the majority of cases, the students whose work was the focus for our evaluation, were working as single researchers in their institution.

This chapter is concerned with two aspects of the coursework undertaken by the individual students or groups of students for their master's degrees:

● the level of support in a school or college for practitioners' research
● the effectiveness of such research in terms of its impact on the individual, the school or college.

From consideration of these two areas it is possible to identify a schema of three levels of change that occurred as a result of the work of these practitioner researchers.

The first area to be considered is the levels of support. However, the extent of support for practitioner researchers depends on the culture of the establishment and this, in turn, is affected by the national culture and accepted ways of behaving.

WIDER CULTURAL FACTORS AND THE IMPACT ON PRACTITIONER RESEARCH

Although some international distance learning students did respond to our survey, the majority of the responses were from UK-based students or from

UK expatriates working abroad. Deference to authority and a desire to avoid causing offence would have been likely to deter some students from any possible dissemination of their work and might stop them offering opinions that might be published.

Students and practitioner researchers in some cultures, for example, many Eastern cultures, will almost certainly experience greater difficulties in obtaining research access than will students in the UK or North America. Where the power distance ratio is high (Hofstede, 1980) subordinates will naturally defer to their superiors in the hierarchy and access to the views of principals through research will be difficult for anyone other than another principal. Referring to research in Hong Kong, Dimmock (1998, p. 372) comments 'rank-and-file teachers often see participation as a privilege granted from above rather than as a right'. However, Dimmock does note that the rapid pace of change in Hong Kong means that younger generations hold different values to 'their more traditional parents and grandparents' (Dimmock, 1998, p. 375).

Where access to senior managers is a problem, it may be easier for a practitioner researcher to avoid interviews and opt for questionnaires or even investigate management practice via analysis of documents such as minutes of meetings and policy statements. Face-to-face interviews with peers or superiors, if granted, may only reveal what the interviewed individuals feel is appropriate to express. The anonymity of questionnaires may actually ensure greater frankness from respondents than could be achieved through an interview. A preference for the more anonymous survey may be just one of the factors linked to a near exclusive use of quantitative research in some countries: 'a recent survey of educational research environments in the developing world suggest that, with the isolated examples of a few countries such as Columbia, the use of qualitative research strategies is still relatively under-developed' (Vulliamy, Lewin and Stephens, 1990, p. 16).

The heavy reliance on qualitative methods in investigating educational management and leadership in Western countries may therefore cause particular difficulties for student researchers whose academic training has been outside the Western tradition and whose background may lead them to think of research as the collection and manipulation of statistical data. Internationally, the collection of research data on education has been largely quantitative and has been for the use of policy-makers (Ross and Mahlck, 1990). All these factors – the relative deference to authority, the expectation of research being large scale and quantitative in nature and the association of research with policy rather than management – mean that individual research within a school or college context may be more difficult in non-Western countries.

Practitioner research in the UK can also be sensitive. Some of the practitioners participating in our investigation reported problems which raise serious ethical issues in relation to practitioner research. Teachers or lecturers researching in their own institution may have to be particularly sensitive to issues such as taking the time of their colleagues in the research process and maintaining anonymity when disseminating research outcomes, something which is especially difficult in a small institution. The insensitive or unscrupulous use of research findings on the part of the researcher, or potentially on the part of the senior management team who receive the findings, is a possibility. The researcher and those supporting site-based practitioner research may be faced with a number of difficulties in collecting, receiving and making use of research data. One such difficulty relating to the dissemination of the data was reported by a researcher respondent to our survey. In this case research on the effectiveness of an interviewing team was found to be 'very, very instructive – it shows how badly a team can work together'. As a result there were no recommendations: 'None – I deemed the report too damning – too negative and have hidden the report from *all* the staff' (quoted in Coleman, 1999a, p. 152).

LEVELS OF SUPPORT FOR PRACTITIONER RESEARCH

In any cultural context the amount of support offered is variable and tends to be largely dependent on the attitudes of the senior management. Judging from our research on our students' own investigations, the prevailing attitudes can be classified as one of the following:

- active endorsement by the senior management to bring about change
- colleague support
- providing practical support
- tolerance/indifference
- hostility/resistance.

Actively endorsing practitioner research to bring about change

In some cases, particularly where multiple research projects were happening (Middlewood, 1999a), the research was completely integrated into a larger school initiative with the full backing of senior management. However, even in the case of a single researcher, with the backing of the senior management team, the work can have a significant impact. In a study of the process of budget decision-making at a secondary school, the teacher researcher reported that: 'This was the first investigation following the appointment of a new headteacher. She was involved in the early stages of the planning and was always the main "audience" for the assignment. The work was therefore closely linked to school development' (quoted in Coleman, 1999a, p. 147).

In the case of one researcher who was a new principal himself, the coursework for the degree was all used to help implement his decision to 'change the culture of the school towards a more collaborative and learner-centred approach' (Coleman, 1999b, p. 37). As a result of his research he felt that his staff knew that their opinions were valued: 'It's telling them you can trust me, I will listen to what you're saying' and that planning could be based on data collected in the school, rather than what he termed 'wishful thinking' (Coleman, 1999b, p. 39). In this case, the opinion of the principal that change was occurring was validated by members of the senior management team.

The support of the senior management team and their *continued* encouragement was seen to be the key factor for the success of school-based groups of practitioners by Middlewood (1999b, p. 118). Other support seen as crucial was having an enthusiastic group co-ordinator; the support of an external (HE) tutor to help to ensure the quality of the research and the careful co-ordination of the different research projects.

Colleague support

In some cases teacher practitioners are in a situation where there is general support for the idea of research but the support seems to emanate from colleagues rather than directly from senior management. Support was reported by a number of respondents to the survey as coming from members of the teaching staff. However, they were felt to be understandably more responsive where the research investigation was relevant to their needs or where it was seen as relevant to the school or college. Reporting on an evaluation of the effectiveness of middle managers, one teacher researcher commented that:
'All were keen to be involved as it was presented to them as an opportunity for reflection leading to improvements'. Another reported that: 'The teachers were usually very willing to participate in the study and had a lot to offer in the way of suggestions as to how to best carry out the survey'. However, the extent of the support did vary: 'The staff were quite helpful although I expected more. I could not run after or remind the staff a second time.' Governors too were sometimes identified as supportive: 'I was given time at Governors' meetings to introduce and feedback on the investigation. The headteacher and Chair of Governors gave it their full support, and were among those interviewed.' (Quotations from Coleman, 1999a, p. 148.)

Practical support

Whilst stopping short of fully endorsing and harnessing the research projects of an individual teacher, the senior management of a school or college may show goodwill by offering practical support. About a quarter of those responding to the survey, reported that they received some form of financial support, varying from payment for printing and paper expenses to partial or full payment of fees for the course. In some cases researchers were given time and allowed release to undertake investigations or to write up the assignment. Other comments related to having clerical support and to being given access to information of a privileged nature. One fortunate practitioner researcher reported that he was granted: 'Access to everything as required and the time provided for the research process; all resources provided by the school' (Coleman, 1999a, p. 148).

Indifference/tolerance

Many of the comments of respondents to the survey were completely positive, but there were those that indicated some ambiguity on the part of the senior management, particularly when the research outcomes were not necessarily welcome: 'The head approved of study although was not keen on the outcomes'; 'For all the work I did and am doing the head is supportive – he condones what I do – but is not keen to read or discuss'. In some cases neutrality from senior management was welcomed: 'I had no interference at all from the head (this was an advantage!)'. (Quotations from Coleman, 1999a, pp. 147–8.)

Hostility/resistance

In some cases overt indifference had the effect of being a complete wet blanket on any potential outcomes from the research. The experience of one lone researcher in a college was of receiving something between indifference and hostility: 'the completed assignment received no response, neither from my Head of Faculty, the Head of School (the subject of the enquiry), nor any member of the College's senior management team' (Coleman, 1999a, p. 152).

The likelihood is that most of these practitioners who responded to our survey were relatively successful in carrying out their research and completing their coursework. The vast majority actually did report some level of support from the senior management and most of them had chosen a topic that they intended would benefit the school or college as well as themselves. Only a few students commented on a lack of support that amounted to hostility and meant that the research would not have any impact: 'no support from headteacher, did not give weight to my research, in spite of it being related directly to the needs of the school. This in turn meant some teachers did not value in-school research' (Coleman, 1999a, p. 148).

Despite the fact that most of the recommendations mentioned by researcher practitioners in the questionnaires appear to have been adopted, problems were reported where the implementation of the recommendations was dependent on the will of the senior management team (SMT). One researcher, although positive about some of the recommendations arising from her research, commented that implementing whole-school change is more difficult as the SMT are resistant to it.

A school which has a bureaucratic, hierarchical structure is unlikely to be affected by the research findings of a teacher who does not have senior responsibility. One such teacher researcher reported that: 'Unfortunately, most of the assignments that I have completed have had very little direct impact on the College. One of the reasons for this, I suspect, is that in hierarchical terms, I am not in a position to follow through any benefits' (quoted in Coleman, 1999c, p. 163).

Obviously there are many ways in which the senior management of a school or college can minimise or eliminate any effects of a small-scale research project. However, when the atmosphere is generally positive, the extent of support has an impact on the effectiveness of the research. Those whose research was in line with interests of the senior management team or whose research was adopted by them were more likely to see practical outcomes from their efforts. However, these outcomes also varied in type and extent. When we questioned our teacher researchers, we were interested in the level and type of support that they received, but also perceptions of the effectiveness of their research in terms of the impact that it had on them as individuals and on their institutions.

EFFECTIVENESS OF PRACTITIONER RESEARCH

If practice and policy are to be informed by research it seems that it can happen on a number of levels. The indications from the survey were, that the recommendations made following a small-scale research investigation were more likely to be adopted when they were relatively short term and practical, particularly when they were directly controlled by the person who had undertaken the research. A researcher whose assignment was investigating the development of a plan for pastoral care in the school reported that: 'The implementation and short term planning recommendations have been adopted. The long term considerations have not been as successful. Staff training, although present, is limited due to financial restraints' (quoted in Coleman, 1999a, p. 150).

Another student working on a marketing strategy reported the adoption of a range of small practical recommendations like the development of a parents' charter and the initiation of a homework club rather than the implementation of a whole-school strategy. One student investigating the deployment, development and integration of non-teaching staff was able to report the decision to involve associate staff in specific ways: 'Associate staff are increasingly involved in training on school INSET days. An associate member of staff has been co-opted on to the school governors' (Coleman, 1999a, p. 151).

Recommendations arising from an assignment on the role of the newly qualified teacher (NQT) mentor in the secondary school, were fully adopted, but most of the changes were in the form of written documentation: 'A more tightly structured/managed induction and mentoring policy is in place for all staff; a better and earlier "matching" system is in place. Mentors have "job descriptions"' (Coleman, 1999a, p. 151).

These were reflections arising from the work of individual practitioner researchers. In the cases of multiple research projects effects were felt to be more far reaching and are discussed more extensively below in relation to the three levels of change.

One factor that is common to the reports of virtually all the researcher practitioners was that, on an individual basis, students reported benefits from the research to themselves, for example through an increased access to accurate information. However, it is possible that this increase in knowledge and understanding could have wide-ranging longer-term effects informing future action and increasing the likelihood of planning and decision-making being based on data derived from valuable in-house research. If an outcome of practitioner research is to be change and improvement, it may be useful to adopt the differentiation used by Huberman (1993 pp. 41–3) who distinguishes between: 'instrumental effects' which are 'changes in tools or methods of daily work; changes in policies or practices at a more institutional level' and 'conceptual effects' which are 'clear conceptual connections between the main findings of the study and the informants' work situation'. The research projects reported by the researcher practitioners (Middlewood, Coleman and Lumby, 1999) indicate that there are three main types of change which may occur as a result of their research. However, they are presented a little differently here to the Huberman categories. It seems as if the research reported by our researcher practitioners, is of three types: one is purely instrumental and small scale, staying within the power of the individual, the second is the impact on the individual which may incorporate the potential for conceptual change and the third, including the development of whole-school policies, is the one most likely to bring about conceptual, long-term and deep-rooted effects.

- Instrumental or small scale change – an individual undertakes a piece of research in an area where he or she has some jurisdiction and is therefore able to act, often in a quite practical way to implement recommendations based on the findings. The outcome here could be termed 'instrumental'.
- Conceptual – potential long-term change – research produces information which has the potential to impact on the individual researcher and on those to whom the research findings are disseminated. It is probable that such data could inform future action and might in the medium or long term bring about 'conceptual effects'.
- Conceptual or whole school or college change – the researcher has the active support of others in the school or college and the backing of senior management is particularly relevant. The research may be as part of a whole-school initiative. Here the outcome is likely to be 'conceptual' in Huberman's (1993) terms and this could include the development of whole-school policy.

Instrumental or small-scale change

Many examples of this first type of institutional effect emerge from our survey data. Individual site-based researchers comment on changes resulting from their research that may or may not be embedded in the school but, at least in the short term, produce benefits to themselves, their teams and their teaching: 'Meetings are much more constructive'; 'Pro-forma devised based on my research to ascertain tutors' development needs/INSET re pastoral care'; 'Exit interviews are conducted' (quoted in Coleman, 1999a, pp. 150–1). Other such changes may include the production of handbooks and departmental policies.

As previously mentioned, the recommendations made following a small-scale research investigation were more likely to be adopted when they were relatively short term and practical, and directly controlled by the person who had undertaken the research. Even with such small-scale changes there may be an impact on the general ethos, but this is very difficult to show.

Conceptual – potential long-term change

The impact of fresh information for example, can lead to insights and may promote reflection leading to future action. Commenting on the benefits of their research projects, individual students completing the questionnaire identified learning outcomes that included the potential for change and improvement. Some of the comments of practitioners indicated this in specific ways: 'I have become a more reflective senior manager and I understand organisational processes better'; 'The process provided considerable clarity as to the place of pastoral care and guidance in the school'; 'a realisation that finance in a school is only significant in terms of its impact on the quality of teaching and learning'; 'I have an improved insight into the wishes and values of parents' (Coleman, 1999a, p. 151).

A more detailed example of the type of research which produces data that could inform management, is research on gender undertaken separately by a primary school and a special school headteacher (Coleman, 1999b, pp. 42–5). For these researchers benefits came from the exploration of leadership style and increased self-knowledge and self confidence. In the case of a male primary head there was insight for him and his research subjects on the complex issues of gender and role, particularly for men working in a largely female environment: '[there is the] need to look at the denial of self for men in certain environments. There is more of an argument for cultural transformation, to make sure that everybody feels they can express both masculine and feminine aspects of their character' (quoted in Coleman, 1999b, p. 44).

Self-knowledge and understanding will impact on the way in which these managers conduct their professional lives. However, knowledge gathering can be focused on a particular issue of change. In the case of a researcher in a tertiary college the actual purpose of the research was to provide information on staff morale and motivation which was intended to be useful for the middle management team: 'the findings did inform ongoing debate and as such contributed to the change process' (quoted in Coleman, 1999a, p. 151).

There is considerable evidence from the questionnaire responses that individual researchers have benefited in terms of increased understanding and confidence and feel better able as a result to apply for promotion. It would seem likely that their increased expertise and understanding will benefit their present and future schools and colleges: 'I now have a broader knowledge of the area which will prepare me for a post as a Deputy Head. I am more aware of the perspectives of others in the school'; 'As a comparatively new first-time Principal I have developed (a) self confidence (b) awareness of the problems perceived by colleagues (c) confidence and the dedication of colleagues' (Coleman, 1999a, p. 151).

Such benefits are reported in relation to work in the classroom, as well as relating to senior management roles: 'Benefits have been in terms of my professional development and the Maths curriculum as I am now tackling changes differently and finding them more successful'; 'I was surprised to find how badly I had communicated the nature of the course to the students' (Coleman, 1999a, p. 152).

Conceptual or whole-school change

When a research project or series of research projects are carried out by a member of the senior management team or, alternatively, have the backing of the senior management team, the recommendations arising from the research have a good chance of being implemented. These are the research projects which are actively endorsed by the senior management. The headteacher/ principal and their deputies are in a particularly strong position to ensure that any research they undertake leads to the implementation of recommendations. As already mentioned, one principal used the whole range of his assignments and dissertation to investigate different aspects of the school with the intention of changing the culture. The headteacher of a First School, researching the induction of new staff was 'in an ideal position to implement her research' (Lumby, 1999a, p. 31) and carrying out the research helped her to establish herself in her new role as well as ensuring a good start to the career of her NQT.

Research on the effect of multiple research projects arising from a group of teachers all following the school-based version of the course, shows the important part that research can play in 'opening doors' (Joyce, 1991) to change and improvement. Examples include the successful launching of a positive rather than negative discipline scheme in one secondary school and the successful review of the homework policy and the partnership with parents in another. In both cases the culture of the school was receptive to such positive changes and once the changes were implemented, efforts were made to institutionalise them through ensuring that they were monitored and evaluated (Middlewood, 1999b). In the case of these schools the development of policies might have been seen as an example of institutional change rather than conceptual change, but the views of the headteachers were that, as a result of the research being undertaken by staff members they were 'making strides towards becoming learning organisations' (Middlewood, 1999b, p. 15) apparently an indication of conceptual change.

OTHER FACTORS AFFECTING THE SUCCESS OF IMPLEMENTATION

The success of research in bringing about change can also depend on a kind of serendipity. A research project might just happen to coincide with a review on the same topic as it did in the case of an individual who investigated a new pay structure at a college just at the point that a merger meant that this had to occur anyway (Lumby, 1999b). In this case, it was felt that the research meant that the changes were better investigated and the outcomes more reliable as a result. School improvement often moves forward on a number of fronts at the same time (Gray, 1998). In some reported cases of practitioner research the individual has found that the impact of research is increased because it is one factor, amongst a range of others that are all leading to change. The deputy head of a girls' school, where recommendations arising from her research on governors was largely implemented, stated that her work acted as a 'catalyst' within a situation where change was seen to be necessary (Coleman, 1999b, p. 37).

The successful implementation of recommendations arising from research depends on the desire for change within the culture of the school or college, and the extent to which the research investigation is allied to the dominant values of that culture and the type of change envisaged. In identifying some of the ways in which improvement can be encouraged, Hopkins (1994) stresses that there should be a common understanding of the vision of the institution, and that collaboration amongst staff is vital for both staff development and school improvement. The effects of multiple research projects were that those participating felt that they had widened their understanding of the school as a whole and benefited from working together in a collaborative way. As a result of their research efforts, the teachers felt empowered, able to criticise and were seen by the senior management to be experiencing more job satisfaction. The headteachers of these schools were aware that the increase in understanding and collaboration as a result of the wide-scale research activity had made their jobs as leaders easier (Middlewood, 1999a). Beare, Caldwell and Millikan (1993, p. 148), in listing current generalisations about leadership in education include: 'Vision must be communicated in a way which secures commitment among members of the organisation.' It seems that the multiple research projects and increased understanding of the research practitioners have helped to do just that.

Micro-political dimensions may also be important. Understanding the power structure of the school or college and ensuring that there is support for the research project may be an important factor in its success and potential impact. The relative success of the research undertaken on building effective learning support in one college, was largely due to the micro-political skills of the researcher who had deliberately set out to build support for the changes implicit in the research amongst the lecturing staff (Lumby, 1999c).

Whilst a collaborative culture enhances the effectiveness of research, and a micro-political culture may be managed to promote research, the culture of the school may also stultify the effects of research, as can be seen in the examples quoted earlier in the chapter where practitioner researchers were working within an indifferent or hostile environment.

CONCLUSION

The degree of impact of practitioner research on practice in education will differ. It may be short term and instrumental and confined to one section of the school or college. Alternatively the impact may be longer term and have conceptual potential where it raises the level of understanding of an individual or group of individuals to inform their management practice. Practitioner research can also be used by or with the senior managers of a school or college as a way of bringing about a change in the ethos of the whole institution. In all cases some benefit is felt in terms of individual professional development. All those interviewed and surveyed testified to the growth in their own knowledge, experience and understanding.

In the case of whole institution change, much will depend on the culture of the institution and on access to micro-political influence. Research is more likely to be successful in achieving its purpose when it is in accord with the thinking of powerful people within the organisation or in line with already identified needs, and is deliberately used or endorsed as part of large-scale organisational change.

The role of the practitioner researcher is unique, as this type of research can combine practical contextual knowledge with the application of theory to bring about differing levels of change in practice. The practitioner researcher can help to bring about both professional and institutional improvement, particularly when harnessed to an institutional will to support change and/or where multiple research projects are occurring. Practitioner research within a school or college can be a potent force in influencing the practice of an individual or a department and, when research projects are actively endorsed, can bring about conceptual change and improvement in institutional practice.

REFERENCES

Beare, H., Caldwell, B. and Millikan, R. (1993) Leadership, in Preedy M. (ed.) *Managing the Effective School*, London: Paul Chapman Publishing.

Coleman, M. (1999a) What makes for effective research in a school or college? in Middlewood, D., Coleman, M. and Lumby, J. (eds) *Practitioner Research in Education: Making a Difference*, London: Paul Chapman Publishing.

Coleman, M. (1999b) Re-appraising roles through research, in Middlewood, D., Coleman, M. and Lumby, J. (eds) *Practitioner Research in Education: Making a Difference*, London: Paul Chapman Publishing.

Coleman, M. (1999c) Conclusions, in Middlewood, D., Coleman, M. and Lumby, J. (eds) *Practitioner Research in Education: Making a Difference*, London: Paul Chapman Publishing.

Dadds, M. (1995) *Passionate Enquiry and School Development*, London: Falmer.

Dadds, M. and Hart, W. (2001) *Doing Practitioner Research Differently*, London: Routledge Falmer.

Dimmock, C. (1998) Restructuring Hong Kong's schools: the applicability of Western theories, policies and practices to an Asian culture, *Educational Management and Administration*, Vol. 26, No. 4, pp. 363–77.

Gray, J. (1998) The contribution of educational research to the cause of school improvement, a professorial lecture, London, Institute of Education.

Halsall, R. (ed.) (1998) *Teacher Research and School Improvement: Opening Doors from the Inside*, Buckingham: Open University Press.

Hofstede, G. (1980) *Culture's Consequences: International Differences in Work-Related Values*, Beverly Hills, CA: Sage.

Hopkins, D. (1994) School improvement in an ERA of change, in Ribbins, P. and Burridge, E. (eds) *Improving Education: Promoting Quality in Schools*, London: Cassell.

Huberman, M. (1993) Changing minds: the dissemination of research and its effects on practice and theory, in Day, C., Calderhead, J. and Denicolo, P. (eds) *Research on Teacher Thinking*, London: Falmer.

Jackson, D. (2001) Leadership and the role of research, in *NCSL in Dialogue*, www.ncsl.org.uk/index.cfm

Joyce, B.R. (1991) The doors to school improvement, *Educational Leadership*, Vol. 48, No. 8, pp. 59–62.

Lomax., P. (2002) Action research for educational management and leadership, in Coleman, M. and Briggs, A.R.J. (eds) *Research Methods in Educational Management and Leadership*, London: Paul Chapman Publishing.

Lumby, J. (1999a) Developing the management of people, in Middlewood, D., Coleman, M. and Lumby, J. (eds) *Practitioner Research in Education: Making a Difference*, London: Paul Chapman Publishing.

Lumby, J. (1999b) Transforming structures and culture, in Middlewood, D., Coleman, M. and Lumby, J. (eds) *Practitioner Research in Education: Making a Difference*, London: Paul Chapman Publishing.

Lumby, J. (1999c) Influencing the management of the curriculum, in Middlewood, D., Coleman, M. and Lumby, J. (eds) *Practitioner Research in Education: Making a Difference*, London: Paul Chapman Publishing.

Middlewood, D., Coleman, M. and Lumby, J. (eds) (1999) *Practitioner Research in Education: Making a Difference*, London: Paul Chapman Publishing.

Middlewood, D. (1999a) Some effects of multiple research projects on the host school staff and their relationships, in Middlewood, D., Coleman, M. and Lumby, J. (eds) *Practitioner Research in Education: Making a Difference*, London: Paul Chapman Publishing.

Middlewood, D. (1999b) Engendering change, in Middlewood, D., Coleman, M. and Lumby, J. (eds) *Practitioner Research in Education: Making a Difference*, London: Paul Chapman Publishing.

Murray, L. and Lawrence, B. (2000) *Practitioner-Based Enquiry: Principles for Postgraduate Research*, London: Falmer.

Ross, K.N. and Mahlck, L. (eds) (1990) *Planning the Quality of Education: The Collection and Use of Data for Informed Decision-Making*, Paris: UNESCO, International Institute for Educational Planning, Pergamon Press.

Southworth, G. (1998) Improving Educational research: ways forward through partnership and development, paper presented at the BERA Annual Conference Symposium on Educational Research – New Directions, August.

Vulliamy, G., Lewin, K. and Stephens, D. (1990) *Doing Educational Research in Developing Countries: Qualitative Strategies*, London: Falmer.

9

Evidence-Informed Policy and Practice in the Learning and Skills Sector

JACKY LUMBY

SETTING THE CONTEXT

The debate about the failures of educational research, initiated in the late 1990s (Hillage *et al.*, 1998; Tooley and Darby, 1998) has led to government, government agencies and practitioners arguing the need for a range of changes, resulting most significantly in a trend which prioritises and lauds applied research (Coffield, 1996). Most academics would agree that there is an ongoing need to keep the state of educational research in review and would wholeheartedly endorse the urgent aim of improving practice and attainment which is at the centre of the debate. At this general level the majority of stakeholders may agree. However, in the detail of what the issues are and how the aim is to be achieved agreement fractures. The proposed goal of a system whereby evidence is produced and communicated in such a way as to inform policy and practice (EIPP) is not so much rejected as seen as problematic along a number of dimensions.

The debate has generally been conducted by reference to schools. Further education has been largely ignored despite its importance to education and training. In research terms the sector is not only historically nearly invisible, but also 'difficult' in that it escapes the assumed boundaries of educational research, ranging as it does since its 2001 conversion to the learning and skills sector (LSS) beyond the conventional education institutions of colleges into teaching and learning in the community and in the workplace. This chapter places the sector within the general debate on EIPP by considering how far research on leadership and management in the LSS does or could inform policy and practice, and discusses the ways in which stakeholders might work singly or together to achieve this aim. It takes as an axiomatic starting point the need to consider carefully and respond to the criticisms, views and requirements of the key customers of research, government and practitioners.

EXISTING RESEARCH ON THE LEARNING
AND SKILLS SECTOR

There are many who have argued that the sector is underresearched (Coffield, 1996; Desforges, 2000; Hughes Taylor and Tight, 1996; Morris, 2001). Others challenge this perspective, for example Martinez (2002) who cites the large body of what he terms 'grey' literature, that is unpublished research in conference papers and dissertations. Stanton (2000) refers to the Brown and Keep (1998) report on vocational education and training in the UK to support his assertion that the volume of research is not an issue. The perspective on the adequacy of the volume of course partly depends on how one defines the research to be included. For some, much of the material produced within institutions, for example, evaluation or action research-based reports is not seen as legitimate research. Others deplore this exclusion as a narrow perspective which misses the very distinctiveness of the sector, its pragmatic and action-orientated nature. There may be a good quantity of unpublished and pragmatically orientated work but certainly much less published work which matches the criteria of rigorous social science methodology.

The debate on the adequacy of the extent of research is broad brush and based on generalisation. Commentary largely does not distinguish between research which focuses on teaching and learning (the majority of the research conducted in institutions), research on leadership and management, and research which links the two. Nor is there often discrimination between research on different parts of the system, for example the differences between research on general further education colleges and sixth form colleges, or research on colleges and workplace learning, or research on young people and adults. Although there are exceptions, writers tend to homogenise discussion of research on the sector and to comment on it as a single body of work. In fact, as Stanton (2000) argues, research is very varied and dispersed. It is varied in focus and in methodology, and its boundaries are unclear. For example, research on staff development in colleges would be classified as educational research. Research on staff development in business where government-funded workplace learning takes place would probably be classified as business research rather than 'educational research'. Such divisions and judgements about boundaries render the research on the sector fluid and contested. Consequently, while commentators on 'educational research' (who are often writing or talking not about education but about a part of it, schools) can be confident that the body of research to which they refer is reasonably homogeneous and defined, those commenting on research on the LSS face the need to consider acutely felt differences in the location and nature of the sector's work and its permeable boundaries.

RESEARCH ON LEADERSHIP AND MANAGEMENT

The literature on leadership and management in the sector is not extensive and is almost exclusively concerned with general further education colleges. The experience of sixth form colleges is largely excluded (Lumby and Briggs, 2002). The empirical base remains thin for much of this work, often based on small-scale studies and self-reported data. It is sometimes concerned with a particular function or functions of management such as marketing, strategy or financial management, or with particular levels of management, such as middle managers, but the bulk of the published research has been concerned with analysing management and leadership within the dominant conceptual framework of managerialism.

The literature on management which followed the incorporation of colleges in 1993 rested on the polarisation of 'oppositional cultures' (Elliott and Crossley, 1997) focusing on a critique of managers. The critique posited the emergence of 'a new type of manager ... with an apparently different value system' (Randle and Brady, 1997, p. 135). The critique was further developed by the argument that such managers had become divorced from students and staff, and had abandoned the traditional values of putting students, rather than funding, first (Hartley, 1997). A hegemony was established which contrasted the new public sector manager, wedded to values closer to those assumed to belong to commercial management, with the professional values of lecturers, who, it was asserted, remained close to teaching and learning and the primacy of the student's needs (Elliott and Crossley, 1997). The research and its analysis since has reflected an ongoing ideological struggle, with much of the writing using emotive language and embodying an attack on government policy and on managers, and arguing largely from the perspective of lecturers, that the latter have been disempowered to the detriment of students.

The purpose in this chapter is not to debate in detail the justification or otherwise for this stance. That has been done elsewhere (Gleeson, 2001; Simkins and Lumby, 2002). Rather it is to explore the micro-political underpinning and its relevance to the degree to which the research is helpful or otherwise in shaping policy or improving practice. The managerialist literature is intrinsically hostile to managers. It is flawed by an absence of discussion of the ideological interpretation and self-interest which may colour the analysis of actions by both managers and lecturers. Put simply, the assumption of unique ownership of professional values by the 'oppositional groups' may ignore a degree of self-interest on both sides. Professionalism can be seen as self-protection, as well as the protection of students. The managerialist literature avoids engagement with the issues of power and control over students. It embodies resistance to the perceived greater power of managers over lecturers by countering with an offensive to retain power over students. The literature therefore presents an argument from an unacknowledged ideological perspective and ignores the rich and complex analysis of concepts such as professionalism and change. As such, it is a long way from a focus on producing practical tools based on knowledge and it is unlikely to influence the leaders and managers who are largely the subject of criticism. The issue in how far this research can have an impact on practice is that in creating, through the literature, a contest to adjudicate who holds the interests of students most at heart and whose actions may best promote those interests, the fact that neither side has the monopoly may be lost to the ultimate detriment of students. It is not the nature of the research but the underlying bias which may weaken the impact of the work. This is one dimension of the unacknowledged allegiances which colour the literature.

A further result of the domination of this framework in the research on leadership and management in the sector is the failure to develop an equivalent body of literature to that on school effectiveness and school improvement. While there is literature on retention and raising achievement, much of this is concerned with strategies at classroom/workshop and individual level. The connections attempted in school effectiveness literature on what characteristics of leadership are related to effectiveness are largely absent from the literature on colleges. The increasing emphasis on learning as central has resulted in a range of college improvement literature, but the relationship drawn between leadership and management practice and improvement is weak. Again, the major thrust is with teaching and learning strategies at the individual and class-room level. The latter, of course, has great value in its own right, but the critical knowledge on the way in which colleges could be managed to be effective and to improve remains underdeveloped, and extrapolating from the literature on schools whose culture and funding are so different, will not meet the case.

The alleged perspectives of managers and lecturers in the managerialist literature underpin one set of allegiances. Drawing on a range of evidence on government commissioned research, Stanton (2000) suggests a second. He argues that there are two main groups involved in researching the sector, those who work for government/government agencies and those in higher education, and that both have vested interests in proving the success or lack of success in policy initiatives. In this context, therefore, government policy is likely to attract a negative response from higher education-based researchers and a positive response from government agency-based researchers. He contrasts the unwillingness of those producing 'official' research to challenge policy with the unwillingness of other researchers to admit initiatives work:

> The price paid for relevance and the possibility of influence may be an inability to make research public or to query the agenda set. This in turn results in those researchers who are not part of the 'official' activities tending to adopt a rival and essentially dissenting perspective, often putting their own objectivity at risk in the process. So from the practitioner's point of view, neither camp is of much use. The official research does not want to hear about flawed assumptions, which may need to be corrected before an initiative can work, and the dissenting research does not want the initiative to work at all.

> (Stanton, 2000, p. 181)

However, such allegiances are not made explicit but embedded in the implied values, the analytical perspective and sometimes the language of the research (Simkins and Lumby, 2002).

The ownership and control of research on the LSS is therefore subject to a struggle for control, with different categories of researchers claiming primary rights or legitimacy. Power struggles are enacted through the analysis and publication of research.

There is a further, more fundamental, dimension of struggle, which attempts to include or exclude categories of researchers from being involved with research at all. It is a common criticism that researchers who have not experienced the sector as a student or by working in it cannot be appropriate researchers, as they lack the necessary knowledge and experience (Stanton, 2000). Not all of those who research law and crime are lawyers or criminals. Neither are all those in medical research practising clinicians. Where the legitimacy of such researchers working in these areas of professional practice is accepted, some within the LSS deny such legitimacy for external researchers in their own field, making a special case which seems to reflect protectionism as much as a convincing rationale. The research undertaken by those based outside the sector is sometimes depicted not only as likely to be inadequate because the researcher has not the prior experience needed, but also ethically questionable, being what Donmoyer (1995, p. 158) refers to as 'the rape model of research' where researchers use staff and students to produce research to their own career advantage and offer no benefit to those who are the subject of research.

For their part, external researchers may equally question the legitimacy of those who research from within the sector. In this case, it is often a debate on the nature of research which is the vehicle to assert their legitimacy and control. Assumed adherence or opposition to the criteria of a particular notion of legitimate social sciences research is a vehicle for contest. Crisp and Starbuck (1997) outline two modes of research: mode one their description pertaining to researchers in higher education and mode two reflecting the philosophy and practice of those who research in the LSS (Table 9.1).

In their model, mode 1 researchers ('traditional university-based research', Crisp and Starbuck, 1997, p. 1) are characterised by adherence to their own sector value systems and norms and are bounded within a single discipline. Mode 2 researchers ('wide range of organisations conducted by all kinds of people' ibid., p. 1) are not bounded by a single discipline and aim to produce 'useful solutions to practical problems'. Mode 1 research is accountable to a university or peers; mode 2 to society. The depiction of each mode contrasts the limited and inward-looking mode 1 with the freer and more practical mode 2. While one might critique and challenge their characterisation and the assumptions it embeds, they argue strongly that the modes of research, that is the underlying approach and methodology, are the means whereby, in their experience, higher education researchers and those in the funding body, the then Further Education (FE) Development Agency, wrested control of a project from those who were FE based within a consortium of colleges and one university. The intention 'to develop co-ownership of research which was of real use to the practitioners' (ibid., p. 3) was not achieved. The firm intention

Table 9.1   Two modes of research

Attribute	Characteristic of Mode 1	Characteristic of Mode 2
Purpose and context of enquiry	Defined by value systems of university academic structures.	Defined by the enquirer's value to one or more stakeholders.
Fit with existing fields or disciplines	Enquiry bounded by existing structures of knowledge. Takes place within a discipline.	Enquiry ranges across two or more disciplines and creates new conceptual frameworks.
Methodology and methods	Legitimacy defined by the cognitive and social norms of a particular academic community. Tendency to value basic or academic research and the established paradigm.	Includes both theoretical and empirical components. Methods derived in an evolving framework aimed at providing useful solutions to practical problems. Theory may not fit established paradigm.
Social accountability	Accountable to university and/or peers within the discipline.	Criteria more widely drawn by diverse groups judging quality against tests of usefulness.

Source: Crisp and Starbuck (1997, p. 2)

to work in mode 2 was thwarted. The underlying issue is not merely methodology, but control of the project.

I have argued that the existence of underlying power struggles has received scant acknowledgement let alone analysis, but a typology of the transparency of underlying values might be attempted. The Johari window (Handy, 1990) might be adapted to arrive at a categorisation using the two spectra of awareness of allegiance and willingness to make such allegiance explicit as in Figure 9.1.

The vast majority of research on the sector falls into the categories of implied or disingenuous, that is, allegiances appear discernible to the reader but are not made explicit by the writer. Analysis of the texts of publication using this framework might reveal more of the current extent of bias. Levačić and Glatter argue in this volume that researchers should not be polemicists and yet Donmoyer (1995, p. 152) refers to Campbell's 1979 characterisation of academic disciplines as 'tribal organisations'. Tribes have strong predilections and allegiances which are the result of a culture which has evolved over time and the socialisation of new members into the culture. If the research on the sector is conducted by tribes, then the inadequacy of a purely rational debate on using evidence to inform policy becomes clear. The whole area of research in the LSS is riven with micro-political turf wars about legitimacy and status.

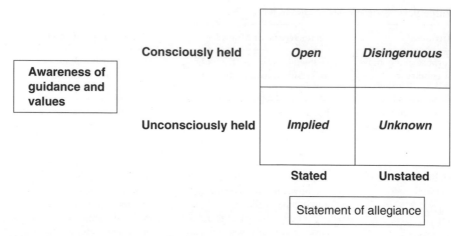

Figure 9.1   Communication of values in research

WHAT DOES THE CUSTOMER WANT?

Accepting that the rational demands of stakeholders may conceal an underlying complexity of micro-political groupings and allegiances, we can return to the start point of this chapter, what does the customer want? Understanding and responding to these demands is essentially a process of marketing (Foskett, 1999). As such, the situation has parallels with the adjustment to marketing philosophy and practice experienced by the LSS. In the late 1980s and early 1990s, a number of criticisms were made of the 'producer capture' (O'Hear, 1991) of education by teachers, specifically in further education, that courses were subject to the same 'marketing myopia' identified by Levitt (1960) and being offered without much consideration of the students' desire for them. The debate which followed made use of quality concepts and as a result listening to the customer received greater emphasis (Davies, 1999; Lumby, 2001). However, it was also argued that in education simply giving customers what they want is too simplistic (West-Burnham, 1992). There are a range of customers, not all of whom will want the same things, and students, as the main direct customers, may wish for things which in the opinion of professionals are impractical or not in their best interests. The appropriate response may not be to automatically provide what is requested. However, neither is it a matter of listening to what the customers want and then telling them they cannot have it. Over time, colleges have come to realise they must listen, negotiate and evolve their products in order to accommodate what customers want with what colleges are able, willing and see as educationally appropriate to provide.

The current criticisms of research signal a parallel revolt against producer capture, alleging that research is being produced with insufficient thought as to who may want it and in what form. The appropriate response may be a similar evolution of an accommodation, listening to customers and then negotiating a response. A number of voices in the sector articulate a range of requests:

> The products of the research have to be useful to all the participants and to be presented in ways that are accessible to them. They have to be seen to solve problems which are real to the practitioners ... For FE college managers, the demands of the 'business' agenda within an ever tightening budgetary regime requires that all activities have to be justified against instrumental measures of value.

> (Crisp and Starbuck, 1997, p. 8)

Further, research must be specific to England or Wales or Scotland (Coffield, 1996), must make clear the findings and resultant practical implications and tools and offer cost-benefit analysis of their implementation. Its impact over time must be measured (Morris, 2001). Some researchers may see providing such outcomes as unproblematic. Others may argue that it is unrealistic or limiting, that theoretical, long-term and cumulative research without apparent immediate impact may influence and change practice and policy in the long term just as significantly (Hammersley, 1997; Saha, Biddle and Anderson, 1995). Both have a point. The situation is complex. Attempts to enforce compliance with a dominant model of instrumental research is fraught with difficulty. For example, the proposed solution to making research 'relevant', that is, insisting researchers respond to problems as experienced by practitioners or policy-makers, side-steps the fact that the way practitioners select problems may be understood as micro-political as well as rational, and may not necessarily be automatically more likely to lead to impact on practice or attainment. Cohen and March (1986, p. 82), in their celebrated garbage can model of decision-making, argue that problems are selected for a whole tranche of reasons, few of which may be rationally connected to workplace processes or outcomes: 'They arise over issues of lifestyle; family; frustrations of work; careers; group relations within the organisation; distribution of status, jobs, money; ideology'. The assumption that, if researchers respond to the problems selected by practitioners and policy-makers, they will be more relevant and therefore have greater impact on attainment is flawed. If the problem has been selected by micro-political reasoning, for example to do with enhancing the status of practitioners or increasing government popularity, it cannot necessarily be seen as more closely linked to impact on attainment.

While responding to practitioners' selection of problems may not be the unproblematic way forward to ensuring greater relevance, neither is ignoring the perspective of those who work in the sector. Difficult though it may be, because it is not clear cut and cannot be prescribed, negotiation and compromise may be the key to establishing genuine partnerships which can begin to weaken the hold of tribal allegiances on research.

WORKING TOGETHER

The field of research on the LSS is contested. Those with influence and power derived from·holding funds, such as funding bodies, or through closeness to central government, such as agencies, are encouraging change in the approach and desired outcomes of research. Partnership has become a requirement, but partnership is a tough task. Both in business and in education the creation and maintenance of partnerships is highly problematic. Macbeth (1995) quotes Pugh's definition of partnership: 'a working relationship that is characterised by a shared sense of purpose, mutual respect and the willingness to negotiate. This implies sharing of information, responsibility, skills, decision-making and accountability' (Pugh, 1989, p. 17).

Hall (1999) points out that not everybody is suited to this mode of working. Individuals vary in the intra-personal arena and some prefer the rewards of autonomy. If forced to collaborate, they may be resentful or withdraw. The requirements of funding bodies may result in enforced shot-gun collaboration, which can be confidently predicted as likely to fail. The danger may be that in attempting to move from the previous producer capture of research by higher education-based researchers, the capture may simply move to another group, the colleges and their allied agencies. One might argue that they have greater legitimacy because they do the work, they support the students, but no one has a monopoly on the responsibility to improve education. Equally, no one has a monopoly on knowing the best way to achieve it. The research on partnerships and change in education suggests that the success of both is dependent on those involved not assuming the high ground, but listening (McCreath and Maclachlan, 1995). Partnership involves change for all.

Given the analysis of the micro-political contest earlier in this chapter, it is unlikely that the struggle for dominance will cease, but if the rhetoric of a need for partnership is to become more of a reality, then a recognition of the multiplicity of motivations for undertaking research and the range of legitimate methodologies and outcomes from the immediate practical to the long-term shift in paradigm or attitude needs to be encompassed and welcomed. Nutley and Webb (2000) offer a typology of ways of understanding the uses of research, based on the work of Weiss (1979):

- Knowledge-driven model – derives from natural sciences. The fact that knowledge exists sets up pressures for its development and use.
- Problem-solving model – involves the direct application of the results of a specific study to a pending decision.
- Interactive model – researchers are just one set of participants among many. The use of research is only one part of a complicated process that also uses experience, political insight, pressure, social technologies and judgement.
- Political model – research as political ammunition; using research to support a predetermined position.

- Tactical model – researchers delaying tactic in order to avoid responsibility for unpopular policy outcomes.
- The Enlightenment model – the indirect influence of research rather than the direct impact of particular findings in the policy process. Thus the concepts and theoretical perspectives that social science engenders pervade the policy-making process (Nutley and Webb, 2000, p. 30).

The current thrust within the LSS is towards the first two understandings: research to produce 'safe knowledge' and research to solve problems. This move is part of the larger trend towards accountability, in research as in all else in education, where the necessity to give an account demands that measurement of change becomes central. The impact of research is not always amenable to numeric calculation. However, those calling for research to be used in these ways have acknowledged awareness of other understandings (Sebba, 2000). They have also recognised that researchers cannot deliver the impact they desire. It is not in their gift (National Education Research Forum, 2000). Research cannot directly raise attainment. It must work indirectly through influencing leaders and managers to establish a culture and systems which support lecturers to improve attainment. This is not to explain to the customers for research that they cannot have what they want and stop there. Customers of research can have what they want in part and also much more. What research can do is support the learning of individuals who participate in or engage with research. It can frame problems, provide information, theories, stimulation, inspiration and suggest tools. It will not be constrained into one mode only. Those in the LSS who have worked so hard to achieve inclusiveness and who have recognised the axiomatic nature of supporting diversity in learners by meeting the needs of a range of different learning styles are well placed to recognise a parallel. There are a range of learning styles which research might support, spanning abstract to concrete engagement and active to reflective responses (Kolb, 1984). Practitioners who wish to use research to learn and thereby change or improve the experience of students will not do so in one style only, in the same way that students will not learn in one style only. The communities involved in researching the sector will not improve attainment by measures to constrain research into one mode or another, nor by enforcing collaboration which ignores differences in motivation, values and predilections. Clark (1996, p. 49) argues that creating a community, research or any other, is dependant on relationships across boundaries but 'there can be no sense of community within or across systems if diversity and distinctiveness is ignored ... Tension between social systems as communities is potentially as creative as it is inevitable'. The different communities who can contribute to research to support the sector have an opportunity to recognise and value diversity, in common with their practice in all other aspects of their endeavour. Partnership and change can then grow organically out of mutual accommodation.

For all the reasons discussed in this chapter, the demands for research in a particular form and the response, whether of acquiescence or opposition may reflect underlying micropolitics. The debate may continue in its current rational form eschewing acknowledgement of the power struggles, or it can become less disingenuous or naive, recognising the need to find a basis for dialogue. Different stakeholders embody different allegiances and values, predilections and desired outcomes. To move forward from this situation, a constructive accommodation is needed, which takes as its goal a greater emphasis on equality amongst stakeholders and less willingness on all sides to assume their single viewpoint necessarily holds or should hold supremacy in deciding the form of research and its consequent value to informing practice and policy. A willingness to embrace plurality may be the key.

ACKNOWLEDGEMENTS

Thanks are due to the University of Leicester for granting study leave during which this chapter was completed and to Ann Briggs for comments on an earlier draft.

REFERENCES

Brown, A. and Keep, E. (1998) Review of VET research in the UK, paper presented to the European COST Conference, University of Newcastle.

Clark, D. (1996) *Schools as Learning Communities*, London: Cassell.

Coffield, F. (1996) Introduction and overview, in Coffield, F. (ed.) *Strategic Research in Further Education*, Durham: University of Durham.

Cohen, M. and March, J. (1986) *Leadership and Ambiguity*, 2nd edn, Boston, MA: Harvard Business Press.

Crisp, P. and Starbuck, B. (1997) Shaping research in further education, paper presented at the First Annual Conference of the Further Education Research Network, Blackpool, December.

Davies, P. (1999) Colleges and customers, in Lumby, J. and Foskett, N. (eds) *Managing External Relations in Schools and Colleges*, London: Paul Chapman Publishing.

Desforges, C. (2000) Putting educational research to use through knowledge transformation, keynote lecture to the Further Education Research Network Conference, Coventry, 12 December.

Donmoyer, R. (1995) Empirical research as solution and problem: two narratives of knowledge, *International Journal of Educational Research*, Vol. 23, No. 2, pp. 151–67.

Elliott, G. and Crossley, M. (1997) Contested values in further education: findings from a case study of the management of change, *Educational Management and Administration*, Vol. 25, No. 1, pp. 79–92.

Foskett, N. (1999) Strategy, external relations and marketing, in Lumby, J. and Foskett, N. (eds) *Managing External Relations in Schools and Colleges*, London: Paul Chapman Publishing.

Gleeson, D. (2001) Style and substance in education leadership: further education as a case in point, *Journal of Education Policy*, Vol. 16, No. 3, pp. 181–96.

Hall, V. (1999) Partnerships, alliances and competition: defining the field, in Lumby, J. and Foskett, N. (eds) *Managing External Relations in Schools and Colleges*, London: Paul Chapman Publishing.

Hammersley, M. (1997) Educational research and teaching: a response to David Hargreaves, TTA lecture, *British Educational Research Journal*, Vol. 23, No. 2, pp. 141–61.

Handy, C. (1990) *Inside Organizations*, London: BBC.

Hartley, D. (1997) The new managerialism in education: a mission impossible? *Cambridge Journal of Education*, Vol. 27, No. 1, pp. 47–57.

Hillage, J., Pearson, R., Anderson, A. and Tamkin, P. (1998) *Excellence in Research on Schools*, London: Department for Education and Employment.

Hughes, C., Taylor, P. and Tight, M. (1996) The ever-changing world of further education: a case for research, *Research in Post-Compulsory Education*, Vol. 1, No. 1, pp. 7–18.

Kolb, D.A. (1984). *Experiential Learning: Experience as the Source of Learning and Development*. Englewood Cliffs, NJ: Prentice-Hall.

Levitt, T. (1960) Marketing myopia, *Harvard Business Review*, Vol. 38, Part 4, July/August.

Lumby, J. (2001) *Managing Further Education Colleges: Learning Enterprise*, London: Paul Chapman Publishing.

Lumby, J. and Briggs, A.R.J., with Wilson, M., Glover, D. and Pell, A. (2002) *Sixth Form Colleges: Policy, Purpose and Practice*, Leicester: Leicester University.

Macbeth, A. (1995) Partnership between parents and teachers in education, in Macbeth, A., McCreath, D. and Aithchison, J. (eds) *Collaborate or Compete? Educational Partnerships in a Market Economy*, London: Falmer.

Martinez, P. (2002) Effectiveness and Improvement: school and college research compared, *Research in Post-Compulsory Education*, Vol. 7, No. 1, pp. 97–118.

McCreath, D. and Maclachlan, K. (1995) Realizing the virtual: new alliances in the market model education game, in Macbeth, A., McCreath, D. and Aithchison, J. (eds) *Collaborate or Compete? Educational Partnerships in a Market Economy*, London: Falmer.

Morris, A. (2001) *National Education Research Forum Consultation: Response from the Learning and Skills Development Agency*, accessed on-line http://www.lsagency.org.uk/PDF/nerf.pdf, 8 January 2002

National Education Research Forum (2000) *Quality of Educational Research: Sub Group Report*, London: National Education Research Forum.

Nutley, S. and Webb, J. (2000) Evidence and the policy process, in Davies, H., Nutley, S. and Smith, P. (eds) *What works? Evidence-Based Policy and Practice in Public Services*, Bristol: Policy Press.

O'Hear, A. (1991) *Education and Democracy: Against the Educational Establishment*, London: Claridge Press.

Pugh, G. (1989) Parents and professionals in pre-school service: is parternership possible? in Wolfendale, S. (ed.) *Parental Involvement: Developing Networks Between School, Home and Community*, London: Cassell.

Randle K. and Brady, N. (1997) Managerialism and professionalism in the Cinderella service, *Journal of Vocational Education and Training*, Vol. 49, No. 1, pp. 121–39.

Saha, L., Biddle, B. and Anderson, D. (1995) Attitudes towards education research knowledge and policymaking among American and Australian School Principals, *International Journal of Educational Research*, Vol. 23, No. 2, pp. 113–26.

Sebba, J. (2000) Developing evidence-informed policy and practice: a national perspective, paper presented to the Sixth International Educational Management and Administration Research Conference, March, Cambridge.

Simkins, T. and Lumby, J. (2002) Cultural transformation in further education: mapping the debate, *Research in Post-Compulsory Education*, Vol. 7, No. 1, pp. 5–8.

Stanton, G. (2000) Research, in Smithers, A. and Robinson, P. (eds) *Further Education Re-Formed*, London: Falmer.

Tooley, J. and Darby, D. (1998) *Educational Research: A Critique*, London: OFSTED.

Weiss, C.H. (1979) The many meanings of research utilisation, *Public Administration Review*, Vol. 39, No. 5 pp. 426–31.

West-Burnham, J. (1992) *Managing Quality in Schools*, London: Longman.

10

Valuable Insights or Further Distractions? Using Evidence-Informed Policy and Practice to Influence School-Based Decisions and Actions

CHRIS DARK

Reason, or the ratio of all we have already known, is not the same that it shall be when we know more.

(William Blake)

Knowledge is of two kinds. We know a subject ourselves, or we know where we can find information upon it.

(Samuel Johnson)

During the last decade the government has taken an instrumental role in centralising educational policy, particularly with regard to schools. Consequently, the objectives and methods of teaching have been, and are, politically determined (Hammersley, 2000; Taylor and Hallgarten, 2000) and result in a great many national strategic initiatives. Examples include the publication of school performance data (PANDA – performance and assessment – reports and league tables), a national curriculum with associated testing procedures and a new school inspection framework (OFSTED, 2000). One outcome of this approach is that school development is now frequently grounded in a managerial perspective. The Green Paper, *Teachers Meeting the Challenge of Change* (DfEE, 1998a), promotes educational strategic policy being informed by insights from good practice. David Hopkins, Head of the Standards and Effectiveness Unit in the Department for Education and Skills (DfES) has recently added his endorsement. He has described the partnership between government and teachers as 'informed professional judgement' characterised by the development of professional learning communities, a focus on pedagogy and increasing networking amongst teachers. These perspectives are relevant to enhancing the status of policy and practice in schools being informed by evidence and imply that teachers need to be involved as consumers and pro-ducers of information. Thus, there is a growing role for enquiry as self-critical and self-confident schools are information-rich and teachers involved in decision-making (Smith and Tomlinson, 1989). The pressure to document and produce evidence can overwhelm, but it can also be a force to help identify good performance, provide focus and target resources. This chapter looks at the impact of evidence-informed policy and practice (EIPP) in two ways. It considers, first, how information and data is used at a micro-level by influenc-ing the organisation and management of Peers School in Oxford. Examples cited include attendance, school self-evaluation, assessment, audit and review, school performance and assessment and using information and evidence across schools. In different ways the priorities and initiatives cited incorporate the use of evidence into their processes, and commonly move from audit to action and then use information for evaluation. Secondly, this chapter explores and advocates by the use of interviews the application of school-based research.

Peers is a coeducational 13–18 specialist technology college and part of a local Education Action Zone. It is situated among large housing estates and draws most of its students from an area characterised by high levels of social and economic disadvantage, a catchment not typical of the city (Noble *et al.*, 1994). Using an EIPP framework implies that coherent and strategic processes are at work, one in which policy is determined by relevant information in the form of evidence. While not claiming that such coherence exists or is for-malised at Peers, I believe we are some way along this continuum. The exam-ples provided here relate to ways in which information is used at Peers.

ATTENDANCE

Consideration of the evidence helps show the nature of a problem and pro-vides a starting point although it does not necessarily find a solution. Taking attendance as an example, I demonstrate how, over a two-year period, we developed a coherent strategy from an information base. Unauthorised absence at Peers had been high for many reasons; transfer at 13 missed the formative Years 7 and 8; many students joined the school with patterns of poor attendance; the external welfare service managed excessive case loads; the school had not taken 'ownership' of attendance procedures and the view among many of the teachers was that the solutions lay elsewhere. In order to tackle the issue, we accessed external funds and used these to establish an elec-tronic registration and data system (BROMCOM). Teachers and support staff were issued with radio-controlled handsets which had a range of functions including sending and receiving attendance data. With the system in place, the scope of the problem emerged and provided a context for consultation with teachers and support staff. In response, an administrator was appointed to manage attendance data and provide staff training in the BROMCOM system. We also appointed a 'rapid response' worker whose role is to liaise with tutors and the Education Social Work Service and carry out case work with individuals and groups of students. This 'rapid response' work is targeted at those students whose attendance is between 80 per cent and 90 per cent, whilst the Education Social Work Service concentrate on those with attendance below 80 per cent. Particular actions are triggered by our data systems and these are then progressed in a case by case way. The electronic system tracks progress and changes in trends for individual students or identified groups and we also use the data generated in a variety of ways to inform our strategies. Two years on, the strategies and systems began to yield results; in 2000 Peers School achieved the most significant reduction in unauthorised absence in the UK (down 6.6 per cent) and increase in attendance (up 4.4 per cent).

SCHOOL SELF-EVALUATION

School self-evaluation helps us to look at what is being achieved and what needs to be done to develop further. The antithesis, external audit, seems to work less well, as Coleman and Collinge (1995, p. 14) note: 'classroom observations by visiting auditors fail to touch the real day to day experiences of children and their teachers'. In this context, it is interesting to note that, in 2000, OFSTED changed its inspection procedure to enable schools to include data from their own monitoring and evaluation in the process to confirm or contest hypotheses. In relation to Peers School, attendance and its upper school intake provides a useful example. There are few upper schools in the UK and therefore no relevant attendance database is available for comparison. As national trends show pupil attendance declines incrementally from Year 7 to Year 11 we wanted to make a comparison that took into account the lack of data relating to the first two of these years. Hence, we used our school data for Years 9–11 to model the missing years and aggregated it with the Year 9–11 data. This then allowed us to make a more appropriate comparison with the national profile.

School self-evaluation enables teachers to be participants rather than observers in the process of determining school performance and to use the evidence to inform their ongoing practice. At Peers, our self-evaluation model draws on insights from teachers, parents, students and governors, and uses the data to influence the development of our systems. We use conversations, group discussions, questionnaires, observations, scrutiny of students' work and student shadowing to generate our evidence. Two school-based professional development groups, each led by an advanced skills teacher, have been set up to consider 'support for learning' and 'support for teaching'. These groups produce criteria for: 'what constituted a good lesson', 'good teaching' and 'good learning' and these are then used in providing feedback from lesson observations.

Similarly, developments in the National Professional Qualification for Headship (NPQH) now require candidates for headship to be competent in the use of performance data to inform school improvement. I asked NPQH Centre Manager for the South Central Region, Roy Arnold, how the course engages with evidence to determine and illustrate key issues for school improvement.

> On joining the programme, course members meet with their tutor and agree, with the headteacher, a focus for the school improvement they will undertake. Areas include: pupils' personal development, attainment, progress, behaviour, attitude to learning and attendance. This focus originates from the school improvement/ development plan and the process involves gaining the evidence, drawing-up action plans, implementing, monitoring and then evaluating over a period of time. Candidates are now more clearly focused about the role of headship and they proceed to final assessment having demonstrated they have information in the form of evidence about each of the standards. Those who completed the process say it has prepared them for addressing the key issues when taking up headship.

AUDIT AND REVIEW

In Oxfordshire, an evaluation framework for school performance using criteria in an evidence base is available with handbook support and electronically accessible templates. Sixty sources of evidence are identified and heads and staff compile information using pro formas about standards in the core subjects, attendance and exclusion data. An annual review is held involving the head (and often the management team as well), the lead LEA adviser, an LEA officer and the chair of governors. The purpose is to validate the quality of the school's approach to self-improvement and integrate it into the development planning process. After consideration of the information profile, the discussion focuses on issues such as how well the school is led and managed; the quality of the curriculum and the opportunities offered to pupils; monitoring the quality of teaching and learning in the school; the care and welfare of pupils; partnership with parents and effective development planning.

The governing body at Peers is actively involved in determining priorities, targets and strategic direction. In this context, a standing committee on monitoring and outcomes has been established with the specific purpose of focusing on areas that are generally considered difficult to quantify. These include issues such as the quality of students' learning experience, parental attitudes, school ethos and balancing qualitative and quantitative indicators. Importantly, this committee undertakes a half-day review several times throughout the school year with the management team. Initially, the committee met regularly throughout the year but after the first cycle it was decided that the number of meetings would be reduced to coincide with key points in the school planning cycle. It was felt that more frequent meetings created pressure on the management team to measure, record and generate data for the purpose of the meeting, rather than in the context of what was happening in the school.

SCHOOL PERFORMANCE AND ASSESSMENT

At Peers, we review the performance of subject areas and individual teachers by undertaking a summative analysis at the end of the Key Stage (KS) using the external results. This process takes place annually in September and is used to determine whole-school priorities and underpin department and subject development plans for the forthcoming year. The data available to the school through the PANDA form is applied to model performance data. This provides a useful indicator of the relative strengths of a department by comparing individual students' grades gained in that subject with average grades in all their other subjects. The difference is calculated for each student in that subject and then averaged over the subject as a whole. Positive averages show relatively good performance while negative scores reflect the opposite situation. Local education authority data show, however, that not all subjects do equally well across the county, and this can also be expressed (for each subject) as an average difference between student performance in that subject with his/her performance in GCSE overall. This figure is then deducted from the school figure in each subject to give a more realistic picture of relative performance within the school. The patterns from the residuals are used as a focus for discussion with faculty leaders, subject leaders and individual teachers about their intended strategies and actions. It is used to establish the objectives and targets for the development plan for each subject (including the evidence provided to confirm success). It is also incorporated into teachers' performance management objectives.

Assessment practice at Peers includes a termly 'checkpoint' in which grades are allocated by each subject teacher for current performance, future targets and homework completion. These are produced by teachers and sent electronically using BROMCOM to the central computer base. A combined report, across all subjects, is produced for each student. However, the data accumulated is further processed in a variety of ways as a means of diagnosing strengths and weaknesses of performance in the school. For example, current performance grades in GCSE courses ('working at') can be aggregated into whole-school performance indicators for 5A*–C, average points. The school can then track its progress in meeting whole-school targets and compare performance with 'like' schools using national benchmarking tables. Students' total point scores can be compared to national expectations (based on their prior attainment at KS3) and this type of value-added comparison helps identify significant under- and over-achievement in the student cohort as a whole and is a basis for focusing intervention strategies on targeted students. When accumulated into an average value-added figure for the whole cohort, it also gives a strong indication of the overall school performance. Perhaps the most powerful technique applied is the use of spreadsheets detailing accumulated assessment data in each subject to compare 'working at' grades, and the rate of progress they represent (from the previous KS) with national expectations of progress available from the DfES Autumn Package. The value-added grade for each student in each subject is easily aggregated, thus providing a good indication of the strength of teaching and learning in that area. Value-added data can be further analysed by different groupings, for example by class/ teacher, by ethnic group, by special need category, to establish more diagnostic information. For any type of analysis, value-added charts indicate the progress of different ability groups relative to national median lines of progress, thus generating evidence of the student progress by ability grouping. Developing practice at Peers has involved overcoming the difficult technical problems of collating and analysing assessment data smoothly after each checkpoint and providing all staff with ready access to relevant spreadsheets in electronic form.

USING INFORMATION AND EVIDENCE ACROSS SCHOOLS

Generating information about achievement and progress has been a focus for the Oxford Education Action Zone (Hamilton Oxford Schools Partnership – HOSP). Established in 1999, it consists of first and middle schools, a pupil referral unit, special schools and a secondary school (Peers). Gloria Walker, Project Director of HOSP illustrates the link between information and practice. The Integrated Support Service (ISS) promotes inclusion in HOSP schools and addresses the former Secretary of State's concern, 'to shift resources from expensive remediation, to cost-effective prevention and early intervention; to shift the emphasis from procedures to practical support' (DfEE, 1998b, p. 5).

Q: How does the Integrated Support Service initiative work and how did you know it was achieving what you thought it was? A: The ISS strand provides an information base to ensure coherent planning about support for students. The scheme tries to maximise the responsiveness, effectiveness and coherence of the LEA pupil support service by promoting multi-agency working with schools in the Zone. It brings together key professionals to profile particular pupils as a part of deciding immediate and long term decisions about how to help them. If the model of working were to be used across the county, then we needed to have a clear evidence base about its efficacy. Evaluation was undertaken by Glenny (2001) using a systems analysis (Checkland and Scholes, 1999). Interviews, baseline data, literature reviews and observation of discussions with the ISS evaluation group were used to gain feedback and a number of benefits detected. Before the ISS scheme was trialled, school assessment processes had to make a case for 'need' in order to make resources available for the student. Nor did the drawn-out assessment process help address this. After the ISS pilot project special needs co-ordinators felt that the process helped improve the co-ordination of pupil support. Schools felt that their time and work was valued because of a tighter focus.

Building common purpose amongst groups of schools and an understanding of the role of information to determine practice is difficult. National Strategies, including Literacy and Numeracy, put pressure on schools, compelling them to address both internal and external demands. Denise Margetts, a former literacy co-ordinator at Peers and currently an LEA adviser considers this issue.

Q: How does implementing a National Strategy engage with the school-based priorities and plans? How do you manage to encourage schools to operate their planning in evidence-based ways? A: In my experience, departmental and whole-school initiatives have become more, rather than less, innovative in response to a national framework. It has created a context for some very creative and solution focused thinking. When I go into schools as a consultant my role is to support this process and help schools to look more closely at the challenges they have identified themselves. The aim is to find information that will provide a clear picture of the issues and then to select points for intervention strategically. For example if a school identifies that Year 8s are not independent writers, then the aim is to plan a series of actions that will achieve measurable changes. Each school will have conducted an audit using or adapting the national model to decide their own priorities. This includes elements such as classroom observation, interviews with teachers in the department and an analysis of data. Interesting conversations with teachers have taken place about what information will be needed and they increasingly look at numbers and data to determine what are the problems. For example, if someone is saying raise results by 5 per cent then the way to make sense of that is to turn it into two pupils in my class and ask what is going to make the difference to those two.

Teachers feel it is important to use not just the test scores, but to look in detail at the children's work. I certainly think the process has empowered teachers giving them a much clearer sense of what's different as a result of their teaching. However, a strategy is required which provides the balance between numbers and real assessments of children's work, pushing teachers to the qualitative, rather than exclusively focusing on the quantitative.

SCHOOL-BASED TEACHER RESEARCH

I have so far emphasised how schools can use information to determine practice, gain better insights and underpin their decision-making. In addition, it is important for teachers to research their own practice with a view to improvement. Fullan (1991, p. 75) sums it up: 'Effective educational change depends on what teachers do and think. It's as simple and as complex as that.' While Pring (2000, p. 160) highlights the link between research and teaching with the obvious connection to learning: 'It is difficult to see how good teaching can be separated from a research stance towards one's own teaching. A stance in which values about teaching are tested out in practice and in which both the values and the practice are a constant focus of reflection in the light of systematically obtained evidence.'

School improvement takes place when teachers talk regularly about learning. The Effective Learning Group (ELG) at John Mason School began in 1991, meeting throughout the year with an emphasis on enquiry and a reflective approach. It operates at 'arms' length' from school policy but with a strong overlap with continuing professional development. Jim Hines, Deputy Head, co-ordinates the group.

Q: How does the ELG group operate, and how has it generated conditions which encourage a research stance in the school? A: The ELG at John Mason School started in 1991 and consists of a working group of teachers who consider the potential and use of school-based research. The group meet approximately ten times a year, have good links with higher education, and currently Richard Pring (Oxford University Department for Educational Studies – OUDES) is chair. There is a strong element of voluntary attendance, with some senior team involvement. There is an emphasis on enquiry and a reflective approach which does tend to reach into the school policy. The ELG determines its own priorities and there is no pressure for it to achieve change in line with the school's development plan, although the outcomes are fed back into the INSET. It was our aim to encourage good reflective teachers and we would happily have people research whatever they want. The principal role is to look at learning and at the classroom level. For example, I am involved to improve my chemistry teaching and for the group, what goes on in classrooms is important. One of our studies aimed to explore the actions teachers can take to improve communication with their students about their learning. The ELG discovered that when teachers and students talked they tended to talk more about bad work and problematic issues, rather than good work and positive issues. The strategies were trialled with 60 Year 9 students and 37 teachers. As a result of the insights gained we acknowledged in school practice that students could identify helpful and unhelpful actions from teachers and were sensitive to the ways teachers treated them. They valued personal written or spoken communication with teachers and could interpret with a great deal of accuracy the intentions behind teacher communications.

Research activities are encouraged by headteachers in the belief that they provide the best mechanism for improving practice in schools. David Wilson, Headteacher of Faringdon Community School, indicated ways in which he tried to affirm this purpose for research across Oxfordshire and within his school.

Q: What are the key issues about developing EIPP? A: We have worked with teachers to generate a higher status for practitioner research by forming collaborative groups such as OEBERN (Oxfordshire Evidence-Based Education and Research Network). Currently two topics are being considered – peer lesson observation and the pupil voice. I prefer small-scale evidence-based activities with a short time-scale and which inform our practice. We have certainly been helped by the new focus of OFSTED about school self-evaluation. Teachers need help to turn generalisable findings into concrete examples, e.g. Inside the Black Box. One teacher undertook a school-based research project and I asked what the rest of the department thought of the work and the findings. He replied that he did not know, feeling the research was insufficiently useful to share with others. Overcoming such resistance is a continual theme. The challenge is to create a culture where professionals are continually looking at their practice and developing their skills to research.

EIPP TENSIONS AND DILEMMAS

During the 1990s I undertook work on inclusion in Russian schools. On visiting each school a common pattern of welcome took place. Headteachers gave information about their schools' worth, including diagrams, charts, graphs and usually accompanied by lengthy explanations. However, it was only when the process was complete and trust had been established that they talked about the real issues facing their schools. My point is that using information about school performance should not be like this. It must be relevant and serve a purpose to those in the school. If, like the situation in the Russian schools, it is a presentation for its own sake, then it is a fruitless distraction.

If evidence is to be used effectively in schools, the following issues and dilemmas are important.

- At present, there is no clear national strategy about the status and role of research. Using information and evidence about school performance requires coherence and it is important to avoid ambivalence amongst teachers who may question its relevance. I do not advocate a single imprimatur, but argue for a dialectical debate about policy and practice amongst the multiple autonomies (the Teacher Training Agency, National Schools Leadership College, General Teaching Council, Department for Education and Skills, higher education, the professional associations).
- The shift in educational discourse towards a focus on learning, as opposed to 'schooling' is significant. The Campaign for Learning (Lucas *et al.*, 2002) has focused on developing 'learning to learn' approaches that are intended to involve and engage learners within their own learning as participants. This stance recognises that they will need to acquire skills to enhance their capacity to learn. Seeking information about how this works is crucial, and such a position endorses a role for teachers as reflective practitioners in the process of review. I asked Campaign for Learning Deputy Director, Toby Greany, about the group's work:

> What proved interesting was that this not only led to raised pupil standards and motivation, but the process itself appears to raise teacher motivation. It encouraged them to refocus on their original motivation for entering the classroom, namely learning. Teachers faced with relentless externally imposed change can use the investigation of their own, and their pupils' learning, as a means of managing that change.

- An opportunity to build collectively upon the experience of others avoids the commonly held view that 'the wheel always needs reinventing'. What seems to help is access to context specific examples, which allow assimilation rather than dissemination of ideas and practice (see Coe, Fitz-Gibbon and Tymm, 2000). Using data about performance in itself may prove to be the most effective way of impacting on how we shape and determine our learning and teaching strategies, but it is necessary to manage the diversity and volume of knowledge available, ensuring that teachers can access the information. Developing standardised systems for holding information would be helpful and, if available electronically, could be readily updated and post scripted by teacher practitioners.

• EIPP in education has been 'borrowed' from medicine, yet the appropriateness of the analogy is uncertain. Chris Husbands, Director of Warwick University Institute of Education, sees comparisons with medicine as problematic:

> My GP tells me that she could not do her job without reading the *British Medical Journal*, feeling that if her professional practice did not reflect this activity she would be a lousy doctor. However, she is not actively involved in research. We need to consider teachers as consumers of research and evidence, and it may be this area which has the best potential for EIPP. This might be achieved, and if so, it's not because we made ourselves like medicine but because we do something else. To this end the Cochrane analogy is not a strong one. Teachers say research does not give them the answers. What I want is for teachers to have the capacity to ask the questions that research can answer.

CONCLUSION

This chapter has endorsed a role for teachers as 'users and producers' of research, encouraging them to be involved in shaping the relationship between information, policy, performance and practice. We need to give teachers the skills associated with finding and reviewing information, in using quantitative and qualitative measures. Their role should not be as spectators but to engage with, test and challenge assumptions for 'we are not truly present in any conversation if we are only silent auditors' (Thompson, 1978, p. iv). However, I also want to ensure that we do not measure for its own sake. Rather, we do so to improve the experience of our students and make our teachers more powerful, effective and assured in their work. I have illustrated how information is used and impacts on our practice at Peers. I know how in different ways evidence informs what we do and what conditions are needed to enable improvement to occur. What I know less well is how to develop a culture and ethos in which teachers can incorporate practitioner research into their pedagogy. Perhaps pressures of accountability and the increased emphasis on school performance may itself prove to be a counter-incentive to a culture of practitioner research. The expertise needed for research and teaching is different but should not deter us from finding the common ground. Teachers deserve opportunities to discover by seeing what everybody has seen and thinking what nobody has thought.

REFERENCES

Checkland, P. and Scholes, J. (1999) *Soft Systems Methodology in Action*, Chichester: John Wiley.

Coe, R., Fitz-Gibbon, C. and Tymms, P. (2000) Promoting evidence-based education: the role of practitioners, round table presented at BERA Conference, Cardiff University, September.

Coleman, P. and Collinge, J. (1995). An inside-out approach to school improvement, paper delivered at the Eighth Annual Congress for School Effectiveness and School Improvement, Leeuwarden.

Department for Education and Employment (DfEE) (1998a) Teachers Meeting the Challenge of Change. Green Paper, London: HMSO.

Department for Education and Employment (DfEE) (1998b) *Excellence for all children: meeting special educational needs*, London: HMSO.

Fullan, M.G. (1991) *The New Meaning of Educational Change*, London: Cassell.

Glenny, G. (2001) *Integrated Support Services Evaluation Report: Hamilton Oxford Schools Partnership*, Oxford: the Centre for Inclusive and Special Education Research, Westminster Institute of Education, Oxford Brookes University.

Hammersley, M. (2000) Diversity or control in educational research, paper to Diversity or Control in Educational Research, City University, January.

Lucas, B., Greany, T., Rodd, J. and Wicks, R. (2002) *Teaching Pupils How To Learn – Research Practice and INSET Resources*, Stafford: Network Educational Press.

Noble, M., Smith, G., Avenell, D., Smith, T. and Sharland, E. (1994) *Rowntree Foundation Changing Patterns of Income and Wealth in Oxford and Oldham*, Oxford: Department of Applied Social Studies and Social Research, University of Oxford.

Office for Standards in Education (OFSTED) (2000) *New Inspection Schedule*, London: OFSTED.

Pring, R. (2000) *Philosophy of Educational Research*, London: Continuum.

Smith, D. and Tomlinson, S. (1989) *The School Effect*, London: Policy Institute.

Taylor, M. and Hallgarten, J. (2000) *Freedom to Modernize*, RSA, Education Futures – Lifelong Learning.

Thompson, E.P. (1978) *The Poverty of Theory and Other Essays*, London: Merlin Press.

11

Leading to Improve: EIPP at a Personal Level

WILL WALE

This chapter focuses on my personal experience as a researcher practitioner, using research into school leadership in secondary schools in the UK to prepare for headship. This experience will be examined within the context of the framework for evidence-informed policy and practice (EIPP) established in this book.

The chapter will consider specifically:

- how I came to research this issue for this purpose
- how the study was set in the context of existing literature
- how the research questions were arrived at
- the nature of the evidence derived from the research and how it might be validated
- how this evidence can be used to inform policy and practice.

The research which forms the subject of this chapter is in the public domain, drawn from an empirical study undertaken as part of a programme of post-graduate work (Levačić and Glatter, Chapter 5 in this volume).

THE STARTING POINT

After a varied career in secondary schools and three years in business management, I was appointed to a deputy headship in an 11–16 comprehensive school. With the career intention of moving to headship, appropriate preparation was a key issue. I was looking to develop my own leadership skills and hence to directly influence policy and practice in the school in which I worked. Initially, I enrolled on the MBA degree in Educational Management at the University of Leicester and began a programme of small-scale research into aspects of secondary school leadership and management. At about the same time (1997), the UK government initiated the National Professional Qualification for Headship (NPQH), with an entirely different competency-based approach to preparation for leadership. I also enrolled on this course and the two qualifications were studied simultaneously, enabling comparisons to be made between each experience of developing skills and preparing for headship.

The research presented here is drawn from the 20,000 word management study I submitted for the MBA degree (Wale, 1998). The title 'Can head-teachers really make a difference?' reflects the focus of the study – the extent to which headteachers can influence their schools in bringing about school improvement. Given my purpose in studying for this qualification, research into the leadership of secondary schools linked to school improvement seemed a natural choice. Although it may appear to be a rather pragmatic and utili-tarian reason for studying the issue, the theory and practice of leadership was of intrinsic interest, not least because it was a motivational factor in leading me to pursue my career in this direction. Additionally, by 1997, school leader-ship and school improvement were taking on considerable significance as related issues in their own right.

The reasons for this are connected with the failure of the structural reforms of the 1980s to raise educational standards, which led to a shift in government policy in the 1990s towards process reforms that included 'school improve-ment' initiatives. Previous attempts at school improvement had focused on a 'bottom-up' whole-school orientated approach to developing classroom prac-tice. This approach underpinned the Technical and Vocational Education Initiative (TVEI) and led to the development of school-based review as a tool for improvement (Hopkins, 1989, p. 116). In 1995, the then Secretary of State, Gillian Shepherd, announced a nationally sponsored school improve-ment project, implying a shift towards a top-down strategy. The Labour government's White Paper, *Excellence in Schools* (DfEE, 1997), continued the project by setting out its priorities for school improvement, including focuses on the quality of teaching and the development of key skills, delivered through strategies for Key Stage 2 initially, and Key Stage 3 subsequently. There has been a historical assumption in UK policy-making that effective headteachers are fundamental to effective schools and hence to delivering school improve-ment. The importance of effective school leadership in bringing about improvement was highlighted by OFSTED (1994, p. 46) and reaffirmed in recent government policy. The 1997 White Paper stated unequivocally that 'the quality of the head often makes the difference between the success and failure of a school. Good heads can transform a school' (DfEE, 1997, p. 46). This transformational view of headship was reinforced by (then) Education Secretary David Blunkett's announcement in March 2000 that schools failing to meet baseline targets on performance faced closure and a 'fresh start' with a new headteacher (TES, 2000, p. 1). Yet the assumption is not universal. In 1998, the Education Select Committee of the House of Commons was quick to point out that effective schools in Switzerland functioned well without heads. Eamonn Kane, Deputy General Secretary of the National Association of Schoolmasters/Union of Women Teachers (NAS/UWT), responded to this by commenting that 'British schools are still hung up by the public school idea of inspirational leaders in the Thomas Arnold mould' (TES, 1998, p. 1). So who is right?

This research attempts to go beyond the assumption of a causal link between effective headteachers and effective schools to consider headteachers' perceptions of their role in the school improvement process. An empirical study was undertaken with serving secondary headteachers to investigate their perceptions of the changing role of headship and the skills, qualities and attributes required to bring about school improvement. Leadership has long since been identified as a deeply personal activity (Bennis, 1989; Covey, 1996). The use of a practitioner-research approach provided a unique opportunity to engage directly with experienced practitioners in the context of their own organisations and to review the extensive body of international literature. One of the aims of this research was to directly influence policy and practice at school level by developing my own skills through the opportunity for systematic investigation and personal reflection. There is a clear contrast between this approach and that of the compliant NPQH model, where practitioner research is limited to documentation of school-based, job-related activities, which are used to demonstrate acquisition of the competencies specified in the *National Standards for Headteachers* (TTA, 1997).

The contrast between the two approaches highlights a paradox between the shift in the policy imperative towards a top-down approach and the need to maintain an evidence base for policy and practice. In reality, perhaps the former is a response to the perceived failure of the latter (Lumby, Chapter 9 in this volume). However, practitioner research provides one way in which the research community, policy-makers and practitioners may be brought together (Levačić and Glatter, Chapter 5 in this volume). Certainly, issues remain in the regulation and systematisation of practitioner research if it is to contribute to a coherent approach to the development of policy and practice.

THE LITERATURE

There is an extensive body of literature on educational leadership. Much of it focuses on the secondary phase of education and a significant amount is international, reflecting the extensive work done in North America and Australia over the last 20 years. An even greater body of work exists relating to management and leadership in the business world. Some writers from the business world have, of course, turned their attention directly to the issues of leading and managing schools – for example, Charles Handy (Handy and Aitkin, 1986). Arguments that business models are irrelevant to non-profit service provision have no place in an open debate on leadership. Arbitrarily excluding any aspect of literature would be detrimental to an effective approach to EIPP. The problems, then, remain that of selection – what to include and what not to – and that of synthesis – how to bring together such a wide range of literature. For the purpose of this study, I drew upon the available body of literature, first, to establish a conceptual framework for the study of leadership and, secondly, to chart the changing nature of headship in England and Wales.

There is a well-established and well-rehearsed theoretical and conceptual framework for the study of leadership. Much of it is based on organisational perspectives using transactional and transformational models. However, the apparent failure of schools to respond adequately to demands for change has led some writers to switch their attention from organisational perspectives to individual or interpersonal ones, making use of psychology to examine personal qualities. Covey's (1996) principle-centred approach is fundamentally personal and pays a great deal of attention to the individual qualities, habits and endowments of the leader. However, if used alone, Covey's approach is deterministic and based on an absolute, rather than a relative, meaning of behaviour. It does not adequately allow for subjective interpretations of behaviour – the phenomenological or perceptual interaction between leader and led. 'Invitational leadership' theory, on the other hand, makes use of an interpersonal perspective that sees the leader acting in the broader context of leadership within the organisation. It starts with the assumption that 'we have the choice to act or react, to behave responsibly or irresponsibly' (Stoll and Fink, 1996, p. 108). The leader creates a context 'in which a person is inclined to act in preferred ways' but is unlikely to be coerced. This approach sees the headteacher inviting 'pupils, teachers and the community with the ultimate view of developing shared leadership' (ibid., p. 108). The invitational relationship is based on four premises:

- *optimism* that people have untapped potential for growth
- *respect* for the individuality of every human being
- *trust* in the behaviour of others
- *intentionality* that actions are supportive and caring (ibid., p. 109).

While this approach emphasises the integrity of these premises in individual behaviour, it accepts that a leader might behave 'situationally as ... manager, facilitator, counsellor or change agent depending on circumstances' (ibid., p. 110).

The development and use of such conceptual models to underpin empirical study is a fundamental part of effective social science research. At practitioner research level, it provides the opportunity for the critical reflection that is vital to developing the degree of understanding required to improve policy and practice.

The second strand of literature I reviewed concerned the changing role of headship. The evidence base is extensive. A survey of educational management journals revealed a plethora of such studies (e.g. Evetts, 1994; Gillborn, 1989; Hughes, 1993; Kerry and Murdoch, 1993; McHugh and McMullen, 1995; Murphy, 1991). Historically, research on the role of headteachers has tended to be either ethnographic, recording and describing the tasks of headship from participant observation (e.g. Hall, Mackay and Morgan, 1986), or subjective, based on a limited number of interviews (e.g. Ribbins and Marland, 1994). Much of the analysis contained in research from Britain,

	Traditional	1960s	1980s	1990s
Public policy imperative	Elitist selection[1]	The comprehensive ideal – social democratic[2]	Local management and public accountability	Improving educational standards
Headship role	Leading pastoral role	Leading professional	Chief executive	Leading professional and chief executive
Dominant leadership and management style	Transactional or transformational, autocratic and charismatic	Transformational, person-orientated and collegial	Transactional, task-orientated and bureaucratic	Transformational, interpersonal and compliant

[1]Lawson and Silver (1973, p. 365).
[2]Garrett (1997, p. 183).

Figure 11.1 Changing headship roles and leadership and management styles

North America and Australia focuses on empirical and normative interpretations of the headteacher's role as 'leading professional' or 'chief executive' and the leadership and management styles required to fulfil these roles.

In reality, the role of headteacher has changed in response to changing national policy. As Anthea Millett, former chief executive of the Teacher Training Agency, put it: 'Demands on headteachers have multiplied in recent years, as they have adapted to managing the national curriculum, assessment and testing, appraisal, financial delegation and regular Ofsted inspection' (Millett, 1997, p. 16).

This theme is developed in Figure 11.1, which sets out a continuum of changing headship roles and leadership and management styles, in response to changing public policy.

The analysis traces development from the nineteenth-century 'headmaster tradition' of Arnold, Thring and Keate, responding to demands for 'elitist selection' and exercising paternal, autocratic and charismatic leadership (Hall, Mackay and Morgan, 1986, p. 3). Change came in the 1960s with demands for social democracy that produced a transformational and collegial style of leadership, fulfilling a leading professional role. Demands for greater public accountability in the 1980s forced headteachers to adopt a role much more akin to that of a chief executive exercising a transactional, task-orientated and bureaucratic style. The focus on standards in the 1990s once again required a change of style, this time towards a transformational and interpersonal one capable of bringing about the degree of change demanded.

The construction of a framework of change and causation (Figure 11.1) brought order to the wide range of studies present in the body of literature and, more importantly, to the complex process of change that has characterised education over the years. The synthesis provided the context for studying headship at the end of the 1990s and enabled the formulation of research questions that were pertinent to real issues facing headteachers at that time.

THE RESEARCH QUESTIONS

The success and validity of any research investigation depends, in part, on the formulation of research questions. The original investigation was based on three research questions that looked at the sources of pressure for improvement, the obstacles to progress, as well as the leadership skills, attributes and strategies required to bring about effective change.

The questions arose in part from my original reasons for undertaking the research (namely to prepare myself for headship and influence practice at school level), in part from the framework established in the review of literature and in part to contribute to the body of evidence that would inform policy and practice in a wider context.

Overall, the findings arising from these questions focused very much on what the respondents perceived to be the changing role of headship as they found themselves forced to meet the challenge of increased pressure for improvement, largely arising from increased accountability, and as they found ways around the obstacles.

In order to present the findings in a coherent and meaningful way within the constraints of this chapter, the three original research questions have been condensed into two:

• How did the headteachers involved in the study see their role changing in response to demands for school improvement created through greater accountability?
• What did they see as the leadership skills, attributes and strategies necessary to bring about effective change?

WHAT COUNTS AS EVIDENCE?

If practitioner research is to make an effective contribution to EIPP, then the evidence generated must be demonstrably valid, perhaps using criteria of the sort adopted by the Cochrane Collaboration in the health service (Levačić and Glatter, Chapter 5 in this volume). To address the issue of validation, this section looks at the design of the investigation and the nature of the evidence generated.

It is generally accepted that school improvement is a complex process, involving not only raising standards, but also improving 'quality' and promoting the ethos of schools (OFSTED, 1994). The relationship between headteachers and school improvement is equally complex. So what research approach and tools would reveal these complexities most effectively? While quantitative methods may be appropriate to the comparative investigation of effective schools or hypothesising about the relationship between leadership and improvement, such methods are limited in shedding light on 'the complexities of human decision-making and behaviour' which may be associated with the process of school improvement (Johnson, 1994, p. 7).

Given these issues, in the context of the purposes and research questions already identified, the research approach and the tools adopted were designed to explore the perceptions of a number of practitioners. Focusing on headteachers' perceptions indicates a 'relativist' approach, accepting a 'subjectivist view of social reality' (Cohen and Manion, 1994, p. 9). At a philosophical level this raises fundamental questions about the nature of truth. As Kierkegaard (1974) put it: 'When the question of truth is raised subjectively, reflection is directed subjectively to the nature of the individual's relationship; if only the mode of this relationship is in the truth, the individual is in the truth'.

This anti-positivist position challenges the existence of objective truth. It sees truth as an intrinsic part of the relationship between individuals and the focus of the specific enquiry. From this perspective, therefore, the reality of the role of headteachers in school improvement lies in their relationship as individuals with their schools and the process of improvement. According to Beck (1979), the practical purpose of social science is 'to understand social reality as different people see it and to demonstrate how their views shape the action which they take within that reality'.

In its epistemology, then, this study is anti-positivist (Cohen and Manion, 1994, p. 9). It is likely that much of the data collected would be qualitative. However, classifying the study as largely qualitative in its approach does not preclude the use of quantitative methods (Bell, 1987, p. 4). Research was therefore based on a survey using semi-structured interviews to explore in depth the perceptions of an opportunity sample of six headteachers – all working within the same town and known to me personally. There are, of course, issues of validity surrounding the use of opportunity samples, which concern the representativeness of the respondents. However, the use of such a sample was for purely practical reasons. Given the constraints of working as a practitioner researcher, it was possible to build hour-long interviews into the busy daily schedules of both the interviewees and myself, simply because of their accessibility to me. The evidence yielded by this method would be largely qualitative. This opportunity sample was set in the broader context of responses to a postal questionnaire sent to all heads in one northern LEA, allowing for a degree of quantitative analysis. This population was chosen because there had been a recent LEA-wide conference for headteachers on school improvement and the survey followed up that conference chronologically with the intention of improving return rates. The population identified for the questionnaire survey may be justified as a probability sample of all headteachers in England and Wales. As such, it can be regarded as a cluster sample, allowing broader generalisations to be drawn from the findings. The use of a large shire authority, encompassing urban and rural settings with wide variations in

Table 11.1 Comparison of respondents' and non-respondents' schools

(a) 5 A*–C rate

5 A*–C Rate 1997	Respondents	%	Non-respond.	%	Respondents as % of total
0–10%	1	1.6	0	0	100
11–20%	5	8.1	2	5.6	71.42
21–30%	12	19.4	7	19.4	63.15
31–40%	10	16.1	9	25.0	52.63
41–50%	9	14.5	10	27.8	47.36
51–60%	13	21.0	6	16.7	68.42
60+%	12	19.4	2	5.6	85.71
	62	100.0	36	100.0	

(b) Percentage point change in 5 A*–C rate, 1994–97

Change, 1994–97 (% points)	Respondents	%	Non-responds.	%	Respondents as % of total
More than 10 pt increase	8	12.9	6	16.7	57.14
5–10 pt increase	21	33.9	7	19.4	75.00
Insignificant change	27	43.5	14	38.9	65.85
5–10 pt decline	5	8.1	7	19.4	41.66
More than 10 pt decline	1	1.6	2	5.6	33.33
	62	100	36	100	

socio-economic conditions, was likely to increase the representativeness of the sample and reduce the risk of sample error (Cohen and Manion, 1994, p. 90).

There were 62 responses to the questionnaire survey sent to the headteachers in this authority, representing 63 per cent of the sample population. Respondents' schools were compared with those of non-respondents to assess how representative respondents were of the sample population. Three criteria were used: size of school, 5 A*–C rate and percentage point change in the 5 A*–C rate. There was no appreciable difference indicated by the first criterion. Differences indicated by the other two criteria are set out in Table 11.1.

The opportunity sample for the in-depth interviews was drawn from headteachers serving in an old cotton manufacturing area with a modern-day multi-ethnic community characterised by high levels of unemployment and social deprivation. Being acutely aware of the issues raised by opportunity samples, profiles of the six respondents are presented in Table 11.2. Compared with contextual analysis of the questionnaire respondents and the LEA as a whole, women were overrepresented and the voluntary-aided sector was underrepresented. The sample was also skewed towards larger schools and those at the lower end of examination performance.

Table 11.2 Interview respondents: contextual data

Respondent	Gend.	Post as head	Years in post	Adv. qual.	School status	No. on roll	5A*–C 1997	Change 1994–97
Alan	Male	First	6–10	None	Comm.	1000–1199	20–29%	Static
Bob	Male	Second	11–15	Master's	Found.	800–999	30–39%	Static
Chris	Female	First	1–3	Master's	Comm.	400–599	20–29%	Declined
David	Male	First	11–15	Master's	Comm.	1000–1199	20–29%	Improved
Erica	Female	First	1–3	Adv Dip	Comm.	1000–1199	30–39%	Improved
Fiona	Female	First	1–3	Master's	Comm.	800–999	10–19%	Improved

Table 11.3 Sources of impetus for school improvement

Factor	Mean	St. Dev.
Commitment to pupils and parents	1.82	1.11
Pupil recruitment	2.61	1.30
OfSTED inspection	3.00	1.39
Publication of performance tables	3.19	1.38
LEA advisers or external consultants	4.23	1.61

Analysis of the findings from each of the research tools raised its own specific issues. The questionnaire was designed to enable quantification and as much of the data as possible was quantified to enable more effective correlation and to allow for a mixture of 'content' and 'grounded theory' analysis, bringing together inductively and holistically the qualitative evidence of the small interview sample with content-analysed quantitative data from the broader sample of questionnaires (Easterby-Smith, Thorpe and Lowe, 1994, pp. 345–47). Where appropriate, statistical techniques were used to aid interpretation and test the validity of the evidence. Tables 11.3 and 11.4 are presented as examples of this methodology.

Table 11.3 presents the responses to a question about where headteachers saw the impetus for improvement to be coming from. Respondents were given the opportunity to rank five factors that had been identified through a pilot survey. In the table, the mean ranking is given and the use of standard deviation calculations indicates a substantial amount of consistency in the ranking. This process enabled greater confidence to be derived about where headteachers perceived the pressures to be coming from.

Table 11.4 presents findings about the usefulness placed on various strategies for achieving school improvement by headteachers. Again, respondents were asked to rank in order a number of factors. Although initial analysis, using standard deviations, again indicated a strong level of agreement, the findings were correlated against a number of contextual factors – school status, number on roll, 5 A*–C rate and percentage change in 5 A*–C rate over a four-year period. Correlation co-efficients were used to provide a measure of significance of these factors by quantifying the comparison between responses classified by

Table 11.4 Strategies for improvement: ranked by school size (NOR)

Less than 800 on roll	More than 800 on roll
Communicating a clear vision for the school	Communicating a clear vision for the school
Regular monitoring of pupil progress	Improving the quality of teaching
Improving the quality of teaching	Development of middle management
Team building	Regular monitoring of pupil progress
Development of middle management	Team building
Target setting for pupils at Key Stage 4	Improving learning environment
Effective annual development planning cycle	Target setting for pupils at Key Stage 4
Mentoring of pupils	Regular monitoring of policy (e.g. homework)
Improving learning environment	Mentoring of pupils
Improving discipline in classrooms	Improving facilities (capital building projects)
Target setting for pupils at Key Stage 3	Effective annual development planning cycle
Regular monitoring of policy (e.g. homework)	Improving learning resources
Effective ways of evaluating development	Effective ways of evaluating development
Improving learning resources	Target setting for pupils at Key Stage 3
Improving facilities (capital building projects)	Improving discipline in classrooms

Note: Correlation co-efficient = 0.801749

each contextual factor. The only factor that revealed a significant degree of disparity was school size and the differences are presented in Table 11.4. Each column indicates the rank ordering according to school size. The correlation coefficient of 0.80 indicates the degree of disparity. This data opens up a further avenue for investigation: why should school size make a difference?

The interviews enabled a much more intimate exploration of headteachers' perceptions of the issues investigated. A semi-structured approach was used with a schedule of five broad questions to enable comparisons between the interviews. Each of the interviews was tape-recorded. Full transcripts were not produced, but verbatim comments were transcribed from the tapes relating to the issues identified for analysis.

In this way clear differences were identified. With regard to the issue of accountability, one of the respondents saw it as a useful tool, something that could be passed on to staff: 'it gives you a bit more grist to your elbow' (Alan). In contrast, another respondent saw external accountability as a slur on her own professionalism and that of her staff: 'I suppose fundamentally we've got a problem with our professional standards ... The idea that we wouldn't be committed to school improvement is actually very insulting' (Erica).

The interviews also clearly allowed me the opportunity to explore in depth the more personal aspects of leadership. Despite discussion of senior management teams, the interviews revealed a personalisation of the leadership role. This may in part be explained by the framing of the investigation that focused on the role of the headteacher as the agent of change. However, it was clear that it was *their* schools they were talking about and responsibility for success or failure lay with them. They were keen to emphasise the importance of personal qualities in defining leadership and management style. As one put it, after vision 'it was down to the personality of the head'. Others developed this point: 'If you look at schools ... you'll make your own judgements about the effectiveness of the head' (Bob); 'The character of a school, or the ethos of the school ... reflects to a large extent the style and leadership of the head' (Fiona); 'Personal relationships are at the heart of all this. Heads set the tone for everything at the end of the day' (David).

An important tool in the process of validating findings is the use of triangulation. This study allowed for an element of triangulation by setting the interview findings against those of the broader postal survey. However, to use Ribbins and Marlands's (1994, p. 6) classification, this was a level 1 study and as such only represents a start in researching this area. Level 2 study – observation of the actions of the head – and level 3 study – seeking the views of other senior managers, classroom teachers and other stakeholders – would be necessary in at least some of the schools involved in this study to fully triangulate and validate the findings.

THE FINDINGS

The findings are summarised below as they relate to the research questions:

1 How did the headteachers involved in the study see their role changing in response to demands for school improvement created through greater accountability?

   • The headteachers in the survey felt that they had *not* been diverted away from educational leadership towards chief executive roles. Most preferred to see themselves as 'leading professionals', though heads of larger schools were more likely to see themselves as 'chief executives'.

   • There were mixed feelings about external accountability and whether it assisted or got in the way of the task of improvement. For many, the moral and value-based imperatives, in the interests of pupils and other stakeholders, were held to be sufficient.

   • There was a clear view that the pressures on heads from a hectic policy agenda created problems and there was a strong feeling that they needed more time to focus on teaching and learning, which was seen as vital to school improvement.

2 What did they see as the leadership skills, attributes and strategies necessary to bring about effective change?

   • The heads demonstrated a clear commitment to their schools, seeing themselves as responsible for their success or failure and not seeing themselves as just organisational managers.

- Linked to this sense of mission, was an orthodox endorsement of vision as fundamental to effective change and improvement. Headteachers need to have a clear view of the direction the school will move in and must be able to articulate this to all stakeholders.
- These heads were acutely aware of the power of culture and the dialectic relationship it has with change and improvement: if you work with culture you can change it; if you can change it, then improvement will be secured.
- In terms of motivating others, there was a clear preference for inclusive approaches and collegial team building. However, they made it equally clear that such approaches are not necessarily democratic and that there had to be strong leadership with the emphasis on control, performance and accountability.
- In terms of leadership style there was no right or wrong; it was more a matter of what worked and that largely depended on a close match between the personality of the head and the context of the school.
- Above all else, the investigation revealed an optimism bordering on faith, expressing itself in a commitment to their pupils and a resilience that, come what may, they and their schools would succeed.

To sum up, the findings of this study echo Hughes's (1993, p. 14) assessment of the role of the headteacher: 'The task is to be honest, while optimistic, and pragmatic while maintaining those statements of vision and overarching direction. Impossible but, nonetheless, essential.'

WHAT CAN WE DO WITH THE FINDINGS?

If practitioner research is to contribute towards an EIPP approach, then its impact on policy and practice at personal, institutional and national levels must be demonstrable. In seeking to demonstrate its impact, three significant problems emerge:

- From the point of view of the practitioner researcher, it is the experience of research as much as the findings that may influence practice.
- Who are the 'we' in the subtitle question?
- How do we demonstrate impact at school level when so many other variables are at play?

Each of these issues is examined in the remaining subsections.

The value of research experience

Research as an activity in itself is an educative process, developing in the researcher a wide range of skills and a depth of understanding it is difficult to achieve in other ways. For example, I found that the experience of research has developed in me greater understanding of the dialectic relationship between leaders and their organisations. Leadership is a complex and highly personal activity that goes well beyond the demonstration of standards required by the National Professional Qualification for Headship. As Warren Bennis (1989, p. 1) put it, the study of leadership is far from being an exact science: 'For one thing, the social world isn't nearly as orderly as the physical world, nor is it as susceptible to rules. For another, people, unlike solids, fluids and gases, are anything but uniform and anything but predictable.'

Investigating the perceptions of practising heads about the changing nature of their role and the skills, attributes and strategies required for successful fulfilment provided ample opportunity to develop an in-depth understanding of the diversity of leadership in schools in England and Wales.

With regard to preparation for headship, there is a qualitative difference between training and education for leadership, the latter requiring greater opportunity to reflect on the complex relationships that underlie transformational leadership if it is to be effective. The uniqueness of the relationship between leader and organisation highlighted by this study calls into question the sufficiency of the compliant model that underpins the Teacher Training Agency's *National Standards for Headteachers* (TTA, 1997) and which forms the basis for the National Professional Qualification for Headship. The availability of a database of empirical studies for aspiring headteachers and the opportunity to carry out personal research each has a key role to play in developing personal skills and understanding based on evidence. To quote Bennis (1989, p. 5) again 'leaders are made, not born, and made more by themselves than by any external means'. There is a need to create opportunities for the individual to explore and reflect.

Who are the 'we'?

Do we mean the wider research community? Do we mean policy-makers and practitioners at local or even national level? If practitioner research is to contribute to EIPP, then findings need to be disseminated. As public domain research, the study presented in this chapter is accessible to the wider research community through the University of Leicester Education Library as an unpublished dissertation (Wale, 1998). Though anyone who has tried to access the wealth of unpublished research in the UK will find it a daunting task, because access is in no way systematised. It could, of course, be published in one of the specialist journals, though it would still remain an 'isolated' set of research findings.

The findings of this study are not ground-breaking in their own right. To some extent they confirm existing orthodoxies, but they do give fresh insights into the issues of preparing aspiring leaders for the challenges that face them. The evidence base that supports these findings, in itself, adds to the depth of understanding of the complex and highly personal nature of leadership.

For the work of myself and other researcher practitioners to have a role in influencing policy, then there has to be a mechanism for disseminating it as part of a coherent body of evidence. Systematic review, including validation of the research, might be a way forward, undertaken by a government sponsored body like the DfES-funded Evidence for Policy and Practice Information Co-ordinating (EPPI) Centre (Levačić and Glatter, Chapter 5 in this volume), to which research studies could be submitted.

Demonstrating impact

Demonstrating the impact of any variable on policy and practice at school level is difficult, simply because it involves attempting to unpack a complex web of cause and effect. This task is made even more difficult where the variable being assessed is a less tangible personal one – the skill and experience of the individual. Huberman (1993, pp. 41–3) identifies three levels at which the work of researcher practitioners may impact on the work situation: 'instrumental effects' on daily work practices, change at institutional level, and 'conceptual effects' that impact on the work situation. Because the study presented in this chapter was not directed at any specific issue or initiative, it is difficult to directly identify 'instrumental' change in work practices. However, the information and knowledge generated will have led to 'conceptual' and institutional outcomes in the medium term.

Circumstances also change. For personal reasons, I was forced to abandon the career move to headship, so that it has not been possible to evaluate the ultimate test of impact – bringing about transformational change in a school of which I was the leader. However, this is not to negate either the experience or the outcomes of this research. I continue to exercise a leadership role in a school 'in challenging circumstances', where the traditional culture is an obstacle to raising standards. Progress has been made in bringing about change and my understanding of cultural issues that arose from this study has undoubtedly played a part in developing the right policies and strategies. As part of this process, I led the successful establishment of Technology College status at the school together with a whole range of other initiatives, each making some use of the experience and findings of this research. Together, these changes have contributed to school improvement and this can be demonstrated in quantitative ways. So, at an institutional and personal level, it would appear that evidence has informed both policy and practice.

Nevertheless, assessment of both the impact of the individual working within a team context and the skills and knowledge of the individual on policy and practice within the school remains, in many ways, subjective. At the time of writing no study has been undertaken to evaluate the impact of the evidence generated by this research on the school – indeed, the design of such an evaluative study would pose a significant challenge.

REFERENCES

Beck, R.N. (1979) *Handbook in Social Philosophy*, New York: Macmillan.

Bell, J. (1987) *Doing Your Research Project*, Buckingham: Open University Press.

Bennis, W. (1989) *On Becoming a Leader*, London: Random Century.

Cohen, L. and Manion, L. (1994) *Research Methods in Education* (4th edn), London: Routledge.

Covey, S.R. (1996) *Principle-Centred Leadership*, New York: Simon and Schuster.

Department for Education and Employment (DfEE) (1997) *Excellence in Schools*, Cm 3681, London: HMSO.

Easterby-Smith, M., Thorpe, R. and Lowe, A. (1994) Analysing qualitative data, in Bennett, N., Glatter, R. and Levačić, R. (eds) *Improving Educational Management*, London: Paul Chapman Publishing.

Evetts, J. (1994) The new headteacher: the changing work culture of secondary headship, *School Organisation*, Vol. 14, No. 1, pp. 34–47.

Garrett, V. (1997) Principals and headteachers as leading professionals, in Ribbins, P. (ed.) *Leaders and Leadership in the School, College and University*, London: Cassell.

Gillborn, D.A. (1989) Talking heads: reflections on secondary headship at a time of rapid educational change, *School Organisation*, Vol. 9, No. 1, pp. 65–83.

Hall, V., Mackay, H. and Morgan, C. (1986) *Headteachers at Work*, Buckingham: Open University Press.

Handy, C. and Aitkin, R. (1986) *Understanding Schools as Organisations*, Harmondsworth: Penguin.

Hopkins, D. (1989) *Evaluation for School Development*, Buckingham: Open University Press.

Huberman, M. (1993) Changing minds: the dissemination of research and its effects on practice and theory, in Day, C., Calderhead, J. and Denicolo, P. (eds) *Research on Teacher Thinking*, London: Falmer.

Hughes, L. (1993) Dimensions, themes and skills: the task of the secondary head-teacher, *Aspects of Education*, Vol. 48, pp. 12–22.

Johnson, D. (1994) *Research Methods in Educational Leadership*, Harlow: Longman.

Kerry, T. and Murdoch, A. (1993) Education managers as leaders: some thoughts on the context of the changing nature of schools, *School Organisation*, Vol. 13, No. 3, pp. 221–30.

Kierkegaard, S. (1974) *Concluding Unscientific Postscript*, Princeton, NJ: Princeton University Press.

Lawson, J. and Silver, H. (1973) *A Social History of Education in England*, London: Methuen.

McHugh, M. and McMullen, L. (1995) Headteacher or manager? Implications for training and development, *School Organisation*, Vol. 15, No. 1, pp. 23–28.

Millett, A. (1997) A head is more than a manager, *Times Educational Supplement*, 21 June, pp. 16.

Murphy, P.J. (1991) School management tomorrow: collaboration – collaboration – collaboration, *School Organisation*, Vol. 11, No. 1, pp. 65–70.

Office for Standards in Education (OFSTED) (1994) *Improving Schools*, London: HMSO.

Ribbins, P. and Marland, M. (1994) *Headship Matters*, Harlow: Longman.

Stoll, L. and Fink, D. (1996) *Changing our Schools*, Buckingham: Open University Press.

Teacher Training Agency (TTA) (1997) *National Standards for Headteachers*, London: Teacher Training Agency.

Times Educational Supplement (TES) (1998) 26 June, p. 1.

Times Educational Supplement (TES) (2000) 3 March, p. 1.

Wale, W. (1998) Can headteachers really make a difference? Secondary headteachers' perceptions of their role in effecting school improvement in a northern LEA, unpublished MBA dissertation, University of Leicester.

12

Leadership Studies in Education: Maps for EPPI Reviews?

PETER RIBBINS AND HELEN GUNTER

INTRODUCTION

Professional researchers in education and in leadership and management in education live in interesting times – with frugal funding and fervent fault finding. On funding, Hillage *et al*. (1998, p. 10) 'estimate that some £65 million a year is spent on educational research, mainly spread over 100 university education departments' or, as Bassey (1997) puts it, 0.17 per cent of the total education budget. As Furlong and White (2002) note: 'even the English budget is estimated to be one of the lowest percentages in the OECD' (1). "Even" because the figures for Scotland at 0.1–0.2 (Nisbet, 1995) and for Wales at about 0.10 (Furlong and White, 2002) are lower still.

On fault finding, various reviews more or less critical of the collective efforts of the field in the UK have been published in recent years and have attracted a great deal of attention. In this chapter we will consider these criticisms. This will lead to an examination of an important response – the evidence for policy and practice information and co-ordinating centre (EPPI-Centre) systematic review approach. We will then argue the need for a map of the field of educational leadership without which, in our view, the systematic review approach as currently interpreted, however rigorously conducted, will be arbitrary in its ambition and partial in its practice. We also believe, for reasons that we shall explain, that it is not only systematic reviewers who need such a map. So, too, does the National College for School Leadership (NCSL). Finally, we will outline three 'mapping typologies' that we have developed, and illustrate using a particular case, how two, taken together, would enable the production of the kind of map we believe is necessary.

CRITICISM OF EDUCATIONAL RESEARCH: REVIEWING THE REVIEWS

The first critical review was presented in an address made in 1996 by David Hargreaves to the Teacher Training Agency (TTA). He branded educational research 'second rate' in so far as it was not cumulative or coherent and was too often inward looking, irrelevant and lacking in impact (Hargreaves, 1996). His views generated a great deal of media, political and other attention and stimulated further reviews sponsored by other government agencies. The most important of these were undertaken by James Tooley (Tooley, 1998) for the Office for Standards in Education (OFSTED) and by Jim Hillage (Hillage et al., 1998) for the Department for Education and Employment (DfEE).

Curiously, both the Tooley and Hillage reports suffered, initially, a similar fate at the hands of the spin doctors of their respective sponsoring agencies. Thus, Edwards (1998, p. 15), in pointing out 'the disparity between (DfEE) press release and the content of the IES (Hillage) report' notes that it (the press release) opened with the statement that: 'Too much educational research is of questionable quality and that which is good is often inaccessible to both teachers and policy makers, according to a comprehensive review commissioned by the DfEE'.

Similarly, Pam Lomax has argued that: 'I don't think that Tooley is the folk devil in this controversy. This role goes to OFSTED's Chief Inspector because of the conclusion (he) appears to draw from the research'. Thus, she points out that while Tooley found 'almost without exception, the research reviewed ... was relevant to practice and/or policy', Woodhead in the Foreword to the report concluded: 'Much that is published is, on this analysis, at best no more than an irrelevance and distraction' (Lomax, 1999, p. 9).

Taking these reviews together, eight sets of criticism, by no means all of which are equally justified, can be identified. Not all the reviews make all the criticisms, but there is some consensus on several of them. First, too much research is producer orientated and dominated. This means that the interests and involvement of users, defined as practitioners and policy-makers, in determining what should be done and by whom and how, and how it should be reported and to whom, is low. It also means that peers and peer review from higher education are accorded too high a status and therefore overly influence too much research and too many researchers. Second, too much research is unrelated to practice and, as such, has little useful to say about 'what works' and why. Third, amongst professional researchers too little regard is had for the knowledge of, or contribution that might be made by, researching professionals. Fourth, too much research is done by too many researchers in too many small institutions making for too much small-scale research that is high on unplanned repetition and low on overall coherence. Fifth, too little, most especially qualitative, research is deliberately replicatory and too much is noncumulative in nature. Attempts to build on previous work are exceptions rather than the norm. Sixth, in determining what should be researched and how this should be conducted, too much emphasis was given to originality and too little to validity and practical value. Seventh, the impact of a great deal of research is very low in part because researchers do not make enough effort to make it accessible to potential users. Eighth, too much research lacks objectivity in so far as it is overtly ideological and politically biased.

Whilst it is uncertain how far such criticisms have shaped rather than simply reflect the views of politicians and civil servants on research in education, what is clear is that they have been used by them. For Chris Woodhead, in his 1999 Annual Report as Chief Inspector:

> The agenda is, or ought to be, obvious. We know what constitutes good teaching and we know what needs to be done to tackle weaknesses ... We know, too, a great deal about leadership skills and why it is that our best headteachers are so effective. Why, then, is so much time and energy wasted in research that complicates what ought to be straightforward ... The challenge now is to expose the emptiness of education theorising that obfuscates the classroom realities that really matter. (As quoted on the back cover page of *Research Intelligence*, 71, March 2000)

The idea that 'we' have the knowledge the Chief Inspector for Schools claims with such conviction is controversial. Not even his political 'masters' at the time seemed in agreement on this. Certainly, it was not a view shared by Charles Clarke, at the time Minister for Schools who, in a meeting with the Policy Group of the British Educational Research Association, referred 'to a widespread ignorance on what works and what doesn't in education' (Bassey, 1999, p. 1). He went on to regret 'the lack of an effective data base that could be used to provide answers to questions about schools, teaching and learning' (ibid). In passing, it might be worth noting the importance the minister, who carried a general responsibility for research, attached to this aspect of his responsibilities. In an opening gambit to the BERA Group he observed: 'I have to tell you that research is my fifth order of priority: you've got half an hour' (ibid.).

Commenting on the Hillage Report, Clarke (1998, p. 8), like the DfEE press office, depicts its findings rather more bleakly than do its authors concluding that: 'research relating to schools is largely irrelevant and inaccessible, rarely informing policy or practice'. His condemnation is catholic – 'this unhelpful state of affairs is the responsibility of all parties concerned – the funders, researchers, policy-makers, teachers and publishers/editorial teams' (ibid). Like Hillage, he identifies three main ways forward:

- A refocusing of research funding by the development of a small number of centres of excellence and by increasing the funding available to specific kinds of research activity including longitudinal studies, literature reviews, randomly controlled trials.
- The development of an information centre along the lines pioneered by the Cochrane Collaboration which was set up 'to improve both the quality of research in the medical field and the effectiveness of communication of findings to clinicians' (ibid., p. 9).
- To increase user involvement in the selection, commissioning and steering process involved in the funding of research.

Such critiques and the proposals that they make for change have generated an energetic debate between members of the educational research community and its internal and external critics. What is involved can be illustrated by reference to a wide-ranging speech on research made by the Secretary of State for Education and Employment to a meeting convened by the Economic and Social Research Council in February 2000 entitled 'Influence or Irrelevance: can social science improve government?' (Blunkett, 2000). What he had to say generated a wide variety of responses from the educational research community.

For Bassey (2001, p. 1) the speech is

> a landmark for educational research ... He has firmly committed the government to 'an open-ended approach to understanding what works and why' and to reliance on social science ... to tell 'what types of policy initiatives are likely to be most effective' ... His ... concern for social justice leads him to understand the need for critical rational debate, for rigorous empirical enquiry, for blue skies work as much as for policy and practice studies ... the new message is clear: the discourse of derision is over, it is a time of hope for those who are prepared to recognise it and robust enough to meet its challenges.

Hammersley (2001a, p. 12) disagrees, suggesting that

> Bassey's positive response ... seems ... a dangerous misjudgement. In my view, the lecture shows clearly the threat to academic autonomy which the Government's attitude towards research represents ... Running through (it) is the view that academic research must become an instrument of government ... this is unacceptable in any liberal society, where the independence of non-governmental institutions must be respected. Moreover, it fails to recognise the essential role that a qualified scepticism can play in the development of knowledge.

Whilst Hammersley and others have advanced their views forcefully, there is reason to doubt how effective they have been in persuading sceptics of their errors. As such, it might be of some consolation to the beleaguered educational research community in the UK to know that it has not been alone in facing the kinds of attack outlined above. A similar controversy has taken place in Australia. This led in 1998 to the Department of Education, Training and Youth Affairs (DETYA) setting up an investigation into the impact of educational research. The findings of this review are reported in *The Impact of Educational Research* (DETYA, 2000).

The need for the review was justified in terms that echo criticisms from the UK but its findings are very different. It concluded that educational research in Australia 'was well recognised internationally and of a vigorous and substantially applied nature' and that there was 'compelling evidence that Australian research ... makes a difference in the worlds of schools, and policy development' (DETYA, 2000, p. 4). A full discussion of the reports of the four groups who undertook the research on which the DETYA (2000) review is based is beyond the scope of this chapter, and is in any case available in Bates (2001).

The DETYA review does not claim that educational research in Australia is flawless. On the contrary, its constituent studies note reservations on quality, impact and the like. But taken together they paint a much more positive portrait than UK reviewers do. This might be explained in very different ways. First it could simply be that educational research is superior in Australia. Second, it could also be that such research is not inferior in the UK but only seems so because the methods used to review it have ensured this result. It seems reasonable to hypothesise that a review conducted along the lines of the Australian study would produce similar findings in the UK. Given this, it is worth being clear about the lessons from Australia. Bates (2001, p. 8) notes five:

> First, while the relationships between research and practice are often indirect, they are significant and numerous. Secondly, by using more sophisticated methodologies which work backwards from practice, many of the ways research contributes to practice can be unravelled. Thirdly, the theory to application paradigm fundamental to so much R&D does not figure strongly in these accounts of educational practice. Fourthly, the models of relationships between the teacher/practitioner, administrator and policy maker that emerges from these studies is far from the hierarchical instruction/compliance model ... so much part of a rational policy making/implementation model of education ... But perhaps the most important conclusion is that ... significant ... research is being conducted.

What ever else might be said there seems a strong case for similar reviews, funded in the same relatively generous way, to be undertaken in the UK.

To argue that the findings of such reviews are influenced by how they are conducted, does not mean being committed to the view that the educational research community in the UK has nothing to learn from its critics. In particular, concerns about inaccessibility and lack of cumulative character may well be justified. With this in mind, the development of an evidence-informed approach to research for policy and practice might help, and it is to this that we turn.

BUILDING ON WHAT IS KNOWN:
THE EPPI REVIEWS APPROACH

Levačić and Glatter (2001, p. 9), in a wide-ranging examination of the approach suggest that 'an important element of evidence-informed policy and practice is the advocacy of far more replicatory research and of research that builds on previous work [and places a] greater emphasis on [the need for] systematic review' of key aspects of what is known. Over the last year, a start has been made to implement such an approach in the study of leadership in education. As Ouston (2001, p. 1) points out.

> SCRELM [Standing Conference for Research in Educational Leadership and Management] has obtained funding for two years from the *Evidence-Informed Policy and Practice in Education Initiative* to set up a School Leadership Research

Group. This Group will prepare systematic reviews in school leadership ... The initiative is based ... at the (EPPI-Centre) ... at the Institute of Education (in London) and funded by the DfEE.

The proposal was made on behalf of SCRELM by Les Bell and Ray Bolam. This indicated that:

The Review Group would aim to conduct systematic reviews on research into leadership and management in primary, secondary and special schools. Its main focus would be on the roles of heads and their senior management teams but, where appropriate, it would review studies involving deputies, heads of departments ... and school governors. As a priority, it is proposed to focus on the distinctive core process of educational leadership ... This would involve reviewing available primary research evidence of all types, emphasising empirical, well designed studies ... from different countries. Reviews would take account of the fact that policy contexts, school types, leadership roles and nomenclature vary between countries and would consider the international generalisability of the research evidence.

(Quoted in Ouston, 2001, p. 1)

Bell and Bolam (2001, p. 1) note that the first year of the programme was planned to be in two stages. The aim of the first stage was 'to map the broad field and identify sub-divisions within it to be the subject of subsequent specific review'. It was anticipated that this could and should build on the 25 papers [in Bush *et al.* (1999); and in a special edition of *Educational Management and Administration* 1999, 27, 3] given at a series of five ESRC-funded seminars on 'Redefining educational management' between June 1997 and May 1999. The 'mapping stage' was expected to 'be completed within six months of the Review Group being established' (Bell and Bolam, 2001, p. 1). In the following six months the first systematic review was to be completed and further themes for review identified. Clearly the group attached great importance to mapping. Before turning to this, we will consider the EPPI process.

Despite its recent origins, EPPI review and the processes it entails have attracted much attention. It is not our intention to summarise the debates EPPI has generated or attempt a comprehensive account of the process. For such an attempt, applicable to education and other areas of social policy, the reader can turn to Levačić and Glatter's chapter in this book and their earlier paper (Levačić and Glatter, 2001). In this evidence-informed policy and practice is described as consisting 'of a set of interrelated processes involving various stakeholders by which research issues are selected, evidence on these collected and validated and communicated and then used or ignored in decision-making by two key players: policy-makers and practitioners' (ibid., p. 6). What is involved is set out in a helpful diagram (ibid., p. 7) justified by the authors by the suggestion that such a 'model of evidence-informed policy and practice may help in distinguishing the key processes, their relationship to each other and the main stakeholders. This enables us to focus on the major components of evidence-informed policy and practice and to locate problems and possibilities in relation to these' (ibid., p. 6).

The systematic review process, as described by the EPPI-Centre at the Institute of Education in London (2001), is set out in two draft documents (*Core Keywording Strategy* and *Review Guidelines*). It entails:

(1) The establishment of a review question
(2) The systematic search for studies: titles and abstracts
(3) The use of inclusion/exclusion criteria for the studies to be systematically reviewed
(4) Coding of the studies using keywording, data extraction and quality assessment
(5) A synthesis of the studies.

By focusing on stage 4 we can illustrate systematic review at work through:

(a) *Keywording*: here the reviewer is asked to categorise the article according to keywords e.g. where was the study carried out, and what is the focus of the topic? The reviewer is asked to categorise the study according to descriptors of eight types:

- Outcome evaluation
- Process evaluation
- Economic evaluation
- Intervention description
- Methods
- Needs Assessment
- Review
- Descriptive study.

(b) *Data extraction and quality assessment*: here the reviewer undertakes a detailed categorisation of the type of study identified from the eight. On this basis, the reviewer selects coded answers regarding the development of the study, the sample, the collection and analysis of the data, the research intervention, the research findings, and the quality of the study.

Whilst its many merits (cumulative character, rigorous process, transparent nature, etc.) have been widely welcomed, concerns about the systematic review approach have also been raised. It is to these, and especially to its lack of clarity about how review questions are to be generated and legitimated, that we now turn.

Wallace (2001a, p. 27), in response to Levačić and Glatter (2001) argues, surely wisely, that we should proceed with caution. Evidence-informed policy and practice, is after all, a new central government policy, and the road to institutional hell over the years of reform has been paved with policy-makers' good intentions. Why should the evidence-informed policy and practice initiative be any less susceptible than other polices to generating unintended consequences for practice that undermine its instigators' good intentions?

We share this view, but our reservations about systematic reviews based on the EPPI-Centre approach are, like Hammersley's (2001a), concerned more with what we see as the underlying ontology and epistemology that structures the practice of the task of reviewing. The technicist approach taken to keywording seems to be more about enabling the data to be stored in a computer efficiently and accessibly than with allowing the richness and plurality of ideas to be revealed. The accumulation of research evidence is not necessarily linear. It can be horizontal, even iterative, and, as such, more like a 'mosaic' which adds, complements and challenges (Hammersley, 2001b, p. 548). Hammersley argues that systematic reviewing is based on a view of the superiority of positivism that is itself a distortion of the positivist position because 'natural science relies on personal or tacit knowledge' (ibid., p. 545). Once we recognise that judgement plays a part then the exercise of discretion, which enables rigour and validity, means that narrative accounts can be rehabilitated. In any case, as Hammersley asks, 'Where is the evidence that systematic reviews produce more valid conclusions than narrative reviews? ... It seems to be assumed that they *must* do because they are "systematic", "explicit". But this prejudges what is to be proven' (ibid., 547). Another assumption, also treated unproblematically, in the systematic review process as described above, is that it is always possible to proceduralise. But what if it is not? On this 'where a process cannot be proceduralised, seeking to reduce it to procedures will lead to distortion; while at the same time exaggerating some readers' impressions of the likely validity of the results' (ibid., 548).

Where does this leave things? We can continue to develop the EPPI-Centre framework and while this is of value it will, as it stands, enable, at best, only a very partial mapping of the field because it privileges particular types of knowledge. Our view is that we can develop alternatives generated from a different position. Before turning to this, we need to say something more on maps and mapping.

THE NEED FOR MAPPING

We would argue that without an appropriate map of the field, any attempt to determine review questions is likely to be arbitrary. We therefore welcome the recognition that the search for a map should take priority in the work of the EPPI Review Group for Leadership and Management in Schools (see above). As such we were glad to have had the opportunity to have been involved in a three-part process led by Geoff Southworth with Bell and Bolam, to progress this: first, to invite a small number of SCRELM members to participate in the process; second, to ask those who were taking part to submit their ideas for a map in written form to other members; third, to hold a one-day seminar in December 2001 at the University of Reading to share and collate ideas. In the event seven papers on maps and mapping the field were exchanged and considered (see Ribbins and Gunter, 2002). This included much illuminating discussion on maps and mapping.

In thinking about this, we begin from the idea that the mapping process is conceptual *and* practical. It is conceptual in that it is concerned with a means by which knowledge production can be understood, and it is practical since the labour of knowledge production in thinking, using and acting has the potential to inform and influence others. The reality of professional practice in real-life situations combined with the struggle over interpretation and meaning leads to the metaphor of mapping. This is so because it provides the language and consequent meanings created by such terms as 'terrain' (Ozga, 2000), 'turf' (Thomson, 2000), and 'field' (Bourdieu, 1990): 'a field is a metaphor for under-standing the intellectual territory which members inhabit, there are spaces where field members locate themselves and their work, and there are boundaries which demarcate those who are within the field from those outside' (Gunter, 1999, p. 230). Dispositions to enter the field and to be accepted assumes border controls. And activity within the field can be characterised as one of association and delineation. As Richardson (1997) demonstrates, a field can be an objective space that is gazed upon, but as field members it is also a place where we are and so we are the 'field' and do not and cannot leave. We play and are players, and are mindful that in our work a field is 'a battleground ... a war zone, as well as an ... inviting expanse, as well as a place where "energy" converts to "matter"' (ibid., p. 4). In proposing a way of mapping the field we are aware that we are engaged in a variety of activities. We also appreciate that in doing so there are structures shaping our capacities in the form of our own personal and profes-sional biographies, how we come to be here at this time on this particular terri-tory and how what we are doing is related to institutional and cultural demands.

Knowledge production has been charted, typically, through gendered, class and age topologies, hence, as we are aware, mapping it is not undertaken on a level playing field and central to the process is a reflexivity that enables the map to be reviewed as an outcome of a situated mapping process. Consequently, a map is the product of process and purpose, and can be small or large scale, realistic or stylised. We are not proposing mapping as the means to present the absolute truth of the study and practice of leadership, since, as Weindling (2001, p. 1) reminds us:

Maps are a selective view of reality and do not show the world as it actually is. The mapmaker chooses what to include and what to exclude ... We are now used to seeing world maps based on the projection developed by Mercator (1512–1594) to represent the globe on a flat two dimensional surface. But it is important to remember that other forms of projection produce different maps.

Hence any process of mapping will produce maps that are themselves contested, and so through dialogue over knowledge claims the purposes and positions in knowledge production can be open to scrutiny and interpretation. Having a sense of self and intellectual community provides possibilities for field members to review purposes and revitalise knowledge claims in ways that facilitate reflexivity and generate possibilities for development.

A consequence of this is that we need always to ask who the mappers are and might be. A central feature of the field of leadership is that it has always been multi-site and hence inclusive of a range of practitioners. Some field members can be characterised as researching professionals in which they enquire about their own and other's practice within a contextual setting, while others are professional researchers in so far as research is their prime professional purpose. Much practitioner activity goes unrecorded except within the recalled professional life, and while researching professionals can publicise their work in a variety of ways, this has not been common. Charting the history of the field through a study of published work by professional researchers and the biographies of field members (Gunter, 1999), shows how the disposition to engage in knowledge production about and for practice is central to the work of those who have legitimised the field in higher education. What this has enabled field members to do is to combine the distinctiveness of practice with research expertise. What is distinctive about this positioning is how through the development of a practitioner–academic habitus the field member can bridge the divide between the purposes of the university and other sites of educational leadership (Gunter, 2002). Working in partnership in practitioner networks nationally and locally the field member can explore the interface between theory, theorising, and practice (see Gunter, 2001; Gunter and Ribbins, 2002; Gunter and Ribbins, 2002a; Ribbins and Gunter, 2002).

While it cannot be incumbent on a mapper to give an account of all the territory in every possible detail, we would expect the choices made to be as inclusive and comprehensive and as open and explicit as possible. In this way who the mappers are, and who the map readers are, can be integrated into the analysis in ways that recognise plurality. Thus, while Fitz (1999, p 314) identifies three basic types of knowledge worker, the academic, the practitioner and the entrepreneur, we hold that there are other groups to be acknowledged if we are to be inclusive and relate our work to democratic development: pupils, parents and the wider community. They are field members, and unless we work for this in our research, school leadership will be the exclusive prerogative of those who are designated as leaders and so remain at a distance from those it is meant to involve. The idea of 'field member' and especially 'knowledge worker' underpins the third of the typologies that we have developed to enable our attempt to map the field. It identifies four positions in knowledge production and these have to do with training, consultancy, expertise and intellectual work. Limitations of space make it impossible for us to discuss this further (see Gunter and Ribbins, 2002). In what follows we will focus on the first and second of our typologies and will say something about how these, taken together, constitute a map of the field.

MAPPING TYPOLOGIES AND MAPS

In producing our mapping typologies and maps, we begin by trying to make our position, and the assumptions that underpin it, plain. To do this is to facilitate understanding and provide spaces through which a typology or map might be refined or challenged by alternative proposals. As we have noted at length elsewhere (Ribbins and Gunter, 2002) six propositions inform our thinking. They stress the need:

- to conceptualise research in educational leadership
- to appreciate the mediated nature of research in educational leadership
- to be aware of variety of purpose in differentiating research in educational leadership
- to be reflexive and critically cumulative
- to be accessible
- to aspire to the highest ethical standards.

At the Reading seminar, we presented an outline 'map' that focused on the knowledge domains underpinning different types of research into leaders, leading and leadership. We developed this initially into a typology of *five domains* (Ribbins and Gunter, 2002) and later of *six knowledge provinces* (Gunter and Ribbins, 2002a). Each *province* has its own orientation: the *conceptual* (epistemological, ontological and moral issues), the *descriptive* (factual reports, usually in some detail), the *humanistic* (lived lives and experiences), the *critical* (power and social justice), the *evaluative* (measuring effectiveness and the conditions for improvement) and the *instrumental* (prescriptions for what works). The provinces are further differentiated as seven *groupings of work* in terms of purpose, focus, context, method, audience, communication and impact (for diagrams summarising Typology One, see Ribbins and Gunter, 2002, pp. 378–9 and Gunter and Ribbins, 2002a, pp. 10–11).

As a result of the discussion at Reading, we came to understand that what we had presented was in effect a one-dimensional typology that could be used as a tool towards the production of a map. A map of the field required a second typology (constituting a second dimension) to set against the first. As such, knowledge provinces express the ways in which the field of leadership in education can be understood by its own knowledge workers and by those outside it. The next question is how these provinces connect with questions of what we know about practice. By practice we mean the realities of being a leader, and doing leading and leadership. Traditionally this has been charted by work focusing on organisational roles, e.g. middle management or headteacher. In addition there is work on those who inhabit these roles, e.g. where they came from and their experiences of being there.

Underpinning this is the application of particular theoretical models for the effective practice of leadership.

At Reading the issue of what leadership is was at the core of most of the maps that were presented. In charting the dimensions of leaders, leading and leadership field members identified themes on the exercise of agency (participation and choice) and impact of structure (roles and rules). By engaging with such themes the mapper has the opportunity to produce a map of research and theory in the field. But this is a vast territory. To develop a focus around these themes, and to produce a second mapping typology, we have pragmatically adopted the 'Ten Propositions of School Leadership' generated by a think-tank for the National College for School Leadership (for a diagram summarising Typology Two, see Gunter and Ribbins, 2002, p. 398–403).

Hopkins (2001, p. 8) groups these ten propositions into three 'reflecting the values, nature, and development and support of school leadership'. This offers an opportunity to be explicit about the knowledge, skills, actions, values and attributes of those that aspire to or are already role incumbents, and the tasks they perform. By setting Typology One (knowledge provinces) against Typology Two (based on the ten propositions), we are able to create a map focused on one part of the leadership territory, i.e. school leadership, and on one reading of what that territory is. This enables a description and analysis *and* a critical evaluation of how the think-tank, as a particular group of field watchers and members, has sought to characterise the field and to influence the National College purpose and agenda through it.

As an example of what we mean, we will focus on the fifth of the think-tank's propositions which holds that leadership is a function that needs to be distributed throughout the school community. If we do so, then it can be seen that the literature contains instrumental work that seeks to enable heads and others to distribute through systems of delegation (Caldwell and Spinks, 1988). There is also evaluative work striving to measure the impact of different levels of leadership within the school on effectiveness (Sammons, Thomas and Mortimore, 1997). What the map does is to enable the search for other positions. We are assisted by the humanistic to understand the contextual setting in which delegation is experienced (Wallace, 2001b), by the critical to ask who is doing the delegating and why (Gronn, 2000), and by the conceptual to consider the moral commitments underpinning practice (Hodgkinson, 1996). The consequences of this inclusive approach for the NCSL, and for those wishing to engage in comprehensive systematic reviews of the field, is that in taking these agendas forward there are a range of questions and issues that need to be at the forefront of dialogue about, amongst other things, research design, improving practice and professional development.

What is involved can also be pointed up by putting together Typology Two with the next strand of the NCSL strategy in relation to the identification, selection and training of educational leaders. Since this is likely to be influential it should be subject to careful scrutiny (NCSL, 2001). What the NCSL is proposing is to build provision around a framework of Five Stages of School

Leadership – *emergent leadership, established leadership, entry to headship, advanced leadership* and *consultant leadership*. Investigating the research literature on leadership careers from the perspective of this framework, whether for a systematic review or not, represents an interesting and necessary activity. In attempting to illustrate the possibilities of our map as a whole we have juxtaposed the five knowledge provinces, proposition five of the ten propositions and the five stages of school leadership (Table 12.1).

What this does is to operationalise the NCSL framework so that in relation to a particular aspect of research into leadership the scope of past and current enquiry can be charted, and the agendas for future work devised. Knowledge workers, as systematic reviewers or not, can use the typology to plot in examples of authors, publications, and key issues. For example, if we take *emergent leadership* we would expect an appreciation of research in the critical province that focuses on evidence, descriptions and explanations of how and why gender has an impact on how and why distribution has been experienced as a power structure. This is in contrast with work in the evaluative province charted to show the emphasis on identifying the ways in which distributive leadership makes an effective and ineffective subject department.

An important outcome of this is the way the process of relating the six knowledge provinces to the five stages of leadership enables the latter to be interrogated. If the NCSL takes an instrumental approach to knowledge production then it will aim to provide a ring binder for each stage with clear types of action. It is possible to integrate specific types of training into the stages and identify from a particular harvesting of the literature the knowledge, skills, and understandings attributable to each stage. The evaluative approach will enhance this by providing evidence of the impact of leadership at the different stages, and by comparing with evidence from outside of education. However, it is still located in the rigidity of a linear model of life and career disputed by evidence generated by the other three provinces. Work in the humanistic province shows lived lives can be described and explained through theorising into stages from the evidence, but this is open to ongoing challenge (Ribbins, 2002). The critical province would ask questions about those who are leaders *and* who is denied leadership because of the workings of oppressive power structures. The conceptual province would facilitate reflection on issues of lived lives and the complexity of choice and purpose.

CONCLUSION

In this chapter we have advocated the need for a mapping process and maps of the field of leadership in education claiming that without this attempts to identify an appropriate set of research questions for systematic reviews will be arbitrary and flawed. To enable this, we have developed two mapping typologies, on *knowledge provinces* and the *practice of leadership* that, taken

Table 12.1 Illustrating the Map of Leadership Research – The Development of School Leaders

Ten Propositions	Five stages of School Leadership NCSL (2001)	Conceptual	Descriptive	Humanistic	Critical	Evaluative	Instrumental
		What we need to think through at each of these stages:	What we need to think through at each of these stages:	What we need to think through at each of these stages:	What we need to think through at each of these stages:	What we need to think through at each of these stages:	What we need to think through at each of these stages:
	Emergent Leadership	(a) Importance of power;	(a) Importance of using a range of sources to produce a detailed factual report.	(a) Experiences of career pathways;	(a) Sources of power that structure the distribution;	(a) Conditions which enable effective distribution to take place;	(a) Key features of distributive leadership;
Proposition 5	Established Leadership	(b) Issue of legitimacy and impact on the morality of distribution.		(b) Head's role in supporting the career pathways of others.	(b) Place of social justice in the distribution process.	(b) How best to measure the impact of these conditions.	(b) Training in distributive leadership.
	Entry into Headship	For example, what does research tell us of the impact of the decision of a deputy head not to apply for headship compared with an experienced head being encouraged to work outside of school as a mentor for a new head?	For example, what does the descriptive account tell us about what those who are distributed leaders do, and what do those who are distributed to actually do?	For example, what does research tell us about the experiences of leadership at the different stages, and the choices made by the individual and the support s/he received?	For example, what does research tell us about the tensions between how men and women experience delegation in relation to the process by how it is done, and the types of work that are delegated?	For example, what does research tell us about how effective collaboration works in ways to develop leadership at different stages in a leadership career?	For example, what does research provide us with that can be abstracted into what distributive leadership means at each stage and what types of training are required to enable it to happen?
	Advanced Leadership						
	Consultant Leadership						

together, amount to such a map. This process has led us to believe that, if they are to be worthwhile, EPPI reviews must be conducted with an intellectual generosity not wholly evident in the protocols and instruments developed for this purpose to date.

REFERENCES

Bassey, M. (1997) Annual expenditure on educational research in the UK, *Research Intelligence*, Vol. 59, pp. 2–3.

Bassey, M. (1999) Editorial, *Research Intelligence*, Vol. 69, p. 1.

Bassey, M. (2001) A time of hope, *Research Intelligence*, Vol. 71, p. 1.

Bates, R. (2001) The impact of educational research: alternative methodologies and conclusions, paper given at the Annual National Conference of the British Educational Research Association, Leeds University, September.

Bell, L. and Bolam, R. (2001) Stage 1: mapping the field, paper presented to the SCRELM Seminar, Reading University, December.

Blunkett, D. (2000) Influence or irrelevance: can social science improve government?, *Research Intelligence*, Vol. 71, pp. 12–22.

Bourdieu, P. (1990) *In Other Words: Essays Towards a Reflexive Sociology*, Trans. M. Adamson, Cambridge: Polity Press.

Bush, T., Bell, l., Bolam, R., Glatter, R. and Ribbins, P. (eds) (1999) *Educational Management: Redefining theory, policy and practice*, London: Paul Chapman Publishing.

Caldwell, B. and Spinks, J. (1988) *The Self Managing School*, Lewes: Falmer.

Clarke, C. (1998) Restructuring educational research to raise standards, *Research Intelligence*, Vol. 66, pp. 8–10.

Department of Education, Training and Youth Affairs (DETYA) (2000) *The Impact of Educational Research*, Canberra: DETYA.

Educational Management and Administration, Special Edition on 'Redefining Educational Management and Leadership', Vol. 4, No. 27, pp. 224–352.

Edwards, A. (1998) A careful review but some lost opportunities, *Research Intelligence*, Vol. 66, pp. 15–17.

Fitz, J. (1999) Reflections on the field of educational management studies, *Educational Administration and Management*, Vol. 27, No. 3, pp. 313–21.

Furlong, J. and White, P. (2002) Educational Research Capacity in Wales, *Research Intelligence*, 78, pp. 15–22.

Gronn, P. (2000) Distributed properties: a new architecture for leadership, *Educational Management and Administration*, Vol. 28, No. 3, pp. 317–38

Gunter, H. (1999) Researching and constructing histories of the field of education management, in Bush, T., Bell, I., Bdam, R., Glatter, R. and Ribbins, P. (eds) *Educational Management: Redefining theory, policy and practice*, London: Paul Chapman Publishing, pp. 229–48.

Gunter, H. (2001) *Leaders and Leadership in Education*, London: Paul Chapman Publishing.

Gunter, H. (2002) Purposes and positions in the field of education management: putting Bourdieu to work, *Educational Management and Administration*, Vol. 30, No. 1, pp. 3–22.

Gunter, H. and Ribbins, P. (2002) Leadership studies in education: towards a map of the field, *Educational Management and Administration*, Vol. 31, No. 1, pp. 387–417.

Gunter, H. and Ribbins, P. (2002a) Challenging orthodoxy in school leadership studies: old maps for new directions? Opening Keynote Lecture given at the first meeting of an ESRC Seminar Series an Challenging the Orthodoxy of School Leadership: Towards a New Theoretical Perspective, University of Warwick, November.

Hammersley, M. (2001a) The sky is never blue for modernizers: the threat posed by David Blunkett's offer of 'partnership'; to social science, *Research Intelligence*, Vol. 72, pp. 12–14.

Hammersley, M. (2001b) On 'systematic' reviews of research literatures: a narrative response to Evans and Benefield, *British Educational Research Journal*, Vol. 27, No. 5, pp. 543–54.

Hargreaves, D. (1996) Teaching as a research-based profession: possibilities and prospects, *Teacher Training Annual Lecture*, London: TTA.

Hillage, J., Pearson, R., Anderson, A. and Tamkin, P. (1998) *Excellence in Research in Schools*, London: Department for Education and Employment.

Hodgkinson, C. (1996) *Administrative Philosophy*, Oxford: Pergamon.

Hopkins, D. (2001) *Think Tank's Report to Governing Council*, Nottingham: NCSL.

Levačić, R. and Glatter, R. (2001) Really good ideas? Developing evidence-informed policy and practice in educational leadership and management, *Educational Management and Administration*, Vol. 29, No. 1, pp. 5–27.

Lomax, P. (1999) Working together for educative community through research, *British Educational Research Journal*, Vol. 25, No. 1, pp. 5–23.

National College for School Leadership (NCSL) (2001) *Leadership Development Framework*, Nottingham: NCSL.

Nisbet, J. (1995) *Pipers and Tunes*, Edinburgh: Scottish Council for Research in Education.

Office for Standards in Education (OFSTED) (1999) *Annual Report of Her Majesty's Chief Inspector of Schools*, London: HMSO.

Ouston, J. (2001) Paper presented to the SCRELM Seminar, Reading University, December.

Ozga, J. (2000) *Policy Research in Educational Settings*, Buckingham: Open University Press.

Ribbins, P. (in press) Biography and the study of school leader careers: towards a humanistic approach, in Brundrett, M., Burton, N. and Smith, R. (eds) *Leadership in Education*, London: Paul Chapman Publishing.

Ribbins, P. and Gunter, H. (2002) Mapping leadership studies in education: towards a typology of knowledge domains, *Educational Management and Administration*, Vol. 30, No. 4. pp. 359–87.

Richardson, L. (1997) *Fields of Play. Constructing an Academic Life*, New Brunswick, NJ: Rutgers University Press.

Sammons, P., Thomas, S. and Mortimore, P. (1997) *Forging Links: Effective Schools and Effective Departments*, London: Paul Chapman Publishing.

Thomson, P. (2000) Move over Rover! An essay/assay of the field of educational management in the UK, *Journal of Education Policy*, Vol. 15, No. 6, pp. 717–32.

Tooley, J., with Darby, D. (1998) *Educational Research: A Review*, London: Office for Standards in Education.

Wallace, M. (2001a) Really good ideas: a rejoinder to Rosalind Levačić and Ron Glatter, *Educational Management and Administration*, Vol. 29, No. 1, pp. 27–35.

Wallace, M. (2001b) Sharing leadership of schools through teamwork: a justifiable risk? *Educational Management and Administration*, Vol. 29, No. 2, pp. 153–67.

Weindling, D. (2001) SCRELM mapping exercise: some notes and preliminary thoughts, paper presented to the SCRELM Seminar, Reading University, December.

Index

Added to a page number, 'f' denotes a figure and 't' denotes a table.